ELVIS PRESLEY

ELVIS PRESLEY

STORIES BEHIND THE SONGS

Volume 1

MATT SHEPHERD

First published in 2018 by Redshank Books

ISBN 978-0-9954834-3-9

A CIP catalogue record for this book is available from The British Library

All images are photos of the author's own record collection

Design by Carnegie Book Production

Printed in the UK by Hobbs the Printer

Redshank Books
Brunel House
Volunteer Way
Faringdon
Oxfordshire
SN7 7YR

Tel: +44 (0)845 873 3837

www.redshankbooks.co.uk

This book is dedicated to my amazing son Charlie.
You make me so proud every day.

And to my wonderful Mum and Dad – thank you for always encouraging me to "Follow That Dream".

To the legend that is Freddy Zapp – thank you for being the best mate ever.

To Zoey Goto and all at Libri – you are all stars.
I can't thank you enough for your support.

Thanks to Dave James for always singing Elvis songs loud and proud.

To Johnny Cowling, fancy a Chinese? Thanks for the laughs and Elvis chats.

To Francis Larkin, a massive Elvis fan and a lovely chap.

ABOUT THE BOOK

I was far too young ever to know who Elvis Presley was while he was alive. I missed out on the rock 'n' roll explosion, the movie years and the unforgettable '68 comeback. I even missed out on the Aloha from Hawaii show and all the mass hysteria when Elvis died more than 40 years ago.

Yet I have always been an Elvis Presley fan. It's deep rooted. His music runs through my veins. Every day I play an Elvis song or twenty. Out of nowhere an Elvis song will appear in my head. My brain is like a 24-hour jukebox that mostly consists of Elvis, Elvis and yet more Elvis.

I was seven years old when I first came across Elvis. I was sitting in front of a television that had just three channels – yep kids, just three! Suddenly before me there was this great-looking, great-singing god – surrounded by girls. Something in my conscience stirred on that day. Was it Elvis or the bikini-wearing co-stars? To be honest, it was probably both…

Soon after I ran home from Bookwell School in Egremont, Cumbria, bypassing the ice-cream van, just so I could catch the last ten minutes of Elvis's 1962 movie *Girls, Girls, Girls.*

Before I moved to Cornwall, my best friend's Mum, Irene Huddart, knocked on my door to offer me a goodbye gift. It was the pink pressing of Elvis's 40 Greatest Hits. I treasured it and still have it to this day.

The first song I ever heard playing on a record player was 'Return to Sender'. At the time I thought Elvis was saying "sinder" and remember naively thinking that must be a place in America.

Luckily, my knowledge of Elvis has improved slightly since then!

For me, it has always been about the music.

There's an Elvis song to suit every mood. People who have said to me over the years "I hate Elvis" – I always reply, "Have you heard everything he did?" It's a fair enough response, mind: some fans prefer the gospel, others the love songs; another group of fans may prefer the Vegas jumpsuit era. There lies the magic of Elvis. He could turn his hand to any genre and tackle it with complete ease.

He may not have been a songwriter but he was an amazing song performer. He could take any track and breathe something new into it. Elvis always gave his all in every song. He even tried his hardest to make the best of the worst movie songs too.

Ever the professional Elvis could and did cover all the main genres. Had he lived beyond his 42 years, there would have been even more musical areas tackled. We can only imagine what Elvis would have achieved beyond 16th August 1977.

Elvis Presley: Stories Behind the Songs is an unusual book, in that it doesn't start at the beginning. I have been asked on numerous occasions why I started in 1969.

For me this was the most crucial period in Elvis's career. He had spent years in the Hollywood wilderness. Once the pioneer and king of the rock 'n' roll movement, Elvis had been reduced to playing pretty much the same role throughout the 1960s – and each time the script was slightly poorer and the soundtrack lower in quality.

However in 1969 he bounced back in a way no-one could have predicted, recording relevant, strong material, often with a 'today' message. The TV comeback may have been in 1968 – that showed the world Elvis could still rock with the best of them.

In 1969, recording once again in Memphis just like he had 15 years earlier, the songs showed the return of Elvis – as a contemporary artist, a major chart force, recording and releasing albums with his strongest material in years.

In this first volume of *Elvis Presley: Stories Behind the Songs*, we start in Memphis, head to Vegas, New York and Hawaii, before returning to Memphis in the 1950s where a young truck driver would realise his dream to become a singer, recording fresh exciting material. These would be the days before RCA, 'Colonel' Tom Parker, TV executives and movie moguls would dig their teeth in and mould Elvis how they wanted him.

He may have been known throughout the world as the King of Rock 'n' Roll but it was gospel music that first ran through the veins of the young Elvis. Some of his early religious recordings feature in this book.

Come with me on a journey through some of the most exciting music Elvis laid down as we tell you the stories behind some of Presley's greatest hits, album tracks, live performances and movie-soundtrack highlights.

ABOUT THE AUTHOR

Matt Shepherd has been a BBC journalist for 24 years. He has produced and presented more than 50 radio shows on Elvis for BBC Radio Cornwall. Matt has also written articles for BBC News Online about the King of Rock 'n' Roll and has appeared on BBC regional television showing local TV reporter David George how to do an Elvis impression.

Last August, on the fortieth anniversary of the passing of Elvis, Matt was interviewed by 20 BBC Local Radio Stations as an Elvis historian and 'super fan'. On the same day, Matt was also interviewed by the BBC World Service and BBC World Television.

Matt has a vast collection of Elvis's records and many of these are used to illustrate the book.

Matt was born in Lancashire and moved to Egremont, Cumbria at an early age. It was here he first discovered Elvis.

Matt has lived in Cornwall for 36 years and is a proud daddy to Charlie.

CONTENTS

INTRODUCTION

From Elvis Presley's first singles on the Sun record label, the early classics on RCA, through the movie years, to the triumphant comeback of 1968 and the glamour of the Vegas ears, across two volumes we will tell the stories behind the songs, the people who wrote them and who else covered the songs.

We'll look at the albums released after Elvis's death including why Felton Jarvis re-recorded backings to several Elvis tracks in 1980, the global success of the remixes 'A Little Less Conversation' and 'Rubberneckin'', the family duets with Lisa Marie Presley, the Christmas songs with the country stars of today and more recently the pairing of Elvis's amazing voice with the talents of the Royal Philharmonic Orchestra for two number-one albums in the UK.

ONE

STUDIO HIGHLIGHTS 1969–1971– THE LEGEND REBORN

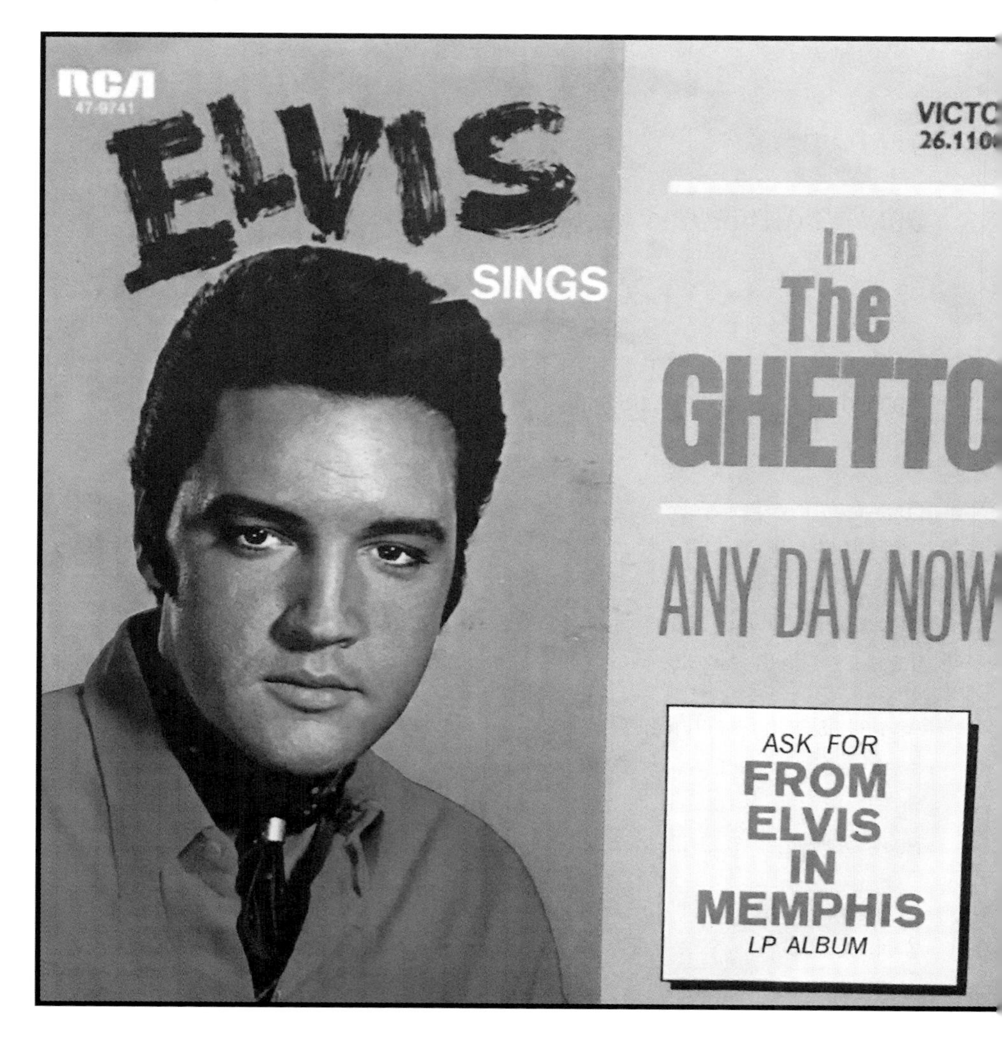

1969

This was such a critical year for Elvis Presley as he came home and recorded in Memphis once again, for the first time since his early, heady days at Sun Studios. The year before, he had proved that he could still perform an electrifying set in front of a live audience after years of making Hollywood movies. However, this had consisted mainly of his hits from the past (with a handful of notable exceptions, such as 'If I Can Dream' and 'Memories').

This time, the venue was American Sound Studios. But could Elvis recapture the Memphis magic and prove himself once again? The executives were nervous. Elvis was as well. But the magic was about to unfold...

JANUARY 1969

DON'T CRY DADDY

On the 15th January 1969 the instrumental track to 'Don't Cry Daddy' was laid down and six days later Elvis added his vocals. The song continued Elvis's comeback, generating strong record sales. Released at the end of 1969, it reached number six in the US and number eight in the UK.

The song was written by Mac Davis. He had already proved to be a successful choice for Elvis, providing strong material like 'Memories' from the *The '68 Comeback Special* and 'A Little Less Conversation', which although initially hidden on the little seen *Live A Little, Love A Little* movie, went on to become a global success when remixed by JXL at the turn of this century. Mac also wrote the classic 'In the Ghetto', which we'll cover shortly.

As well as being a songwriter, Davis enjoyed success as a singer. Many of his songs did well in both the country and popular music charts, including 'Baby, Don't Get Hooked on Me' (a number-one Grammy-nominated success), 'One Hell of a Woman' and 'Stop and Smell the Roses'.

Over the years, he has written hits for Kenny Rogers ('Somethin's Burnin''), Bobby Goldsboro ('Watchin' Scotty Grow') and Gallery ('I Believe in Music').

O.C. Smith, Freddie Hart, Ray Price, Lou Rawls, Dolly Parton and Rascal Flatts are among the others to have benefited from the writing talents of Davis.

Hit songs Mac wrote and recorded himself include 'My Bestest Friend', 'It's Hard to Be Humble' and 'Texas in My Rearview Mirror'. His successful TV series, *The Mac Davis Show* on NBC, and many TV specials over the years enabled him to be selected as the Academy of Country Music's Entertainer of the Year and the People's Choice Award's very first Favourite Male Singer.

As for movies, Mac co-starred with Nick Nolte in one of the greatest football movies of all time, *North Dallas Forty*, and went on to enjoy starring roles in *The Sting II*, *Cheaper to Keep Her* and the family film *Possums*.

In 1997 Lisa Marie Presley made a video of 'Don't Cry Daddy', which she sings as a duet with her famous Dad. This video was presented on 16th August 1997 at the tribute concert that marked the twentieth anniversary of Elvis's death.

Elvis made live recordings of the song during his second season in Las Vegas, in February 1970, and several of these have since been released. During the dinner show on 13th August 1970 at the International Hotel, he recorded a version that led seamlessly into 'In the Ghetto'.

FROM A JACK TO A KING

Elvis had the amazing knack of taking an already established hit and adding further magic to it. Another example is the Ned Miller track 'From a Jack to a King'. Elvis would record the track on 21st January 1969 at American Sound Studio in Memphis.

The song would feature on the double LP *From Memphis to Vegas/From Vegas to Memphis*, which was released in October 1969 by RCA Records. The album was unusual at the time because sides one and two captured Elvis live on stage at the International Hotel in Vegas, 24th–26th of August, while sides three and four were taken from Elvis's mammoth studio recording sessions of January and February 1969. Full of strong material, it is no surprise that the double LP was certified gold in December 1969, just two months after its release. The double LP was then released as two single LPs in November 1970, another unusual step at the time.

Ned Miller's version of 'From a Jack to a King' had originally been released in 1957 but it failed to drum up the support of the record-buying public. Its release was probably buried under the huge amount of rock 'n' roll being issued at the time and being snapped up by teenagers. However, Miller had faith in the track and managed to persuade his record company, Capitol Records, to re-release it five years later.

Miller was right to keep the pressure on his label. On its re-release in 1962 the song became a crossover hit, peaking at number two on the Billboard US country chart. It made number six on the US Pop chart and peaked at number three in the Adult Contemporary charts. Miller's version reached number one on the Irish singles chart, while peaking at number two on the UK singles chart. It was the sixth most-played single of 1963 in the United Kingdom.

His faith in the song definitely paid off, but it would be the highlight of his career. Miller never repeated its success and, by the time Elvis recorded 'From a Jack to a King', Ned Miller was considering retirement from recording. In the '70s he stopped completely. In his obit in the *New York Times* it said: "Mr. Miller considered himself a songwriter more than a singer and had such bad stage fright that he sometimes asked friends to perform under his name." The obit quotes Ned Miller as saying: "If you love shows and like to perform, it's a great business, but if you don't, you shouldn't be in it." Ned Miller passed away in 2016 at the age of 90 years old.

Country legend Jim Reeves also recorded 'From a Jack to a King', enjoying great success with his version in South Africa. Fast forward to 1988 and country music artist Ricky Van Shelton enjoyed his fifth consecutive number one on the Billboard Hot Country singles chart with his version.

Elvis takes a casual approach to the song, but it is a committed performance: he loses himself totally in the song and seems to love every second. Ned Miller's version was a huge hit, but Elvis's take seems to elevate the song further. It feels like it's taken from a jamming session, with Elvis's voice displaying a reckless abandon, but don't be deceived: Elvis is in total control and the end product is a polished take by a man in total control. Apparently, it was one of Vernon Presley's favourite songs. If so, his son did him proud.

Presley also enjoyed singing another Ned Miller composition in private – 'Dark Moon'. But more about that in a future edition.

GENTLE ON MY MIND

By the time Elvis recorded 'Gentle on My Mind' it was already becoming a country standard, even though it was still a relatively new song. The late Glen Campbell's version has received over five million plays on the radio. Campbell used 'Gentle on My Mind' as the theme to his television variety show, *The Glen Campbell Goodtime Hour*, between 1969 and 1972. However, Dean Martin's version, recorded in 1968, was the more successful chart-wise.

According to Shane Brown in *Elvis Presley – A Listener's Guide*, recordings by John Hartford and Glen Campbell had been pure unadulterated country. However, Elvis's take was a heavier sound, mixing rock and gospel with country. 'Gentle on My Mind', written by John Hartford, was tackled by Elvis at American Sound Studios in Memphis in January 1969 and the song featured on the award-winning album *From Elvis in Memphis*.

John Hartford won Grammy awards in three different decades and recorded a catalogue of more than 30 albums. According to his obituary, which appeared in papers in 2001, he was born on 30th December 1937 in New York. He grew up in St. Louis where he acquired a lifelong love of riverboats. After achieving some success as a professional musician, Hartford found time to pursue his love of riverboat lore, even working for a time as a boat captain.

A talented multi-instrumentalist, Hartford was also drawn to the music of Flatt and Scruggs. He moved to Nashville in 1965 and released his debut album, *John Hartford Looks at Life*, in 1966. His own version of 'Gentle on My Mind' went to number 60 in 1967 on the Billboard country chart.

Glen Campbell's recording of the song went to number 30 in the country chart and number 62 in the pop chart in the same year. A year later, Campbell released the song again and it climbed to number 39 on the country chart.

The song's popularity is best measured by the number of times it has been recorded: between 400 and 600 times. It has been performed more than six million times. The most random cover of 'Gentle on My Mind' was by the actor Leonard Nimoy. Have a search online, it is out there – and once you've heard it, you will never forget it!

In an archive interview Hartford said he wrote 'Gentle on My Mind' after going to see *Doctor Zhivago*. In Dorothy Horstman's book *Sing Your Heart Out Country Boy*, Hartford said: "I have never really understood commercial music like I've wanted to. I have no idea, except for the message in that song, why it was a hit."

HEY JUDE

Next a song that was a huge hit for the Beatles. Elvis tackled this more as a jamming session, but it still found its way onto an album.

Paul McCartney originally wrote 'Hey Jude' as 'Hey Jules' and it was about John Lennon's son Julian, who was then just five years old. This was a difficult time for the young Lennon as his parents were going through a divorce. Paul was very close to the youngster and wrote the song to comfort him. The title was later changed to Jude.

In an interview for Steve Turner's book, *The Stories Behind Every Beatles Song*, Julian Lennon talked about a conversation with Paul McCartney in New York in 1987. Julian said:

> Paul and I used to hang out quite a bit – more than Dad and I did. There seem to be far more pictures of me and Paul playing at that age than me and Dad. I've never really wanted to know the truth of how Dad was and how he was with me. There was some very negative stuff – like when he said that I'd come out of a whisky bottle on a Saturday night.

> That's tough to deal with. You think, where's the love in that? It surprises me whenever I hear the song. It's strange to think someone has written a song about you. It still touches me.

Coming in at a grand total of seven minutes and 11 seconds, 'Hey Jude' was a long song to be released as a single at that time. Most groups wouldn't have got away with it – but this was the Beatles and they were immune from any rules regarding single timings! It was also the first song released on Apple Records, which was a record label owned by the Beatles themselves. The track was recorded at Trident Studios, London, on 31st July and 1st August 1968. According to songfacts.com, the "na na na" fadeout in 'Hey Jude' takes up four minutes of the track. The chorus is repeated 19 times!

Elvis's performance of the track has divided fans: some love it, some really dislike it. A quick glance at the comments on the songbase on elvisnews.com further backs this up. Cruiser621 says: "Without a doubt, next to 'Do the Clam', this song 'Hey Jude' is the absolute worst song Elvis Presley ever recorded. I can't believe RCA in its infinite wisdom dragged this thing from the vaults and put it on his album *Elvis Now* where it really stood out as a sore thumb. Horrible vocal. Absolutely Atrocious." Whereas burninglove92 says: "This was just an informal recording, Elvis just jamming with it, and in my opinion it surpasses the Beatles' version. Elvis shows a unique vocal performance and the ending with his 'Jude Jude Jude Jude' is just amazing, sung with pure passion."

Elvis's version was recorded on 22nd January 1969. However, it wasn't released until three years later on a real mop-up album hilariously titled *Elvis Now*. There was nothing 'now' about it, with the most recent recording having been made on 20th May 1971. The oldest track on there was 'Hey Jude'. Despite Elvis not knowing all the words to the song, it still lasts for four and a half minutes.

If you don't take it too seriously and avoid comparing it to the Beatles' master version, then it can be quite an enjoyable listen to Elvis in a laid-back studio environment.

I'LL HOLD YOU IN MY HEART

Elvis recorded 'I'll Hold You in My Heart' in 1969. However, it was first recorded in 1947 by Eddy Arnold, who enjoyed huge success with the song he had co-written with Hall Horton and Tommy Dilbeck. Arnold's version went to number one on the country charts and stayed there for 21 weeks, making it the second-longest-running number-one country hit of all time.

Eddy Arnold became a pioneer of the 'Nashville Sound', also called 'Countrypolitan', which was a mixture of country and pop styles. His crossover success paved the way for later singers such as Kenny Rogers. In an archive interview, which was featured in his obit in newspapers, Arnold said: "I sing a little country, I sing a little pop and I sing a little folk, and it all goes together."

Eddy Arnold was elected to the Country Music Hall of Fame in 1966. The following year, he was the first person to receive the Entertainer of the Year Award from the Country Music Association. Most of his hits were created in association with the famed guitarist Chet Atkins, who was the producer on most of Arnold's recording sessions. The late Dinah Shore once described Arnold's voice as "warm butter and syrup being poured over wonderful buttermilk pancakes."

Elvis also recorded 'Make the World Go Away', which was another huge hit for Eddy Arnold. Presley recorded 'I'll Hold You in My Heart' on 22nd January 1969. It can be found on the album *From Elvis in Memphis*.

I'M MOVIN' ON

Next, see "That big eight wheeler a rollin' down the track?" That's the opening line of our next tune, 'I'm Moving On'.

The song is a 1950 country standard written by Hank Snow. It was one of three songs in the history of the Billboard country charts to spend 21 weeks at number one. The others were 1947's 'I'll Hold You in My Heart (Till I Can Hold You in My Arms)' by Eddy Arnold (featured above as Elvis also recorded it) and 1955's 'In the Jailhouse Now' by Webb Pierce.

'I'm Movin' On' was covered in 1959 by Ray Charles, who used congas and maracas to give the track a taste of Spain. Al Hirt also covered the track, including it on his 1963 album, *Honey in the Horn*. And famed UK band the Rolling Stones did a live version on their album *December's Children*.

Hank Snow was born Clarence Eugene 'Hank' Snow on 9th May 1914 in the sleepy fishing village of Brooklyn, Queens County, on Nova Scotia's South Shore. According to his website (www.hanksnow.com) the young Snow quickly developed excellent skills as a musician and entertainer at kitchen parties and neighbourhood picnics. His professional career started at CHNS Radio in Halifax in 1933 where he had his own radio show. He changed his name to 'Hank, The Yodeling Ranger' because it sounded more Western.

Throughout the 1930s and '40s, Snow toured the Maritimes and western Canada playing at county fairs and local radio stations. On 2nd September 1935, he married Minnie Blanche Aalders, who stayed with Hank through all the hard, travelling years and beyond. Hank and Minnie had one son together, Jimmie Rodgers Snow (named after Hank's idol Jimmie Rodgers), who also travelled with them and eventually joined Hank on stage on numerous occasions.

In 1936 Hank Snow made his first recording in Montreal with RCA Victor's Bluebird label and signed a contract that would last 47 years, the longest continuous contract in the history of the recording industry. Snow was to be a major influence in the young Elvis's life. Both Hank and Elvis recorded 'A Fool Such as I' as well as 'I'm Movin' On'. A regular at the Grand Ole Opry, in 1954 Snow persuaded the directors to allow a young Elvis Presley to appear on stage.

Snow used Presley as his opening act and introduced him to Colonel Tom Parker. In August 1955, Snow and Parker formed the management team, Hank Snow Attractions. This partnership signed a management contract with Presley but before long, Snow was out and Parker had full control over the rock singer's career. Forty years after leaving Parker, Snow was still steaming about his treatment. He said: "I have worked with several managers over the years and have had respect for them all except one. Tom Parker [he refuses to recognise the title 'Colonel'] was the most egotistical, obnoxious human being I've ever had dealings with."

Elvis recorded 'I'm Movin' On' overnight into 15th January 1969 at American Sound in Memphis. On the same night he tackled 'Gentle on My Mind' and 'Don't Cry Daddy'. 'I'm Movin' On' appeared on the album *From Elvis in Memphis.* It was also one of the tracks taken by Felton Jarvis for his 1980 *Guitar Man* album project. It saw Presley's voice being used with more modern backings that the producer felt were more suitable for the 1980s. More about that project in a future edition...

IN THE GHETTO

Elvis worked on the recording of 'In the Ghetto' on 21st and into 22nd January 1969. The song will forever be associated with Elvis, but it was not originally written as a song for the King. Songwriter Mac Davis said that he'd never really dreamed of pitching this particular song to Elvis. Davis had been working on 'In the Ghetto' for several years. As a child he was friends with a little boy in Texas whose family lived in very poor conditions. Mac Davis later said he could never understand why his family lived in better conditions than his friend did. As a result, Mac had always wanted to write a song about the situation. The original title was 'The Vicious Circle'.

In interviews Mac Davis has said: "I didn't write the song for anyone in particular, but later while I was working on an album in Memphis, Chips Moman called me and said Elvis was recording and asked me if I had any songs for him. So I sent him a tape with 19 songs on it and Elvis recorded the first three songs on the tape, 'In the Ghetto', 'Don't Cry Daddy' and another song they didn't release titled 'Poor Man's Gold'."

After years of recording on the Hollywood Sound Stage and in Nashville, Elvis's friends like Marty Lacker encouraged him to record at American Sound Studio. The small studio was in a then-rundown neighbourhood and was operated by Chips Moman, who had already been garnering praise as a producer long before Elvis walked into the building.

Elvis had a busy night on the 21st January 1969. As well as 'In the Ghetto', he also worked on 'My Little Friend', 'Mama Liked the Roses', 'Don't Cry Daddy',

'Long Black Limousine', 'I'm Movin' On', 'Inherit the Wind' and 'Poor Man's Gold', which wasn't released at the time.

Just like 'If I Can Dream', recorded in the previous year, 'In the Ghetto' was a message song, which no doubt made Elvis's manager Colonel Tom Parker very nervous. He never wanted 'his boy' to record anything that could be deemed as controversial – how quickly Parker had forgotten the impact Elvis had had in the 1950s!

'In the Ghetto' tells of a boy who is born to a mother who already struggles with a large family. The young child grows up hungry and angry; he steals and fights, finds a gun and steals a car, but his attempts to run ultimately lead to him being shot and killed just as his own child is born. The listener is led to believe the newborn will meet the same fate, continuing the cycle of poverty and violence.

The famous singers, from several genres, who have since recorded 'In the Ghetto' make a huge list and include Sammy Davis Jr., Dolly Parton, Bobbie Gentry, Nick Cave and Merle Haggard – and even the songwriter Mac Davis recorded a version of the song for a greatest hits album released in 1979.

The Presley connection to the song continued in recent years, too, when the track was recorded in 2007 by Lisa Marie Presley as a duet with her father. This was to raise money for the Presley Charitable Foundation, a non-profit philanthropic organisation dedicated to improving people's lives with real solutions. It was created by Lisa Marie Presley in August 2007 and aims to offer rent-free housing, child day care, career and financial counselling and other tools to help families break the cycle of poverty. You can find out more about it by visiting: http://www.presleycharitablefoundation.org/index.php.

'In the Ghetto' was Presley's first top-10 hit in the US in four years, peaking at number three, and his first UK top-10 hit in three years, peaking at number two. It hit number one on Cashbox. It was also a number-one hit in West Germany, Ireland, Norway, Australia and New Zealand. Just after the *'68 Comeback Special*, Elvis said he would never again record a song he didn't believe in. He was true to his word when it came to songs like 'In the Ghetto', a song that remains as relevant today as it was when Elvis recorded it back in January 1969...

'Suspicious Minds' was a product of a 23rd January 1969 session that took place between 4 am and 7 am. It took eight takes to produce the final song, in which the lead vocal track was overdubbed by Presley himself later that same night. Elvis's publishing company, along with his manager, Colonel Tom Parker, tried to get their usual cut of the royalties from this and threatened to stop the recording if they didn't. Elvis insisted on recording the song regardless and it went on to become a monster hit for him. This song was inducted into the Grammy Hall of Fame in 1999 and is widely regarded as the single that revived Presley's career success, following his '68 Comeback Special.

In the UK, Elvis had a hit with this song three times. First in 1969 when it was originally released; then in 2001 when a live version recorded at the International Hotel, Las Vegas, in August 1970 was issued and went to number 15; then again in 2007 when it was reissued to commemorate the thirtieth anniversary of Elvis's death, going to number 11.

Presley first performed 'Suspicious Minds' at the Las Vegas International Hotel (later renamed the Hilton) on July 31 1969, and the 45 rpm single was released 26 days later. The studio version is a knock out but the live version takes the track to an even more unforgettable level with Elvis giving his all on the track both vocally and physically. The live version of 'Suspicious Minds' was performed during the filming of the movie *That's the Way It Is*.

YOU'LL THINK OF ME

When you've got a classic A-side single like 'Suspicious Minds' it's easy to forget that the B-side is really strong material too. 'You'll Think of Me' was featured on Elvis's 1969 double album, *From Memphis to Vegas/From Vegas to Memphis*. It was also that very B-side of 'Suspicious Minds'.

Presley recorded 'You'll Think of Me' on 14th January 1969 at the American Sound Studio in Memphis. The song was written by Mort Shuman who, along with his song-writing partner, Doc Pomus, contributed several successful songs to Elvis from the late 1950s onwards. 'A Mess of Blues', 'Little Sister', 'Surrender', 'Viva Las Vegas' and 'His Latest Flame' were all written by Pomus and Shuman for Elvis. The pair wrote hits for other stars of the time including

'You Are My Baby' for Ray Charles, 'A Teenager in Love' for Dion and 'Can't Get Used to Losing You' for Andy Williams. For classic soul band, the Drifters, Pomus and Shuman wrote 'This Magic Moment', 'Sweets for My Sweet' and 'Save the Last Dance for Me'.

In an archive interview on mortshuman.com, Shuman said:

> For many people, the most important aspect of my songwriting career was the number of songs I wrote for Elvis (16 or 20 or anything in between, it all depends on who's counting and so much for the archives). It didn't matter that there were some other songs which were more important and of which I am somewhat prouder, or that many of the Presley songs were illustriously unknown film fodder and deservedly so. It didn't and doesn't matter that there are others who wrote at least twice as many for him as I did, people like Ben Wiseman, but perhaps it's because Ben never wrote a definitive Elvis song that his name is not mentioned along with Doc [Pomus] and Jerry [Leiber] and Mike [Stoller] and Otis [Blackwell] and myself, I guess.

You can read the full interview here: http://www.mortshuman.com/mort_on_elvis.php.

In one of the earliest appraisals of Elvis's recording output, *Elvis Presley: A Study in Music*, Robert Matthew-Walker said of 'You'll Think of Me': "There is a strangely disconnected opening which gradually builds to the basic tempo. The song, which lasts almost four minutes, is long for the material, but Presley manages to hold it together through the layers of sound."

The single 'Suspicious Minds' with 'You'll Think of Me' on the B-side enjoyed immense success. It was certified gold by RIAA for sales of one million copies in the United States on 28th October 1969. On 27th March 1992, it was certified platinum. The single went to the top of the charts in the USA, Canada, Australia and Belgium, and just missed out on reaching number one in the UK, stalling at number two. Elvis would have to wait until the summer of 1970 to score his next UK number one with 'The Wonder of You'. His previous number-one hit in the UK had been five years earlier with 'Crying in the Chapel'.

FEBRUARY 1969

AFTER LOVING YOU

The marathon sessions of January and February 1969 captured a rejuvenated Elvis Presley singing with a confidence that had been hiding for several years. According to Ernst Jorgensen, Elvis had been practising Eddy Arnold's 1962 hit, 'After Loving You', for years. He'd informed his publishers that he planned to record it at the February 1969 sessions. Elvis sang the song with the same passion he'd brought to 'One Night' back in the 1950s. Vocally he pushed it as hard as he could.

Not only had Eddy Arnold recorded the track but another country great, Jim Reeves, put out his own version. The song was written by Eddie Miller and Johnny Lantz. Eddie Miller's first published song, written in the mid-1930s, was 'I Love You Honey'. In 1946 he wrote what was to become his biggest hit, 'Release Me', though at first he could not get anyone to record it. Eventually he recorded it himself. Subsequently, it was covered by several singers and became a big hit.

Della Reese recorded 'After Loving You' in 1965 and two years later Bobby Vinton, who had scored big hits with 'Blue Velvet' and 'Roses are Red', also had a stab at the track

Recorded on 18th February 1969, 'After Loving You' was released on *From Elvis in Memphis*.

AND THE GRASS WON'T PAY NO MIND

While there were many powerful tracks recorded during Elvis's prolific recording period of 1969 to 1971, he also tackled some quieter, but equally memorable tracks.

As well as performing Neil Diamond's 'Sweet Caroline' in concert, Elvis also recorded Diamond's 'And the Grass Won't Pay No Mind' in 1969. Diamond was one of the world-famous Brill Building songwriters. His first success as a songwriter came in November 1965 with 'Sunday and Me', a top-20 hit for Jay and the Americans. Greater success as a writer followed with 'I'm a Believer', 'A Little Bit Me, A Little Bit You', 'Look Out (Here Comes Tomorrow)' and 'Love to Love', all performed by the Monkees. Diamond had composed those songs for himself; however, the cover versions were released before his own. 'I'm a Believer' was voted the Popular Music Song of the Year in 1966. Diamond also recorded his own version of 'And the Grass Won't Pay No Mind'

Elvis first tackled the song on 18th February 1969 at American Sound studio. On the same day he recorded 'Power of My Love' and 'After Loving You'. Then on 26th September 1969 he returned to the song during a session at RCA's Studio A in Nashville.

In an interview with Elvis.com.au, the Australian website, Neil Diamond said:

> I did see him perform live in Vegas, I had never seen him before. You know, he was Elvis Presley and I was awed. He was an amazing, amazing live performer. He was electric and he was wonderful and halfway through his show, he introduced me. I was in the audience and he introduced me and it's like worshipping a god and that god is saying, 'Oh, stand up. I like this person. World, why don't you meet him?' So I stood up and the audience started to cheer and they started to say, 'Get up on stage. You know, sing together'. No, I couldn't possibly. It's – and he saw I was uncomfortable with it. He said, 'Well, he's on holiday now, so leave him alone. Let him enjoy the show'. And they did.

Interviewer Andrew Denton asked: "Does a part of you regret that you didn't take that opportunity to hop up and sing with Elvis?" Neil Diamond replied:

> You know I thought about it over the years, what would I do, what songs would we do, and it's not a good idea to come up and sing with another performer when it's their show and it's their band, I do know that. And I'm glad I didn't, because I don't think it would have been a good idea to touch that, you know, the hem of the god. He was amazing. He was warm and very generous to me, and I think it's best left at that.

You can read the full interview here: https://www.elvis.com.au/presley/neil-diamond-elvis-presley.shtml.

Other notable artists who recorded Neil Diamond's songs include Lulu, who covered 'The Boat That I Row'. Deep Purple performed their version of 'Kentucky Woman' and Cliff Richard released versions of 'I'll Come Running', 'Solitary Man', 'Girl, You'll Be a Woman Soon', 'I Got the Feelin' (Oh No No)' and 'Just Another Guy'.

According to the song-base on Elvisnews.com, one fan described Presley's version of 'And the Grass Won't Pay No Mind' as: "An overlooked slice of top drawer quality material from Elvis. He sounds quite different in this tune. Different for the better, very relaxed and interested. This song as sung by Elvis makes me think of a hot summer day by a stream in the countryside with a beautiful girl in the long grass."

Recently the track was featured on the million-selling album, *If I Can Dream*, which paired Elvis with The UK-based Royal Philharmonic Orchestra. The new overdubs were recorded at London's Abbey Road Studios, famously home to the Beatles in the 1960s.

ANY DAY NOW

While 1968 saw Elvis bounce back as an amazing performer thanks to the NBC Comeback Special, it was early 1969 when Elvis the singer re-emerged, performing meaningful songs for the first time in years.

Memphis has been an important part of Elvis's life for so many reasons, including recording highlights. It was at the local Sun Studios that the young Elvis's career was launched on an unsuspecting 1950s record-buying public. The area also provided the backdrop for Elvis's major studio sessions of 1969 – this time at American Sound Studios. Any of the Elvis tracks recorded during those marathon sessions could have provided strong A-side single material. But for now let's take a look at a track that proved to be a great album song and a B-side – 'Any Day Now'.

The track was originally recorded by South Carolina R&B singer Chuck Jackson. It peaked at number 23 in the Billboard Hot 100 in 1962. It had been written that year by Burt Bacharach and Bob Hilliard. Bacharach went on to become a six-time Grammy Award winner and a three-time Academy Award winner. He's probably best known for his countless hits produced with Hal David. Bob Hilliard worked at the famous Tin Pan Alley, as well as enjoying success on Broadway. His talents also helped to provide hits like 'Our Day Will Come', 'Tower of Strength' and that novelty song 'Seven Little Girls'.

Next to record 'Any Day Now' was UK artist Alan Price. He'd originally enjoyed major success with the Animals. Who could forget 'House of the Rising Sun'? Price's version of 'Any Day Now', recorded in 1965, failed to chart.

Elvis recorded his take on the track on 20th February 1969. Presley had previously recorded at the American Sound Studio in January 1969. A further six sessions were then planned to run from 17th to 22nd February. On the same day he recorded 'Any Day Now', Elvis also laid down 'It Keeps Right on a-Hurtin'' and 'If I'm a Fool (For Loving You)'.

IF I'M A FOOL (FOR LOVING YOU)

Elvis's album career had its strange moments. At a time when the full-priced LPs like the fabulous *From Elvis in Memphis* were flying off the shelves in record stores around the world, songs from the same sessions were bizarrely being made available on budget albums.

The LP *Let's Be Friends* was released on RCA's Camden label in 1970 when Elvis had returned to the peak of his powers. It's an unusual album in that it features songs Elvis had recently recorded, including Bobby Darin's 'I'll Be There' and 'If I'm a Fool (For Loving You)'. The latter was track two on the budget album. It was recorded on 20th February 1969 during those now-legendary Memphis sessions.

The song was written by Stan Kesler, whose own career had also started at Sun Studios. It wasn't the first time Elvis had recorded songs from the pen of Kesler. While at Sun in the 1950s, the young rock and roll star had covered 'I'm Left,

You're Right, She's Gone' and 'I Forgot to Remember to Forget'. Kesler played on hits by Jerry Lee Lewis and Carl Perkins, two other stars on the Sun record label. He also tried his hand as a producer, with one of his biggest successes being the '60s party anthem 'Wooly Bully', which became a hit for Sam the Sham & the Pharaohs.

There are only nine tracks on the album *Let's Be Friends* but it's one of the strongest released for the budget market.

'If I'm a Fool (For Loving You)' is an underrated song that sees Elvis in tender country mood, backed by the same excellent Memphis musicians who appeared on tracks like 'In the Ghetto' and 'Don't Cry Daddy'.

IT KEEPS RIGHT ON A-HURTIN'

'It Keeps Right on a-Hurtin'' had already been a hit for its composer Johnny Tillotson when Elvis put his magnificent voice on the song during the hugely successful Memphis recording sessions. It was recorded on 20th February 1969 at American Sound Studios in Memphis. The song would be the penultimate track on side one of *From Elvis in Memphis*.

Tillotson had already enjoyed a UK number one and US number two with 'Poetry in Motion' in 1960. His original version of 'It Keeps Right on a-Hurtin'' reached number three in the US in 1962. However the song failed to repeat the UK success of 'Poetry in Motion' when it stalled at number 31. In fact the highest place Tillotson would see in the UK charts after 'Poetry in Motion' was number 24 with 'Send Me the Pillow You Dream On', a number 17 hit in the US.

The origins of 'It Keeps Right on a-Hurtin' are particularly sad. The young Tillotson wrote the song about his own father who had a terminal illness. Presley himself was no stranger to the pain of losing a parent, having lost his beloved mother Gladys in 1958. Some of his friends say the trauma of that tragic loss never left him. Maybe this is why he could relate to the song and gave a brilliant performance.

According to an interview with Johnny Tillotson carried out on the great website elvis.com.au, Elvis had known about 'It Keeps Right on a-Hurtin" since the song came out in the early 1960s. Tillotson said: "So when he went to Memphis to do *From Elvis in Memphis*, he just decided he wanted to do it. And 112 people recorded the song, and I love every one of them, but when I got the news that Elvis had recorded 'It Keeps Right on a-Hurtin', I was ecstatic. One of the nice things, when I'd be appearing in Las Vegas, for example, Joe Esposito, his right hand man, and sometimes Colonel Parker and all the guys, they would extend every courtesy to me and they would always tell Elvis 'Johnny's in the audience'."

Johnny Tillotson praised Elvis's passion for his music and his impeccable manners. He said: "I never saw anyone that had such joy and passion for music, and had such a good time, and didn't take himself terribly serious on stage. I think that's why so many of the men could relate to him as well, you know, as well as all the ladies. But he was also always so courteous. I would take friends up and he would all say 'Yes ma'am, no ma'am'. He gave my daughter, Kelly, one of the teddy bears. And one of my favourite treasures from Elvis is a signed picture that says 'To Johnny with love and respect, Elvis Presley'." You can read the full interview carried out by elvis.com.au at the following link: http://www.elvis.com.au/presley/interview-johnny-tillotson.shtml.

The song would earn Johnny Tillotson his first Grammy nomination in the Best Country and Western Recording category. Since Tillotson recorded the track more than 100 singers have tackled it.

ONLY THE STRONG SURVIVE

On 19th February 1969 Elvis was back in the recording studios at American Sound in Memphis to record a relatively new track, 'Only the Strong Survive'.

It had been recorded just the year before by one of the song's composers, Jerry Butler. Ironically just after Elvis had recorded it, the song was released as a single by Butler and became huge. It was the most successful single of Jerry Butler's career, reaching number four on the Billboard Hot 100 and peaking at number one for two weeks on the Billboard Black Singles Chart, in March and

TWO

BACK ON STAGE – LIVE HIGHLIGHTS, 1969–1974

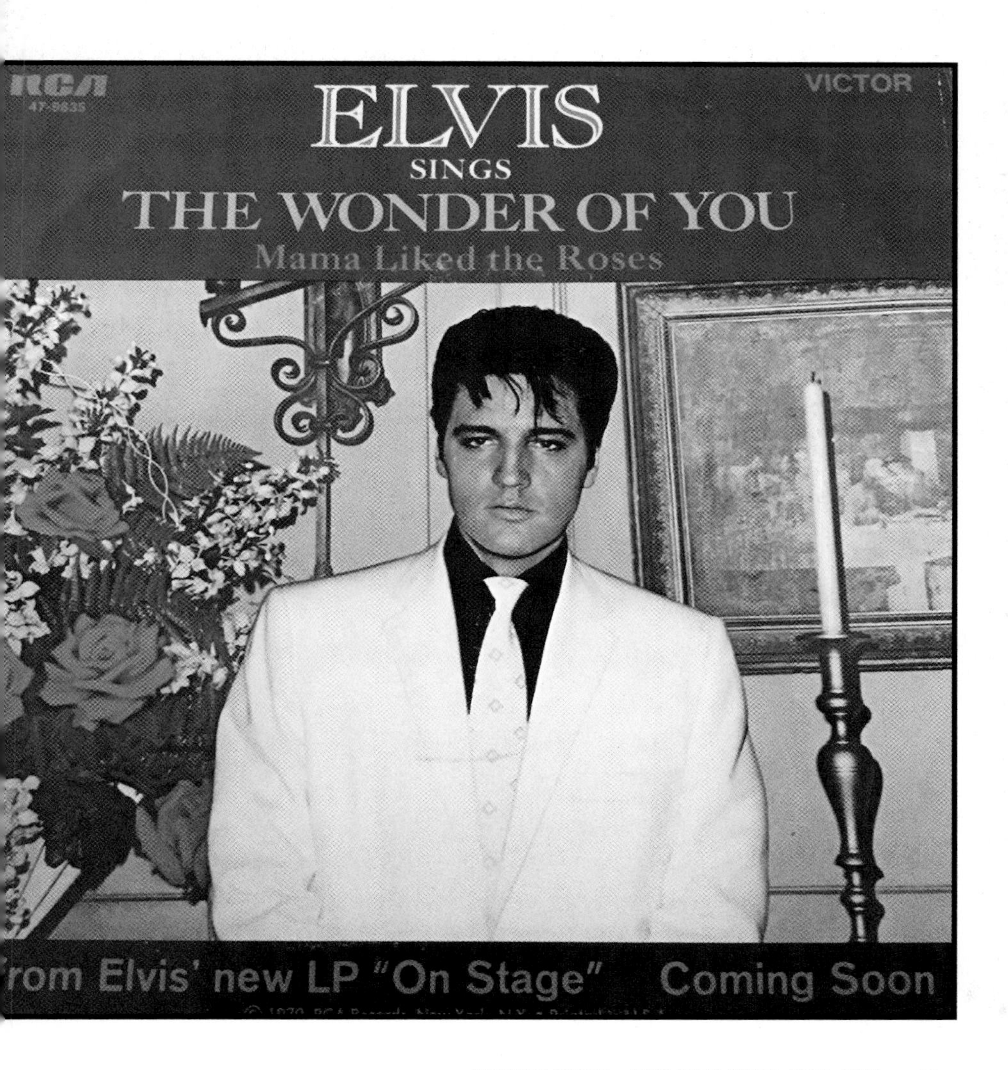

22nd–26th August 1969, International Hotel, Las Vegas

I CAN'T STOP LOVING YOU

Even though his version was a cover, this song will forever be associated with Ray Charles.

'I Can't Stop Loving You' was written and originally recorded by the country singer Don Gibson on 30th December 1957. Released on RCA records in 1958 it became a double A-side smash, being paired with 'Oh, Lonesome Me'. Gibson became known as the 'Sad Poet'. He gained the nickname because of his tendency to compose songs about lost love and loneliness, including 'Don't Tell Me Your Troubles', 'Sea of Heartbreak', 'Lonesome Number One' and 'I Can Mend Your Broken Heart'. In the late '60s, Gibson joined forces with singer Dottie West, which produced hits like 'Rings of Gold' and 'There's a Story Goin' Round'.

In the early '60s, R&B giant Ray Charles turned his hand to country music, recording his version of 'I Can't Stop Loving You'. The song was released as part of Charles' *Modern Sounds in Country and Western Music*. It became a huge hit when it was released as a single, reaching number one on the Billboard Hot 100 in 1962 where it remained for five weeks. In the UK, the track enjoyed a two-week stay at number one.

Kitty Wells recorded the track before Ray Charles and so did the great Roy Orbison.

Elvis performed the song live from 1969 right through to his final tours in 1977. His version appeared on the RCA release *Elvis in Person at the International Hotel, Las Vegas, Nevada* when RCA captured the King in fine form between 24th and 26th August 1969.

MY BABE

Elvis may have been the King of Rock and Roll but with his amazing talent he was able to create expert performances in so many other genres: gospel, country, pop, ballads, folk – and after growing up in Tupelo and Memphis, the boy could really sing the blues, as he proved on many stand-out performances. It is a shame that Elvis never created a pure R&B concept album, as he had done with country and gospel LPs.

'My Babe' was tackled by Elvis on his return to live performances, but by then a number of other people had recorded the song.

It was written by Willie Dixon for Little Walter. Dixon's songs have been recorded by several artists over the years. His most famous compositions include 'Hoochie Coochie Man', 'I Just Want to Make Love to You', 'Little Red Rooster' and 'You Can't Judge a Book by the Cover'. The songs were performed by the likes of Muddy Waters, Howlin' Wolf, Etta James and Bo Diddley. They were released on Chess Records or its sister label Checker Records.

'My Babe' was first released in 1955 by Little Walter, a blues singer and harmonica virtuoso, one of the most influential harmonica improvisers of the late twentieth century. He had made his first recording, 'I Just Keep Loving You', in 1947 for a local label, Ora Nelle. Soon he was working with the likes of Muddy Waters. During the 1950s, Little Walter successfully sent 14 songs to the top 10 on the R&B charts, including 'Mean Old World', 'You Better Watch Yourself' and 'My Babe'. Although the '50s had brought him great success, the following decade wasn't kind and Little Walter succumbed to alcoholism and inactivity. In 1968, he was involved in a street fight and later died, at age 37, from head injuries.

The song 'My Babe' became a favourite with artists who came after Little Walter's main chart success including the Everly Brothers, Ricky Nelson and Gene Vincent, who recorded the song as 'My Baby Don't 'Low'.

On 25th August 1969, RCA recorded several concerts at the International Hotel in Vegas, marking Elvis's return to live performance. The results of the recordings can be heard on *From Memphis to Vegas/From Vegas to Memphis*, released in October 1969.

Elvis's recording of 'My Babe' was one of the first examples of the TCB band working together live on stage. The legendary musicians included James

Burton and John Wilkinson on electric guitar, Jerry Scheff on bass and Ronnie Tutt providing the driving force on the drums.

RUNAWAY

When Elvis returned to Vegas, it became *the* ticket in town and all the big stars wanted to make sure they were seen there including the likes of Frank Sinatra, Sammy Davis Jnr, Tom Jones and Elvis's co-star in *G.I. Blues*, Juliet Prowse. In 1969 Elvis performed his first show at the International to a full house and he went on to perform regular engagements at the huge complex for seven years – a total of 837 consecutive sold-out performances in front of 2.5 million people.

By February 1970, the onstage nerves were disappearing and Elvis's confidence was building with every performance. RCA was there to record Elvis's on stage highlights for a new album in 1970. The recordings were made chiefly between 17th and 19th February 1970 at the International Hotel, Paradise, Nevada. There were only 10 tracks on the LP and a couple of those were from a previous engagement in 1969.

'Runaway' was one of those tracks and one night Del Shannon was in the crowd to hear Elvis perform the cover. The Facebook group 'All Things Del Shannon' refers to an interview that Shannon gave to Bob Costas in 1989. He said: "When I was producing Brian Hyland, Elvis's office called and said 'We're up in Las Vegas with Elvis and he's doing "Runaway" in his act and he would like you to be his guest'. So we went up there and Elvis said 'I'd like to introduce Del, are you out there?!' and the spotlight couldn't find where I was sitting. Then Brian Hyland who is a really shy guy got up in the middle of all these people and yelled out 'He's over here!!!!!' and he pointed down at me and I took a bow. We did talk with Elvis for a couple of hours after the show and he wasn't drunk or bombed or anything, I think I was much more drunk. Elvis Presley was the best looking man I've ever seen in my life. Maybe it was his make up, I dunno, but seeing him in person was amazing."

Shannon had scored a worldwide hit with 'Runaway'. The producers sped up the recording. 'Runaway' was released in February 1961 and was immediately successful. On 10th April of that year, Shannon appeared on Dick Clark's *American Bandstand*, which helped to catapult it to the number one spot on the Billboard charts where it remained for four weeks. When Del Shannon was interviewed by David Letterman in 1986, he said that at its height 'Runaway' was selling as many as 80,000 singles per day!

Among others covering the song were the Beach Boys in 1965 – the Hawthorne California band recorded a live version of 'Runaway' in Chicago. However, it didn't get released until 2013 when it appeared on the *Made in California* box set. John Mayall included a cover of this song on his first album, the live *John Mayall Plays John Mayall* (Decca LK 4680). In 1977, Bonnie Raitt included a bluesy version of the song on her album *Sweet Forgiveness*. Also released as a single, it reached number 57 on the U.S. Billboard Hot 100. Even Del Shannon himself re-recorded the song in 1967 as 'Runaway '67' but that version failed to do anything in the charts.

WORDS

The song 'Words' has been covered by many artists over the years, ranging from its writers, the Bee Gees, to Irish boyband Boyzone who in 1996 took the song to number one in the UK charts. 'Words' was the Bee Gees' third UK top-10 hit, reaching number eight, and in a UK television special on ITV in December 2011 it was voted fourth in the Nation's Favourite Bee Gees Song.

Bee Gee Barry Gibb said in an archive interview: "'Words' was written by me at Adams Row when I was staying at Robert Stigwood's place. A lot of people began to cover that song, so over the years it's become a bit like 'To Love Somebody'. I didn't know it wasn't on an album – that's strange how it used to work in those days. We used to bang singles out one after another." Robin Gibb said: "'Words' reflects a mood. It was written after an argument. Barry had been arguing with someone, I had been arguing with someone, and happened to be in the same mood. They were just words. That is what the song is all about; words can make you happy or words can make you sad".

The song was originally written for UK singer Cliff Richard, but he never got round to recording it as he wasn't making an album at the time. Rather than wasting the song, the Bee Gees decided to record it themselves in 1967. Barry Gibb said: "Robin and I were in the studios at nine o'clock in the morning, and Robin kept on falling asleep over the piano. I wanted him to write the piano part of the song and play it because I'm not much of a pianist, but he just couldn't keep his eyes open, so I ended up doing it myself".

When Bee Gee Maurice Gibb heard Elvis was doing their song back in 1969, he said: "Elvis has done the song just as I imagined he would. I like it because it's more uptempo and rock 'n' roll-ish."

Elvis was recorded live in concert at the International Hotel by RCA on 25th August and 'Words' was one of the songs that made it onto the album *Elvis in Person at the International Hotel, Las Vegas, Nevada*, also known as *Elvis from Memphis to Vegas.*

16th–19th February 1970 – International Hotel, Las Vegas

POLK SALAD ANNIE

Tony Joe White wrote and performed our next track, 'Polk Salad Annie'. The song describes the lifestyle of a poor rural Southern girl and her family. Traditionally, the term to describe the type of food highlighted in the song is polk or poke sallet, a cooked greens dish made from polk weed. Now before you go rushing out to buy some, this isn't something you will find in your local stores. The polk weed is actually toxic in its raw state. If you were ever to eat this, you would need to boil it several times before consuming.

White explains in the song's folksy introduction that polk is "a plant that grows out in the woods and the fields, and it looks something like a turnip green." He then introduces Annie, a woman who made polk salad for her family, since that's all they could afford to eat.

White grew up in Oak Grove, Louisiana near the Mississippi River and wrote what he called 'swamp songs' about the folks from the area. In an interview published on songfacts.com, White said: "Annie, she could have been one of maybe three or four girls along that river there because all the girls were kinda tomboys." White has even admitted he'd eaten what he was writing about. He said: "I ate a bunch of it growing up on the cotton farm. It grows wild, and you pick it a certain time during the year, and you boil it and cook it like greens. My mother said it had a lot of iron in it and stuff for us kids, so it was something that tasted real good to me back then. I still eat some every spring."

Elvis Presley performed the track at many of his 1970s concerts. A performance on 18th February 1970 at the International Hotel in Las Vegas was included on his live album *On Stage*. Tony Joe White admitted that it was "a real thrill" that Elvis recorded 'Polk Salad Annie', since White had performed a lot of Elvis songs when he first started out.

According to songfacts.com, Elvis arranged for White, who was living in Memphis at the time, to fly to Vegas so he could be in the audience for the concerts that were compiled into *On Stage*. White may have hung out with Elvis back stage and enjoyed playing instruments together but they didn't perform the song together on stage. White did however perform a version in a duet with Johnny Cash on the 8th April 1970 edition of *The Johnny Cash Show*. This performance has been released on a DVD entitled *The Best of the Johnny Cash Show*.

SWEET CAROLINE

Neil Diamond has enjoyed several decades as a top recording artist, although his career started with him writing songs for others. One of his earliest successes as a singer–songwriter was 'Sweet Caroline'.

It had long been thought that 'Sweet Caroline' was an ode to the young daughter of the late US President, John F. Kennedy. In recent years, Neil Diamond revealed the true inspiration behind the 1969 song was his then wife Marcia Murphey – but the name didn't quite fit. In an archive interview, Diamond explained he knew of Caroline Kennedy, then aged 11, at the time, but said: "I was writing a song in Memphis, Tennessee, for a session. I needed a three-syllable name. The song was about my wife at the time – her name was Marcia – and I couldn't get a 'Marcia' rhyme. Sweet Caroline – yes! That was it. And that's what it's been."

However in 2007, Diamond, who was born in Brooklyn, New York, performed the song to Miss Kennedy at her 50th birthday celebrations.

Neil Diamond officially released the track on 16th September 1969. It was arranged by Charles Calello and recorded at American Sound Studio in Memphis, Tennessee, where Elvis recorded some of his greatest songs. 'Sweet Caroline' reached number four on the Billboard chart and eventually went platinum for sales of one-million singles. In the autumn of 1969, Diamond performed 'Sweet Caroline' on several television shows. It later reached number eight on the UK singles chart in 1971.

Countless artists have recorded the track over the years, including Frank Sinatra, Roy Orbison and the soul legends, the Drifters.

Elvis's version of 'Sweet Caroline' was performed at a faster tempo then Diamond's original. Presley was captured live on stage on 18th February 1970 performing his version. The song was included on the album *On Stage*.

THE WONDER OF YOU

This track remains both a favourite with fans and also a karaoke favourite. It put Elvis back at the top of the UK charts as well as selling well in several other countries.

'The Wonder of You' was written by singer and composer Baker Knight. During his career he wrote more than 800 songs. Knight's tracks were recorded by several artists including Hank Williams Jr and Hank Snow. He was a major contributor to the careers of Ricky Nelson and Dean Martin. Nelson recorded 14 of Baker Knight's songs and Martin put his unforgettable style to 12 of his tracks.

In an archive interview, Baker Knight explained how he was recommended to Ricky Nelson by Sharon Sheeley, who had been the long-term girlfriend of Eddie Cochran. Knight said: "I was surprised when Ricky Nelson came knocking at my door. He told me that he had heard from Sharon that I had some songs he might like. So I picked up my guitar and went to work." Baker said he played the teen idol what he thought were his best numbers. However, Nelson offered no response. A few minutes later the singer thanked him and left.

Knight thought he had blown his chances, but just two hours later there was another knock on the door. Standing there was Nelson's attorney armed with a publishing contract and an advance cheque for $2,000. A few months later, Nelson scored a major hit with Knight's 'Lonesome Town'. Ricky went on to enjoy success with other songs like 'I Got a Feeling', 'Never be Anyone Else but You' and 'Sweeter than You', all penned by Knight.

It was while Baker Knight was in hospital recovering from an ulcer that he started to write what would become 'The Wonder of You'. In past interviews Knight has said: "I guess I was on a spiritual search, and while I was laying in my hospital bed, I just started writing a song, trying to sort out my relationship with God. In truth, the song was very poorly put together at that point, but it was a prayer of thanks for God not giving up on me. I finished it when I went back to L.A."

The first person to record the song was Vince Edwards, an actor who played the lead in the TV show *Ben Casey*. He didn't score a hit with the song. Soon after, Ray Peterson recorded the track. He'd just landed a contract with RCA Victor. Peterson's version of 'The Wonder of You' peaked at number 25 on Billboard's Hot 100 chart. He enjoyed further success with his next single 'Tell Laura I Love Her'.

Elvis fell in love with Peterson's version of 'The Wonder of You' long before he himself recorded it. He even invited Peterson onto a movie set to talk about the song. As Knight recalled: "Elvis took Ray out to lunch, almost asking permission to cut the number." Permission was naturally granted over lunch, but it was another decade before Elvis would record the song.

In an old interview, Knight recalled receiving a very important phone call. He said: "I had just gotten a divorce, was living in an apartment in Ventura. I was always a night person and slept during the day. Anyway, the phone rang 7:30 in the morning. I couldn't imagine who would be calling me at that time. On the line was one of the folks in Elvis's band, Glen Hardin. He asked me if I could give him the words to 'The Wonder of You'. Elvis needed them because he had decided to do the song on stage that very night." In the next few minutes, the lyrics were passed on down a phone line. Elvis received them and spent the day learning the words. He then sang the song on stage that very night – in February 1970. How's that for speedy!

The song was released as a single on 20th April 1970, backed by the song 'Mama Liked the Roses'. In the United States, both songs charted at number nine in the spring of 1970. 'The Wonder of You' was one of his most successful records in the UK ever, topping the UK singles chart for six weeks in the summer of 1970. It also stayed at number one in the Irish charts for three weeks that same year. 'The Wonder of You' would enjoy further success as the title of the second album produced with Elvis and the Royal Philharmonic Orchestra. Released in October 2016, the album went straight to the top of the UK charts. 'The Wonder of You' was then released as a single in December 2016, with a video featuring the world-famous supermodel Kate Moss. A source was quoted in UK newspapers as saying: "Kate is a huge Elvis fan and the opportunity was simply too good to turn down."

13th–15th August 1970 – International Hotel, Las Vegas

I JUST CAN'T HELP BELIEVIN'

Elvis Presley spent the summer of 1969 and February of 1970 in Las Vegas, playing well over 50 shows at the International Hotel. On 14th July 1970 he went to the MGM lot in Culver City, California, to start rehearsals for his third run, scheduled to begin on 10th August and be filmed for a new documentary, *Elvis: That's the Way It Is*.

One of the great songs that came from the third season in Vegas was 'I Just Can't Help Believin''. The track was written by Barry Mann and Cynthia Weil. The husband-and-wife team created many unforgettable songs, winning several Grammy Awards as well as Academy Award nominations for their compositions for film. As their Rock & Roll Hall of Fame biography puts it: "From epic ballads ('On Broadway', 'You've Lost That Lovin' Feelin'') to outright rockers ('Kicks', 'We've Gotta Get Out of This Place') they placed an emphasis on meaningful lyrics in their song writing. With Weil writing the words and Mann the music, they came up with a number of songs that addressed such serious subjects like economic divides ('Uptown') and the difficult reality of making it in the big city ('On Broadway'). 'We Gotta Get Out of This Place' became an anthem for the Vietnam soldiers, anti-war protesters and young people who viewed it as an anthem of greater opportunities."

'I Just Can't Help Believin'' was recorded by B.J. Thomas and became a big hit for him in 1970, reaching number nine on the Billboard Hot 100 singles chart. It gained further success, enjoying one week at number one on the easy listening chart. Others beating Elvis to the song recordings-wise included Bobby Vee, who released it on his 1969 *Gates, Grills and Railings* LP. Bobby Doyle released it as a single in 1969 on the Warner Brothers label. And how about this: the song was even recorded by Leonard Nimoy in his 1969 album *The Touch of Leonard Nimoy*. Yes, we know you really want to hear it as well... Feel free to do a Google search. It is out there!

Elvis's classic version of 'I Just Can't Help Believin'' also enjoyed chart success. It was released as a single in the UK in November 1971, finally peaking at number six. It enjoyed further success in the charts in Germany and Spain, with the B-side 'How the Web Was Woven'.

PATCH IT UP

Next a show-stopping moment from Elvis's return to the live stage, which was captured on camera for the silver screen – 'Patch It Up'.

The track was written by Eddie Rabbitt and Rory Bourke. Rabbitt began his career as a songwriter. As well as 'Patch It Up', he wrote 'Kentucky Rain', which Elvis also recorded. Later on in the 1970s, Rabbitt put his own voice on his songs including 'Every Which Way but Loose' from the film of the same name starring Clint Eastwood (although the star of the show was arguably Clyde the orang-utan). He also enjoyed success with 'I Love a Rainy Night'. Rory Bourke enjoyed success when his songs were recorded by the likes of Olivia Newton John and Lynn Anderson. His biggest success was with a song he co-wrote for Charlie Rich, 'The Most Beautiful Girl', which became a huge smash in the country and pop charts.

Back to 'Patch It Up'. Presley's version came from the Elvis Summer Festival starting on 10th August 1970. The performance was filmed for the MGM movie *That's the Way It Is*. It produced a soundtrack LP that was the first soundtrack long player Elvis had released since the movie *Speedway*. The version of 'Patch It Up' that appears on the soundtrack LP was recorded on 12th August 1970. It's a powerful four-minute track that bounces out of your speakers.

Elvis is in great control vocally and certainly owns the stage in the filmed version of the track. You can almost visualise Elvis performing the track: arms flying, legs shaking and vocals soaring as he thrills his audience. Check out the footage on the *That's the Way It Is* DVD or see a clip on YouTube. It shows just how brilliant a visual performer Elvis was.

YOU'VE LOST THAT LOVIN' FEELIN'

Made famous by the Righteous Brothers, here's a classic that Elvis covered during his prolific recording period of 1969–71.

The husband-and-wife song-writing team of Barry Mann and Cynthia Weil wrote this song at the request of Phil Spector, who was looking for a hit for an act he had just signed to his Philles label: the Righteous Brothers. The duo, Bill Medley and Bobby Hatfield, had enjoyed minor success before signing with Spector.

Mann and Weil apparently gained their inspiration for 'You've Lost that Lovin' Feelin'' from the Motown classic 'Baby I Need Your Loving', which had been a hit for the Four Tops. Uncertain of a hit-making title for the song, the composers gave it the working title 'You've Lost that Lovin' Feelin''. However, the songwriters didn't need to think of a better title as Spector loved it. The song went to number one for the Righteous Brothers – a first-ever number one for Mann and Weil.

According to the website songfacts.com, the opening line, "You never close your eyes any more when I kiss your lips," was inspired by the Paris Sisters song 'I Love How You Love Me', which begins, "I love how your eyes close whenever you kiss me."

Spector put the time on the single's label as 3:05 so that radio stations would play it. The actual length is 3:50 but this was a period when all songs had to be short. By the time the radio producers had worked out the trick, the song had already become a massive hit!

'You've Lost that Lovin' Feelin'' has been covered by numerous artists. A 1965 hit version by Cilla Black reached number two in the UK singles chart. Dionne Warwick took her version to number 16 on the Billboard Hot 100 chart in 1969. A 1971 duet version by singers Roberta Flack and Donny Hathaway peaked at number 30 on the Billboard R&B singles chart. Long John Baldry charted at number two in Australia with his 1979 remake and a 1980 version by Hall and Oates reached number 12 on the US Hot 100.

Elvis's version of 'You've Lost that Lovin' Feelin'' was captured on film for *That's the Way It Is*. The film shows the song's dramatic opening, with Elvis resplendent in a white jumpsuit, with his back to the audience and the spotlight showing just the back of his head and shoulders when he starts the song. This continues for almost a minute until the chorus when Elvis dramatically spins around to face the crowd. He always was a great performer! The film and its soundtrack are still available to buy and are essential viewing and listening for Elvis fans. They show Elvis could still command the stage as he entered his third decade as a recording artist.

10th June 1972 – Madison Square Garden, New York

NEVER BEEN TO SPAIN

Before *Aloha*, there was another major success on stage for Elvis. He took New York by storm when he performed all-sold-out shows at Madison Square Garden. We'll take a more in-depth look at that concert in a future edition, but for now let's take a track from that successful run of concerts, which culminated in a best-selling album.

'Never Been to Spain' was a contemporary track for Elvis to record. Written by Hoyt Axton and released by Three Dog Night at the end of 1971, it became a huge hit for the band. Composer Hoyt Axton first became known in the early 1960s as a folk singer on the West Coast. He also became famous for his song-writing, composing tracks like 'Joy to the World', 'The Pusher', 'No No Song', 'Greenback Dollar', 'Della and the Dealer' and, of course, 'Never Been to Spain'.

But how did Three Dog Night get their name? Well, the official commentary included in the CD set *Celebrate: The Three Dog Night Story, 1964–1975* reveals that vocalist Danny Hutton's girlfriend, actress June Fairchild (best known as the 'Ajax Lady' from the Cheech and Chong movie *Up in Smoke*) suggested the name. It came about after she had read an article about indigenous Australians, in which it was explained that on cold nights they would customarily sleep in a hole in the ground while embracing a dingo (feral dog). The colder the night, the more dogs. If it was freezing, it became known as a 'three dog night'.

On the songbase on elvisnews.com, fans comment on Elvis's countless performances. Visit the website here: http://www.elvisnews.com. Of 'Never Been to Spain', TCB1974 said: "This is a powerhouse performance by our man and one of the good songs that were added to his live repertoire. The text seems to be written by someone who was psychedelic but for some reason it works and is a great song. Four stars from me." And Jack409 said: "While I'm a fan of Three Dog Night, the King's version of 'Never Been to Spain' outclasses theirs."

THE IMPOSSIBLE DREAM

In Las Vegas in 1971, Elvis introduced his version of 'The Impossible Dream' for the first time. On some nights it even replaced 'Can't Help Falling in Love' as the closing song – it was very unusual for Elvis to end his concerts with anything but the classic, 'Blue Hawaii'. The best-known version of 'The

Impossible Dream' comes from Elvis's hugely successful shows at New York's Madison Square Garden.

Often subtitled 'The Quest', 'The Impossible Dream' was composed by Mitch Leigh, with lyrics written by Joe Darion. The song became popular when it was included in the 1965 Broadway musical *Man of La Mancha*. It was also used in the film version starring Peter O'Toole, which came out in 1972.

The song's composer Mitch Leigh began his career as a jazz musician. He earned additional money by writing commercials for radio and television. In the mid-1960s, he joined forces with lyricist Joe Darion and writer Dale Wasserman to produce a musical version of a TV play the latter had written in the late 1950s called *I, Don Quixote*. The musical became *Man of La Mancha*. It opened on Broadway and enjoyed a hugely successful run of 2,328 performances. Mitch Leigh was awarded a Tony Award for his work on *Man of La Mancha* and received an award from the Songwriter's Hall of Fame for 'The Impossible Dream'.

The first version of the song released was in 1965, featuring Richard Kiley, on the original Broadway cast album of *Man of La Mancha*. The following year Ol' Blue Eyes himself, Frank Sinatra, included the track on his album *That's Life*. In 1967, Motown stars, the Temptations, featured a version on their release *The Temptations in a Mellow Mood*. Jack Jones, Scott Walker, Andy Williams, Cher, the Smothers Brothers and Roberta Flack all recorded versions of the song before Elvis started featuring it in his live performances. Even Hammer Horror movie king Christopher Lee recorded a version on his album *Revelation*... and indeed it was!

1973 – Honolulu International Center Arena, Hawaii – Aloha from Hawaii

AN AMERICAN TRILOGY

We visit now the global success that was the *Aloha from Hawaii* show. This live recording brings together three nineteenth-century American songs performed by the ultimate American legend: 'An American Trilogy' performed by Elvis.

'An American Trilogy' blends 'Dixie', 'Battle Hymn of the Republic' and 'All My Trials'. 'Dixie' had originally been written as a song in its own right back in 1859. It was written by Dan Emmett. It was apparently first performed in South Carolina in December 1860. The words for 'Battle Hymn of the Republic' can be traced back to the Willward Hotel in Washington DC. It was written by Julia Ward Howe. A friend had suggested she write new words to go with an already existing tune: 'John Brown's Body'. The words were composed in December 1861. The composer of 'All My Trials' isn't known. Before Elvis, the Kingston Trio recorded the song in 1959.

This fabulous medley of songs was first brought together by Mickey Newbury. He became an acclaimed songwriter during the 1960s, writing hits for Don Gibson and Kenny Rogers. He enjoyed a top-30 hit with 'An American Trilogy' in 1972. Soon after, Elvis performed his take on the medley, which has become the definitive version. Newbury was inducted into the Nashville Songwriter's Hall of Fame in 1980. Over a 30-year period he recorded 15 albums. His final one was a mail-order-only album in 1996 called *Lulled by the Moonlight*. Kris Kristofferson once said of Mickey Newbury: "I learned more about song writing from him than any other writer. He was my hero and still is."

Elvis began to feature 'An American Trilogy' heavily in his concerts from 1972. He can be seen singing it in the movie *Elvis on Tour*. It appeared on the Madison Square Garden album later in 1972. 'Trilogy' could then be seen around the world just a few months later thanks to the *Aloha* show at the start of 1973.

'An American Trilogy' was released as a single by RCA backed by 'The First Time Ever I Saw Your Face'. In the UK the song peaked at number eight. In 2007 when several Elvis singles were re-released, it made number 12. In the US, surprisingly it didn't fare as well, making only the lower regions of the Billboard Hot 100. It fared better in the easy listening charts, reaching number 31.

The official single release was a version recorded in Las Vegas in February 1972. The flute player on the official single release was Jimmy Mulidore. He had moved to Las Vegas in 1957 to pursue a career in music. He soon started working with some of the biggest stars in the business, including Frank Sinatra,

Dean Martin, Sammy Davis Jr and Lena Horne. His studio performances can be heard on albums by Sinatra, Nat King Cole, Barbra Streisand, Dino and many more. Another Elvis link for Jimmy Mulidore is that he built up a close relationship with Ann Margret, conducting for her several times throughout her career. Ann was the unforgettable co-star in the Elvis movie *Viva Las Vegas*. The two became close friends and remained so until Presley's death in 1977.

In a *Rolling Stone* magazine interview in 2015, Priscilla Presley said of 'Trilogy': "I was driving down Sunset Boulevard and I heard Mickey Newbury's version. I made a U-turn and went back to the house. I said to Elvis there's a song you really should listen to. He just sat there at the desk. He put his head down and kind of nodded to it. He closed his eyes and said 'Damn, damn good song'. And the next thing I know we're back in Vegas and he ate it up and spit it out." Soon after he made sure the whole world knew about the medley when he performed it to his global audience in the *Aloha* show.

I'LL REMEMBER YOU

As well as attracting a global audience, the *Aloha from Hawaii* show raised thousands and thousands of dollars for charity, specifically the Kui Lee Cancer Fund. Kui Lee was a singer songwriter who achieved great success in his short life. He initially became the 1960s golden boy artist of Hawaii. Lee then achieved wider success when Don Ho began performing and recording Lee's compositions. Ho always made a point of promoting Kui Lee whenever he performed his material.

Lee achieved international fame towards the end of his life. *The Extraordinary Kui Lee* was the only album released during his lifetime. Highlights from that album included 'Days of My Youth' and 'I'll Remember You' – the latter of which Elvis recorded both in the studio and as a live track during his Hawaiian show in January 1973.

Kui Lee was born in Shanghai, China on 31st July 1932. His parents moved to Hawaii when he was five. Since his parents were entertainers, he also entered the entertainment world of Hawaii. Lee later went to New York where he met his wife, Nani Naone. They had four children together before the Lees returned to

Hawaii in the early 1960s. In Hawaii, Lee learned to sing and compose songs and started his own band, which played some of the famous nightspots of Hawaii, including the Waikiki Shell.

Kui Lee was just 34 years old when he died from lymph gland cancer. The Kui Lee Cancer Fund had been created shortly before Elvis's huge concert by Hawaii veteran newspaper columnist, Eddie Sherman. Tickets for Elvis's satellite show could only be obtained by making a donation to the Kui Lee Cancer Fund. Tickets for the dress rehearsal, which later became known as the 'Alternative Aloha', went on sale after the main show sold out.

Not only was the *Aloha* concert a huge success for Elvis, the Kui Lee Cancer Fund received a much larger cheque than they had expected. The total earnings of the concert were $75,000. The money was donated to the Kui Lee Cancer Fund. The original estimate had been around $25,000. Elvis and Colonel Tom Parker contributed to the money raised. They each paid for their own $100 ticket.

Today there is a statue of Elvis outside the Neal Blaisdell Center, the present name for the Honolulu International Center Arena, where Elvis had performed *Aloha from Hawaii.* There is a plaque at the bottom which says: "Elvis Aloha From Hawaii. The World's first satellite TV concert. Jan 14th, 1973. With supreme talent and sincere humility, Elvis Presley made his gift the world's. Thank you, thank you very much".

I'M SO LONESOME I COULD CRY

Now a song Elvis introduced as "probably the saddest song I've ever heard", 'I'm So Lonesome I Could Cry'. Elvis sang the track during his *Aloha* satellite show, but its roots go way back to the 1940s when it was written and recorded by country legend Hank Williams. His initial thought was that the words could be spoken over music rather than sung.

The song is all about loneliness and is believed to have been based on Hank's thoughts about his often-difficult relationship with his wife, Audrey Sheppard. In the book, *Hank Williams: A Biography*, author Colin Escott says that the despair in Williams' voice can also be heard in the song's backing. Escott says: "Jerry Byrd played a solo of unusual simplicity, subtly adjusting tone and volume. Hank sang with unshakable conviction." It was released as the B-side to the ironically jovial 'My Bucket's Got a Hole in It'. At the time, up-tempo numbers were seen as more appropriate for the often lucrative jukebox trade in the 1940s and early '50s.

Singer k.d. lang said in an archive interview: "I think 'I'm So Lonesome I Could Cry' is one of the most classic American songs ever written." *Rolling Stone* magazine said: "In tracks like 'I'm So Lonesome I Could Cry' Williams expressed intense personal emotions with country's traditional plainspoken directness, a then revolutionary approach that has come to define the genre…"

In 1966 B.J. Thomas scored a number-eight Billboard pop singles hit with his version of the song. After Leon Russell and Terry Bradshaw had hits with the track, Jerry Lee Lewis recorded his own take in 1982. However, Andy Williams, Cousin Roy, Helen Merrill, Ronnie Hawkins, Johnny Cash, Tab Hunter, Mark Dinning, Diana Trask, Ferlin Husky, Connie Stevens, Johnny Tillotson, Dean Martin, Hank Williams Jr, Hank Locklin, Del Shannon and countless others recorded the song before Elvis performed his version in January 1973 for his global audience.

IT'S OVER

Speaking of *Aloha*, here is another show-stopping moment from that concert called 'It's Over'

'It's Over' is not to be confused with the equally powerful song by Roy Orbison. The track Elvis performed in Hawaii in 1973 was the song that was written by Jimmie Rodgers. He scored a hit with the track in 1966, but Rodgers' career had started in the previous decade.

In the summer of 1957, Jimmie Rodgers had recorded a song called 'Honeycomb'. The tune was Rodgers' biggest hit, staying on the top of the charts for four weeks and clocking up sales of more than one-million copies, earning Rodgers a gold disc. The following year, he had a number of other hits enjoying top-10 success. These include: 'Kisses Sweeter than Wine', 'Oh-Oh, I'm Falling in Love Again' and 'Are You Really Mine'. His biggest hit in the UK was 'English Country Garden', which reached number five in the chart in June 1962. That seemed to be it, chart-wise, for Rodgers until 1966 when he returned to the charts with 'It's Over'.

On 1st December 1967, Jimmie Rodgers suffered traumatic head injuries after the car he was driving was stopped by an off-duty police officer near the San Diego Freeway. The singer had a fractured skull and required several surgeries. Rodgers himself later said he had no specific memory of how he had been injured, but he did recall that he had seen blindingly bright lights from a car behind him. Years of recovery were to follow with only the occasional recording and performance.

After years out of the mainstream spotlight, Jimmie Rodgers appeared in a 1999 video, *Rock & Roll Graffiti* by American Public Television. During the programme he admitted his injuries and illness meant that he could hardly sing. However, the great performer did manage to do his old hit 'Honeycomb'. Rodgers returned to his home in Washington in 2011 and 2012, performing to sell-out crowds.

Sandwiched between rock and roll classics like 'Johnny B. Goode' and 'Blue Suede Shoes', Elvis performed his rendition of 'It's Over' during the *Aloha* show. Other people to record the song include Eddy Arnold and Glen Campbell.

JOHNNY B. GOODE

Next a rock and roll classic. 'Johnny B. Goode' was written by the great Chuck Berry while he was on tour in 1958 in New Orleans. Berry himself says in interviews that the song is autobiographical: a poor boy from the deep South with little education who masters the electric guitar and becomes the leader of a rock and roll band. The truth is that Berry grew up in Saint Louis.

'Johnny B. Goode' was recorded in 1958 with a band that included the legendary bassist Willie Dixon. Berry may have turned up at gigs with back-up bands that he'd never seen or rehearsed with, but when it came to his studio recordings he insisted on the best. 'Johnny B. Goode' was produced by Leonard and Phil Chess who were behind the success of record label Chess Records. Berry's version of the song enjoyed 15 weeks on the American charts; however, it peaked at number eight.

Acts ranging from AC/DC to the Beatles and the Beach Boys, John Denver, Conway Twitty through to B.B. King and even Alvin and the Chipmunks have all recorded 'Johnny B. Goode'. According to an article in a 2007 edition of the *Guardian* newspaper, 'Johnny B. Goode' was "Probably the first song ever written about how much money a musician could make by playing the guitar [and] no song in the history of rock 'n' roll more jubilantly celebrates the downmarket socioeconomic roots of the genre." The newspaper highlighted the fact the song was also inserted into a capsule and blasted into outer space. You can't help but wonder what extra-terrestrials would make of this character called Johnny B. Goode! They must be rocking on some far-out planet…

Elvis's version of 'Johnny B. Goode' was taken at a frantic pace, coming in at around 100 seconds! It was included in the *Aloha from Hawaii* concert, sandwiched between two love songs ('Love Me' and 'It's Over') and proved Elvis could still rock out – and rightly so, with the likes of rock-and-roll guitarist James Burton by his side. Hold on to your hats when you listen to it as this song doesn't hang around.

STEAMROLLER BLUES

We're going all bluesy for another highlight from the *Aloha* show. 'Steamroller Blues' was written by James Taylor, appearing on his successful album *Sweet Baby James* in 1970. The song painted a humorous side to the singer–songwriter who has become well known for his deeply personal lyrics. With lines like: "I'm a steamroller baby, I'm bound to roll all over you", "I'm a napalm bomb for you, baby" and "I'm a churnin' urn of burnin' funk."

What was Taylor's reason for writing 'Steamroller Blues'? In an interview he revealed he had heard "one too many pretentious white blues bands" and he composed 'Steamroller' to mock them. This is further backed up by *Rolling*

Stone Album Guide critic, Mark Coleman, who says Taylor "effectively mocks the straining pomposity of then-current white bluesmen".

James Taylor has gone on to become a five-time Grammy Award winner. Among his other successes are selling more than 100 million records. His 1976 *Greatest Hits* album was awarded Diamond status and has gone on to sell in the millions. In fact, every album Taylor released from 1977 to 2006 sold over a million copies. In 2000, he was inducted into the Rock & Roll Hall of Fame.

Among those to record 'Steamroller Blues' are Billy Dean on his 1994 album *Fire in the Dark* and soul star Isaac Hayes, who sang the song on an episode of the never-to-be-forgotten 1980s TV show, *The A-Team*.

Elvis included 'Steamroller Blues' in his *Aloha* show and it is yet another classic moment from that unforgettable concert. Recently, the Royal Philharmonic Orchestra provided backing for the song on the 2015 Elvis album *If I Can Dream*. We'll look at that album in a later volume.

WELCOME TO MY WORLD

We stay in Hawaii in January 1973 for a country song from the *Aloha* show.

'Welcome to My World' had already become a well-known track by 1973, having been recorded by country legend Jim Reeves in 1962. 'Welcome to My World' was written by Ray Winkler and John Hathcock, and was recorded by many artists including Faron Young. Irish country stars also recorded the track including Daniel O' Donnell and the duo Foster and Allen. By the time Elvis featured the track in his global January 1973 show, it had already been covered by Dean Martin in 1965. Faron Young, Wilma Burgess and Ricky Nelson all did versions in 1966. Kitty Wells did the track in 1967 and Eddy Arnold covered the song in 1971.

The traditional love song took inspiration from the Bible for the bridge of the track with globally known lines like "Knock and the door will open; Seek and you will find."

Jim Reeves' version was released as a single in early 1964, and reached number two on the Billboard Hot Country singles chart that spring. The song would become one of Reeves's last major hits in his lifetime, as he was tragically killed in a plane crash on 31st July 1964.

As well as featuring in Elvis's *Aloha* concert, 'Welcome to My World' was also the title of a compilation album by Elvis that was released by RCA Records in early 1977, just months before his death. This album went on to be certified gold on 30th September 1977 and platinum on 14th January 1983 by the RIAA. According to *Elvis: The Illustrated Record* by Roy Carr and Mick Farren, all but one track on this album had been previously released. That one track is 'I Can't Stop Loving You', recorded during the afternoon performance at Madison Square Garden on 10th June 1972. The entire concert was later released on CD.

'Welcome to My World' was certified gold on 30th September 1977 and platinum on 14th January 1983. Although the '70s Elvis was represented on the album, one track, 'Your Cheatin' Heart', dated back to 1st February 1958.

WHAT NOW MY LOVE

And now, a show-stopping moment from a global success. In the press conference to announce the *Aloha from Hawaii* show, Elvis said the live shows were "my favourite part of the business." He also said it was hard to comprehend such a large audience. In a further press conference, in November 1972, in Hawaii, Elvis said he wanted the satellite show to be "pure entertainment. No messages, just try to make people happy."

'What Now My Love' was one of those moments of "pure entertainment". The melody comes from a French song called 'Et Maintenant' ('And Now'). Carl Sigman, who wrote several hits by putting English lyrics to foreign melodies, was called on to do the same with this one. His son Michael was interviewed about his father. In the archive interview he said: "Spurred by Beatlemania, recording artists started penning their own material the way the Beatles did. The need declined accordingly for Tin Pan Alley writers, who could only thrive by writing songs for others to record. Like his cohorts, Carl felt the effects of this change, but he refused to be left behind. He continued to prove his place in a parallel pop universe, as well as his adeptness with European tunes, including his most important foreign assignment to date. That assignment called for him to write a lyric to French composer Gilbert Becaud's 'Et Maintenant' ('And Now')." He continued: "Carl quickly came up with the English words 'What Now My Love', a rough translation of the French title, to go with the opening notes of the melody. But what he did with that 'translation' was wholly original. 'What Now My Love', a dramatic story of lost love and desperation, was, with 'Ebb Tide' and 'It's All in The Game', one of the songs that, for Carl, transcended craftsmanship into the realm of inspirational art."

According to the website americansongwriter.com: "Knowing great singers would always need great songs, he continued to create standards such as 'Ebb Tide', a hit in 1953 by Vic Damone, and more famously in 1965 for the Righteous Brothers – with monumental wall-of-sound production by Phil Spector. 'Shangri-La', co-written with Matt Malneck and Robert Maxwell, was a hit first for the Four Coins and again in 1969 for the Lettermen. Frank Sinatra recorded 15 of his songs and Elvis recorded Sigman's 'Fool', co-written with James Last." You can read more about Carl Sigman here: https://americansongwriter.com/2009/05/american-icons-carl-sigman/.

Famous conductor and arranger Nelson Riddle was brought in to produce an early album by Welsh superstar Shirley Bassey. The album, called *Let's Face the Music*, included Bassey's version of 'What Now My Love' that went on to be a huge hit for her, reaching the top five in the UK. Jane Morgan hit the top 30 in the US with her rendition and countless cover versions were to follow. Sonny and Cher did a hip, guitar-based rendition and even the Muppets featuring Miss Piggy did a version!

Elvis's take on 'What Now My Love' showed to a global audience that here was a man who could rise to immense challenges and tackle them with the greatest ease and professionalism. Recently it was one of the tracks featured on the UK number-one album that paired Elvis with the Royal Philharmonic Orchestra.

Carl Sigman's son, Michael, recalled a funny moment on a golf course many years ago. He said: "One time a golf partner asked Dad to name some of

THREE

JUNE 1970 – RCA STUDIOS IN NASHVILLE

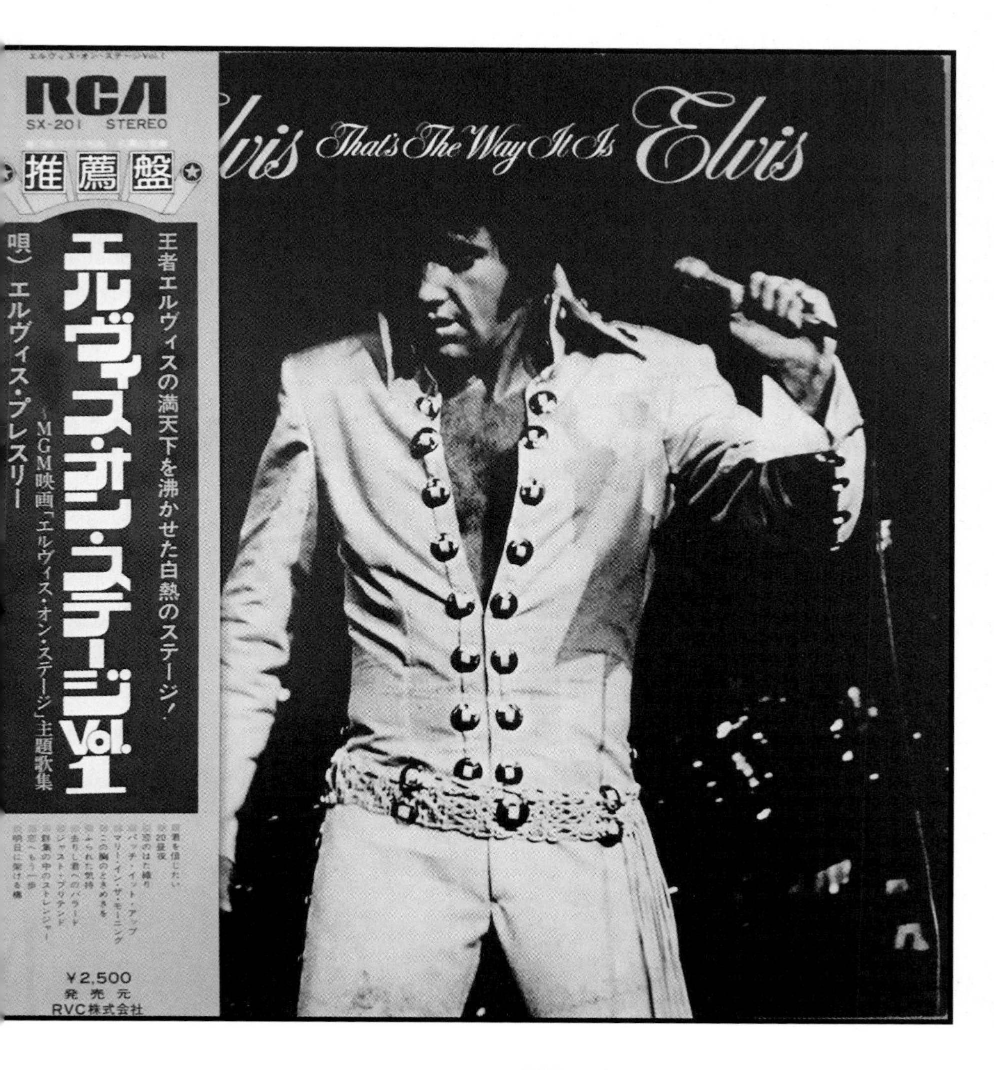

BRIDGE OVER TROUBLED WATER

More than 50 artists have recorded the next song we're going to feature and it certainly was one of the all-time classics of the last century.

'Bridge over Troubled Water' is forever associated with the singing duo Paul Simon and Art Garfunkel. They had been friends for many years before they hit the big time in the 1960s. They had met as children and started to spend all their spare time working on perfecting their harmonies. The duo made no secret of the fact they were huge fans of the Everly Brothers, eventually sharing a stage with them in more recent years.

Their first release was not as Simon and Garfunkel, but under the name Tom and Jerry – no cats or mice were involved in the recording though! The teenagers enjoyed minor success with 'Hey Schoolgirl', doing their best to sound like their idols Don and Phil Everly. As the '60s got underway, the duo enjoyed chart and album success; however, by the time they started recording the *Bridge over Troubled Water* album they were close to splitting up. Their often rocky relationship had led to artistic disagreements.

Their final studio record, *Bridge over Troubled Water*, was their most successful, becoming one of the world's best-selling albums. The song 'Bridge over Troubled Water' was composed by Paul Simon, beginning with just a piano. From the word go you can really hear the gospel tinge in the song – could this be what attracted Elvis to the track?

Released at the end of January 1970, Simon and Garfunkel's version of 'Bridge over Troubled Water' reached number one on the Billboard Hot 100 chart on 28th February 1970 and stayed at the top of the chart for six weeks. It enjoyed worldwide success as a single and an album, and was a track the duo performed countless times during their several reunion tours. But was Elvis influenced by that version of the song? It's been debated in online chatrooms by fans before and there are some who think it was B.J. Thomas's cover, also recorded in 1970, that moved Elvis more. Some of the 50 or so artists who have recorded the song include Willie Nelson, Johnny Cash, Aretha Franklin, Bobby Darin, Bon Jovi, Elton John and Quincy Jones.

Elvis Presley recorded his version of the song in Nashville on 5th June 1970 and it formed part of the album *That's the Way It Is*, the soundtrack for the film of the same name. He included it in his set list for his next engagement in Las Vegas, which was filmed. The song was included in the original theatrical release. Legend has it that during that summer season in Vegas, Paul Simon attended one of the shows and, after seeing Elvis perform the song, apparently said: "That's it, we might as well all give up now."

'Bridge over Troubled Water' remained a popular choice in concerts for Elvis and was always a great opportunity to showcase his majestic voice. The song appeared in the set list in the Elvis Madison Square Garden shows and Presley can be seen once again on the big screen singing the song, as part of the *Elvis on Tour* film, which went on to receive a Golden Globe. He even sang it on his final tour – just six weeks before his death.

In his book, *Elvis Presley: A Study in Music*, Robert Matthew-Walker wrote of the song: "Presley's outstanding singing is not disguised. This is a fabulous version, burning with sincerity and power, and finding depths not revealed by the composers." More recently the song was one of those chosen for the album *If I Can Dream*, which paired Elvis's voice with the Royal Philharmonic Orchestra. The album, released in Autumn 2015, did particularly well in the UK, where it hit the top of the charts, leading to a follow-up album called *The Wonder of You* in October 2016, which also reached the number-one position.

FUNNY HOW TIME SLIPS AWAY

Next a song penned by country music legend Willie Nelson. 'Funny How Time Slips Away' is one of many classics written by Nelson, another stand-out track being 'Crazy', which was a huge hit for Patsy Cline.

Willie Nelson was born on 29th April 1933 in Abbott, Texas. He rose to prominence at the end of the 1960s and contributed to the 'outlaw country' subgenre, which challenged the conservatism of Nashville. Nelson got his first guitar at the early age of six and soon started writing his own songs. A few years later, he played his first professional gig with a local polka band.

In 1960, Nelson moved to the country music capital: Nashville, Tennessee. He got a job as a songwriter for Pamper Music, earning about $50 a week. The next year, two of Nelson's songs became hits for other artists – Faron Young's version of 'Hello Walls' and Patsy Cline's legendary rendition of 'Crazy'. With his gritty, road-house sound, Nelson did not fit into the traditional Nashville country music scene. Nelson moved back to Texas and continued writing and recording, and working with the likes of Kris Kristofferson and Waylon Jennings. He also kept recording albums, but he stuck to making his own kind of country music. *Shotgun Willie* (1973) is considered to be one of his greatest albums of all time.

'Funny How Time Slips Away' was written by Willie Nelson and first recorded by country singer Billy Walker. Walker's version peaked at number 23 on the Hot C&W Sides chart. Before Elvis recorded the song, many other artists tackled it including Jimmy Elledge who, in 1961, released a version peaking at number 22 on the Billboard Hot 100. In 1964, Joe Hinton had a major crossover hit with his version, which went to number one on the Cash Box R&B chart and number 13 on the Billboard Hot 100 pop chart in the US. The following year saw the Supremes release a version on their album, *The Supremes Sing Country, Western & Pop*. Then in 1967 Harry James released a version on his album *Our Leader* which featured the voice of Ernie Andrews.

After all those versions, Elvis recorded the track on 7th June 1970 as part of a five-day recording session in RCA's Studio B in Nashville. The highly productive session yielded 35 usable tracks. Elvis also often included the song in his live shows. It was an opportunity for him to turn on the auditorium lights so he could look at the crowd that had been looking so adoringly at him. Although in truth, he probably could only see the first few rows as those stage lights were certainly bright.

'Funny How Time Slips Away' appeared as part of the song list to the historic run of concerts at Madison Square Garden in 1972. It was also recorded when Elvis appeared live on stage in 1974 in Memphis. It didn't feature on the original 1974 album, but did make an appearance on the Follow That Dream label's expanded version when it was released in 2004. In 2014, that version appeared on a Sony Legacy release of the concert.

I REALLY DON'T WANT TO KNOW

This song was written in 1953, with music by Don Robertson and lyrics by Howard Barnes. One of the earliest and best-known versions of the song was recorded by Les Paul and Mary Ford in 1953, which became one of the top-100 songs of 1954. Andy Williams released a version on his 1963 album, *Days of Wine and Roses and Other TV Requests*. It was also recorded by Eddy Arnold.

Elvis's version appeared on *Elvis Country* as the closing track on side one. It was recorded on 7th June 1970. Elvis expert Harley Payette wrote an essay for elvis.com.au, the website of the official Elvis Presley Fan Club of Australia, about Elvis's concept album, *Elvis Country*. He wrote:

> Then, almost out of the blue, Elvis tore into Don Robertson's ballad 'I Really Don't Want to Know', a number that had been a hit for Eddie Arnold, Les Paul and Mary Ford, and Tommy Edwards, and that had always defined the poppiest edge of country music. But Elvis didn't perform it like a pop number. He didn't perform it as a country number either. He sang it like it was blues. It was the same type of reinvention he used at Sun on 'Blue Moon of Kentucky' and 'That's All Right' all those years ago. Now instead of Sam Phillips recognizing the moment and catching it for posterity, it was Elvis himself. The song set him on a fit of inspiration. Next thing he laid into an absolutely rocking version of Bob Wills' standard 'Faded Love'.

Elvis also covered the song live in concert, including on his final tour, which was captured on cameras by CBS, although that was a much shorter version clocking in at under two minutes.

I WASHED MY HANDS IN MUDDY WATER

Concept albums became a big thing from the mid-1960s onwards. It started with *Pet Sounds* by the Beach Boys in 1966 and was followed a year later by the classic *Sgt Pepper* project by the Beatles.

Elvis dabbled with the idea of concept albums at the beginning of the '70s. 'I Washed My Hands in Muddy Water' came from the album, *Elvis Country*. It was originally a hit in 1965 for Stonewall Jackson. His version reached number eight on the Hot Country Songs Chart.

The following year Johnny Rivers did a version of the song, which reached number 19 on the Billboard Hot 100. The song was written by Cowboy Joe Babcock. At last count, the song's different versions had sold more than four-million records combined. In 1968, Cowboy Joe joined the *Hee Haw* nationally syndicated television show and was an original cast member doing vocal backing with the Nashville Edition. *Hee Haw* started on CBS-TV as a summer 1969 replacement for *The Smothers Brothers Comedy Hour*. The show was dropped in 1971; however, the producers were convinced that it still had a long life ahead of it, so they put together a syndication deal for the show. They were right to do so. The syndicated show went on for about 20 years. Cowboy Joe also emerged as the lead vocalist with the Hee Haw Gospel Quartet. He also formed another group called the Hee Haw Cowboy Quartet, with the aim of paying tribute to the cowboy stars he had listened to as a child.

The bulk of the *Elvis Country* album came from five days of recording sessions in June 1970. Nearly every style of country music is represented: bluegrass, honky tonk, Western swing and rockabilly. It's a great album and shows what Elvis could achieve when he concentrated on the idea of a concept album. Elvis also enjoyed success with his gospel albums. Many fans would have liked Elvis to have done a folk concept album as he recorded several folk-style songs during the early '70s. *Elvis Country* has parts of the song 'I Was Born about 10,000 Years Ago' mixed in between each track. If you've never heard the album, it's well worth searching out as one of Presley's most cohesive sets. The original album was released with a postcard showing Elvis as a child with his parents. The album, with the postcard still intact, has become highly collectable among fans of Presley.

JUST PRETEND

'Just Pretend' is classic 1970s Vegas Elvis showing off his immense vocal talents. It was written by Mervyn Guy Fletcher and Doug Flett, who wrote several hits for other artists. It wasn't the first time the duo had seen their lyrics recorded by Elvis. They wrote 'Wonderful World', which appeared in the opening sequences of the film *Live a Little, Love a Little*. It showed a carefree Elvis driving around the dunes in a beach buggy. For once his hair was naturally blowing around all over the place as well! The duo was also responsible for 'The Fair's Movin' On', which appeared on the B-side of Elvis's 1969 single 'Clean Up Your Own Back Yard'.

Earlier in life, Fletcher had enjoyed a chance meeting that led to him working with studio maverick Joe Meek. His experiences with Joe opened the door for him into the industry. Fletcher recalled in an *M-Magazine* article: "It was a complete immersion into Joe's way of recording. He was known either as a genius or a lunatic, and I think there was a little bit of both in him. He was like the English equivalent of Phil Spector, except he was recording in a flat in North London. He had a home studio way before anyone else." The fledgling songwriter and artist sang on over 100 singles made by Joe Meek in his domestic hit factory.

Meek was a troubled genius whose life ended tragically when he shot and killed his landlady and himself. Big record companies at the time had tried their hardest to block Meek and his never-ending ideas for single releases. He became extremely frustrated and suffered from deep paranoia, along with a dependence on pills, which may have all contributed to the tragic events of 3rd February 1967.

'Just Pretend' featured in *Elvis: That's The Way It Is*. It was recorded on 6th June 1970. Elvis was captured performing the song live on 11th and 12th August and even performed the song as late as 1975, that version being available on the *Live in Las Vegas* box set. The Australian Elvis Presley Fan Club describes 'Just Pretend' as "a lost gem. This delicate song of seeking to regain lost love is given a superb interpretation by Elvis."

In December 2016, Guy Fletcher was awarded a gold disc for his song-writing work on the Elvis and the Royal Philharmonic Orchestra number-one album, *The Wonder of You*. Guy and his composer colleague Doug Flett received accolades for 'Just Pretend' at a surprise party at PRS for Music's central London office. PRS for Music Limited (formerly the MCPS-PRS Alliance Limited) is the UK's leading collection society. It undertakes collective rights management for musical works by its 118,000 members.

'Just Pretend' features twice on the 2016 album, *The Wonder of You*, with award-winning German artist Helene Fischer singing alongside Elvis's original take for a reworking of the song. Fletcher told *M Magazine*: "I was aware that the album had achieved considerable sales but I had absolutely no idea it merited a Gold Disc. Any writer would be thrilled, as I was. It was such a lovely surprise."

LOVE LETTERS

(Love Letters from Elvis LP Version)

Next a classic love song that Elvis recorded in the studio on two separate occasions.

Written by Edward Heyman and Victor Young, 'Love Letters' was first recorded back in 1945. The song originally appeared, without lyrics, in the movie of the same name and was nominated for the Academy Award for Best Song for 1945. Edward Heyman was born in 1907. He was an American lyricist and producer, best known for his lyrics to 'Body and Soul', 'When I Fall in Love' and 'For Sentimental Reasons'. He also contributed to a number of songs for films. Victor Young was born in Chicago on 8th August 1900. In the mid-1930s, he moved to Hollywood where he supplied backing for popular singers, including Bing Crosby. His composer credits include 'When I Fall in Love', 'Blue Star (The 'Medic' Theme)', 'Moonlight Serenade (Summer Love)' from the motion picture *The Star* (1952), 'Sweet Sue, Just You', 'Can't We Talk it Over', 'Street of Dreams', 'My Foolish Heart' and 'I Don't Stand a Ghost of a Chance with You'.

Several people recorded 'Love Letters' before Elvis put his voice to it. Back in 1945, Dick Haymes scored a hit with the song; then nine years later the great

Peggy Lee did a version. Nat King Cole recorded the song in December 1956 for his 1957 album *Love is the Thing.* In the 1960s, Ketty Lester recorded 'Love Letters' enjoying top-10 success in America and the UK.

Elvis reached number six in the UK with his first version of 'Love Letters'. It only reached number 19 in the Billboard Hot 100. While it was normal for Elvis's label to record and release live versions of his songs, it was rare for Elvis to revisit a song in the studio. He did this with 'Blue Suede Shoes' when it was featured in the movie *GI Blues.* In 1965, overdubs were added to two songs Elvis had recorded ten years previously ('When it Rains it Really Pours' and 'Tomorrow Night') for the album *Elvis for Everyone.*

He revisited 'Love Letters' in June 1970 in Nashville and it formed the title of the album *Love Letters from Elvis.* The LP was made up of leftovers from Elvis's marathon sessions in Nashville. Most of the other 35 songs recorded during those sessions had been used in Elvis's 1970 albums *That's the Way It Is* and *Elvis Country (I'm 10,000 Years Old).* Felton Jarvis, Elvis's producer had to remix and overdub the remains to bring them up to scratch. Out of the albums released during the prolific period of 1969–1971, critics dubbed *Love Letters from Elvis* the weakest. (Although, it has to be said that a weak album during this period was definitely stronger than a lot of the movie soundtracks of the previous decade!) The album failed to crack the top 20 of the Billboard album charts. However, it did better in the UK reaching number seven. The full-priced album's release was sandwiched between two budget albums: *You'll Never Walk Alone* and *C'mon Everybody.*

'Love Letters' was a song Elvis revisited on stage during the '70s, even performing it as late as the famous New Year's Eve concert in 1976 at Pittsburgh.

MAKE THE WORLD GO AWAY

This is a great country song composed by Hank Cochran. He wrote the track while he was on a date at a movie theatre in 1960. Whatever he was watching inspired him to write the song. He left the theatre quickly and a matter of minutes later had composed 'Make the World Go Away'.

Rock and roll fans will remember that Hank teamed up with a young Eddie Cochran in 1954 to form the Cochran Brothers. The duo weren't related. Hank was doing most of the lead vocals, while Eddie supplied lead guitar. Occasionally, Eddie would lend a little harmony support. Just a few short years later, Eddie brought us such unforgettable tracks as 'C'mon Everybody', 'Summertime Blues' and 'Somethin' Else'.

'Make the World Go Away' enjoyed big chart success on several occasions. Ray Price scored large with the song. Timi Yuro enjoyed success with the song in 1963. Two years later it was the turn of Eddy Arnold. The next decade saw Donny and Marie Osmond score a hit with the track in 1975.

In between those chart versions, Elvis Presley recorded 'Make the World Go Away'. It was chosen as the final track of the *Elvis Country* album, being recorded on 7th June 1970. On the same night, Elvis worked on 'When I'm Over You', 'I Really Don't Want to Know', 'Faded Love', 'Tomorrow Never Comes', 'The Next Step Is Love', 'Funny How Time Slips Away', 'I Washed My Hands in Muddy Water' and 'Love Letters'. Elvis and his band certainly worked hard on that night!

Other people who recorded 'Make the World Go Away' included Jim Reeves, who performed the song at his last recording session in July 1964. Dean Martin, Tom Jones, Engelbert Humperdinck, Jimmie Rogers, Charly McClain, Mickey Gilley and Martina McBride have all covered the track over the years.

MARY IN THE MORNING

'Mary in the Morning' was written by songwriter Michael Rashkow and the singer Johnny Cymbal. The latter is probably best remembered for his rock 'n' roll hit, 'Mr. Bass Man'. This was followed by 'Dum Dum De Dum', but this stalled at number 77 in the Billboard. There was further disappointment when the next single, 'Teenage Heaven', made it to number 58 in the US. However, the same track did reach the top of the charts in Sweden.

Cymbal was also a prolific song writer, publishing more than 200 songs. As 'Mr Bass Man' proved, he was a great singer but he always saw himself first and foremost as a composer. Rashkow and Cymbal wrote numerous other songs including 'Julie on My Mind' which gained its biggest success in the Caribbean Islands.

'Mary in the Morning' was recorded by a number of artists including Ed Ames in 1967. Glen Campbell also did the song, but Al Martino had the most success with the track, gaining a number-one hit on the easy listening charts in July 1967.

Elvis recorded his version of 'Mary in the Morning' on 5th June 1970 in recording sessions that produced the soundtrack album, *Elvis: That's the Way It Is*. On the same day he recorded 'Stranger in the Crowd', 'How the Web Was Woven' and 'Bridge over Troubled Water' – a very successful day then! 'Mary in the Morning' was one of eight studio tracks included on the album. There were four live tracks featured as well.

On the songbase on elvisnews.com, fan reviewer ElvisSacramento said of 'Mary in the Morning': "This is surely one of the most beautiful ballads that I've ever heard and Elvis's rendition of this song is the greatest rendition of it that I've ever heard. Elvis should have sung it at some of his 1970s concerts too. This song really should have been a hit for Elvis, but it sadly wasn't."

TOMORROW NEVER COMES

Next a track that tested Elvis's vocal abilities to the extreme, a song that had a real Roy Orbison feel to it, 'Tomorrow Never Comes'. Like many of Orbison's tracks, the song starts quiet and then begins to build and build until, just when you think it can't get any more powerful, bang! Elvis hits unbelievable notes and holds them for what seems like forever.

Just listening to the track you can hear Elvis is totally committed to it. It begs the question, why wasn't it released as a single? I think it would have been massive! What are your thoughts? Feel free to add your thoughts to the *Elvis Presley: Stories Behind the Songs* Facebook page. It would be great to hear from you.

After working on 'When I'm Over You', 'I Really Don't Want to Know' and 'Faded Love' in RCA's Studio B in Nashville, Elvis turned his attention to 'Tomorrow Never Comes'. It was a productive evening on 7th June 1970.

Let's look at the song's two composers. Ernest Tubb, nicknamed the Texas Troubadour, was one of the pioneers of country music and was born on 9th February 1914. In 1936, Tubb contacted Jimmie Rodgers' widow to ask for an autographed photo. A friendship developed and she was instrumental in getting Tubb a recording contract with RCA, later to be Elvis's main record label. Tubb was also responsible for the Ernest Tubb Record Shop in Nashville, which opened in May 1947.

Johnny Bond, the co-writer of 'Tomorrow Never Comes', was born in Enville, Oklahoma. He got his first break working for Jimmy Wakely in the late 1930s and went on to join Gene Autry's Melody Ranch in 1940. In 1965, he scored his biggest hit with the comic 'Ten Little Bottles', which spent four weeks at number two in America.

On elvisnews.com's songbase, fan ElvisSacramento wrote: "This song is a definitely true masterpiece and the best rendition of it is definitely Elvis's rendition. Elvis's recording of it should surely be much better known than it actually is. Elvis used the full power of his vocal abilities for this gem. I've never skipped it. 5 Stars."

B.J Thomas, Glen Campbell and Slim Whitman were among the others who covered 'Tomorrow Never Comes'.

THERE GOES MY EVERYTHING

'There Goes My Everything' was written by Dallas Frazier and published in 1965. The following year Jack Greene did a version which saw him enjoy a seven-week stay at the top of the US country music chart.

Songwriter Dallas Frazier hailed from Oklahoma. As a teenager, he played with Ferlin Husky and appeared on the programme *Hometown Jamboree*. How's this for impressive? In 1954, at the ripe old age of 14, Frazier released his first single, 'Space Command'. In 1957, a song Frazier composed called 'Alley Oop' went to number one for the rock and roll band the Hollywood Argyles.

Engelbert Humperdinck had a huge hit with 'There Goes My Everything' in 1967. It reached number 20 on the Billboard Hot 100 and in the UK it just missed out on a number-one placing, stalling at number two. Engelbert, or to give him his real name, Arnold George Dorsey, was born in India. His family moved to Leicester, England when he was ten years old. But where did that amazing name, Engelbert Humperdinck, come from? Well, Arnold Dorsey had been struggling to make it as a star for ten years using the name of Gerry Dorsey. Tom Jones' manager, Gordon Mills, suggested the name change, which was borrowed from the German nineteenth-century composer of operas such as *Hansel and Gretel*. The name change was a pure gold idea. In 1967, both 'Release Me' and 'The Last Waltz' topped the UK music charts ensuring Engelbert earned two million sellers in just one year.

In an interview on the website elvispresleyfansofnashville.com, Engelbert Humperdinck spoke of his friendship with Elvis. He said:

> When you watched Elvis work on stage, you saw that reality come through. He never took his image seriously and often made fun of himself. That was the great thing about him. He had a great deal of humility and I learned all sorts of messages just watching him. I remember once teasing him and said, "You know Elvis, you stole my sideburns." He replied in that beautiful Southern accent of his, "Well, if it looks good on you, it'll look good on me."

Elvis's version of 'There Goes My Everything' was recorded on 8th June 1970. The track opened side two of *Elvis Country (I'm 10,000 Years Old)* and was the B-side of the single 'I Really Don't Want to Know', which was released on 8th December 1970 and peaked at number 21 on the Billboard Hot 100.

In a future volume we'll look at Elvis's version of 'He Is My Everything' which was performed to exactly the same tune as 'There Goes My Everything'.

YOU DON'T HAVE TO SAY YOU LOVE ME

'You Don't Have to Say You Love Me' was a great way for Elvis to show off his vocals when he left behind the movie years and took back his musical throne. Elvis was one of very few artists who could take a song made famous by the great Dusty Springfield and still do it justice.

Dusty Springfield was born Mary O'Brien in North London, England. As a child, her friends saw her as a tomboy who loved to play football with the boys, so she was given the nickname Dusty and it stuck throughout her life. Later, her distinctive smoky voice earned her the nickname the White Queen of Soul. Like Elvis she also recorded some great work in Memphis. Also like Presley, Springfield successfully turned her voice to numerous genres including rock, pop, folk and country.

She had her first taste of success with her brother Tom and friend Mike Hurst. In the early 1960s, they became the Springfields. The group enjoyed some chart success but Dusty left soon after to pursue what was to become a highly successful career. Her hits included 'I Only Wanna Be with You', 'Son of a Preacher Man', 'I Close My Eyes and Count to Ten' and of course 'You Don't Have to Say You Love Me'. A fan of the Motown sound that was sweeping the United States, Springfield helped introduce Britain to soul music through the British TV programme *Ready Steady Go*, which devoted shows to the music stars of Detroit.

'You Don't Have to Say You Love Me' was originally an Italian song composed by Pino Donnagio. Springfield heard Donnagio perform it at the San Remo festival and asked her friend Vicki Wickham, who produced *Ready Steady Go*, to write some English lyrics for it. With the help of the Yardbirds' manager, Simon Napier-Bell, she did.

In the book *1,000 UK #1 Hits* by Jon Kutner and Spencer Leigh, Simon Napier-Bell is quoted as saying: "Vicki and I used to eat together, and she told me that Dusty wanted a lyric for this song. We went back to her flat and started working on it. We wanted to go to a trendy disco so we had about an hour to write it. We wrote the chorus and then we wrote the verse in a taxi to wherever we were going. It was the first pop lyric I'd written, although I've always been interested in poetry and good literature."

The song had a much more profound effect on the singer. Dusty said that she cried when she first heard the song. 'You Don't Have to Say You Love Me' was recorded by Elvis Presley for his 1970 album release, *That's the Way It Is*. The song was issued as the second single on 6th October 1970. The track had been recorded in the evening of 6th June 1970 in Studio B of RCA Studios, Nashville, being the third of seven songs recorded that night. The session's producer Felton Jarvis felt that the second take was good enough to serve as the master track but Presley insisted on a third and final take.

In America, the track peaked at number 11 in the Billboard Hot 100. However, it gave Elvis another number one in the US easy listening chart. Elvis's version became an international smash, reaching number six in Canada, number seven in Australia, number nine in the UK and number 17 in Ireland.

Whereas Dusty Springfield's take has an instrumental introduction before she bursts into the song, Elvis goes for it vocally straightaway and the impact is fantastic!

September 1970 – Nashville

SNOWBIRD

According to songfacts.com, Anne Murray recorded 'Snowbird' after watching its composer, Gene MacLellan, perform it on Canadian TV. It was only the second song MacLellan had ever written and he penned it in just 25 minutes. He also recorded it for his own 1970 album, *Street Corner Preacher*, and included an additional verse:

> My mind says that I only want to be
> A wanderer and just like you I'm longing to be free
> But in my heart I know it's just a lie
> For without her love the vision of my happiness will die

It was to become Anne Murray's first hit and was the first ever gold record by a Canadian solo female artist.

How Gene MacLellan actually wrote Snowbird is a topic of great debate back at his home on Prince Edward Island. According to MacLellan biographer David Sheffield: "The legend of Snowbird is huge... every third person on PEI has a version of how and where the song was written. While there are similarities between the stories, the one thing they have in common is that the teller believes that their version is the truth."

Among those who recorded the track are Bing Crosby, who joined Count Basie for a version, and Al Martino, Loretta Lynn and Lynn Anderson.

No matter how happily Anne Murray sings it, it is a sad song. The composer writes of missing days gone by in the lines "When I was young my heart was young then, too/And anything that it would tell me, that's the thing that I would do" and the subsequent desire to get away from himself. "And if I could you know that I would fly away with you."

Elvis had already had a massive recording session in June 1970 at RCA's Studio B in Nashville. He was back at the studio in September of that year to record 'Snowbird'. As well as recording 'Snowbird', Elvis also sang 'Put Your Hand in the Hand' which was also composed by Gene MacLellan. Elvis had recorded this song at the previous June session.

'Snowbird' was the opening track on *Elvis Country (I'm 10,000 Years Old)*. The album itself would be certified gold on 1st December 1977.

WHOLE LOTTA SHAKIN' GOING ON

Next a rock and roll classic that lit up the charts in the 1950s, but that Elvis didn't get round to recording until many years later.

'Whole Lotta Shakin' Going On' will forever be associated with the man they dubbed 'the killer' – Jerry Lee Lewis. He wasn't the first to record it though. Big Maybelle has that honour. The song was written by Dave 'Curlee' Williams and usually credited to him and James Faye 'Roy' Hall. There has been a dispute over the years. Roy Hall made a recording of the song in September 1955 for Decca Records and maintained that he had written it and had secured the legal copyright as co-writer under the pseudonym 'Sunny David'. However, a Decca sample copy of Hall's recording lists Dave Williams as the sole writer.

One thing that isn't up for question is who produced Big Maybelle's recording of the song. It was a man whose career spans six decades in the entertainment industry and enjoyed an incredible 79 Grammy Award nominations – Quincy Jones. In the mid-1950s, when Big Maybelle recorded 'Whole Lotta Shakin…', Quincy Jones also produced acts like Ray Charles, Dinah Washington, Count Basie, Duke Ellington and Sarah Vaughan. Later, Quincy Jones was the producer, with Michael Jackson, of Jacko's solo albums *Off the Wall*, *Thriller* and *Bad*.

Jerry Lee Lewis was no stranger to 'Whole Lotta Shakin' Going On' when he tackled it at his second recording session for the famous Sun recording studios in February 1957. The star had been performing the track as part of his live set while touring around America. Sun Producer Jack Clement was in charge of the session. Clement also worked with Roy Orbison, Carl Perkins and Johnny Cash while they were under contract at Sun. Another rock and roll legend recorded the track too – Little Richard – and his version appeared on an album called *The Fabulous Little Richard*.

On 22nd September 1970 at RCA Studio B in Nashville, Elvis recorded his version of 'Whole Lotta Shakin…'. Mary and Ginger Holladay provided backing vocals along with the usual backing vocalists. They had first worked with Elvis on his huge smash 'In the Ghetto'. In an archive interview, Ginger Holladay said of Elvis: "He was just larger than life. No kidding. When he would walk into the recording room you knew he was there, even if you had your back turned and headphones on. That's the kind of energy and presence he had."

The track proved that given the right material, Elvis could still rock out with the best of them. He had taken a song from the '50s and made it sound contemporary in the 1970s.

Love Letters
from
ELVIS

FOUR

1971–2 – BACK IN THE STUDIO

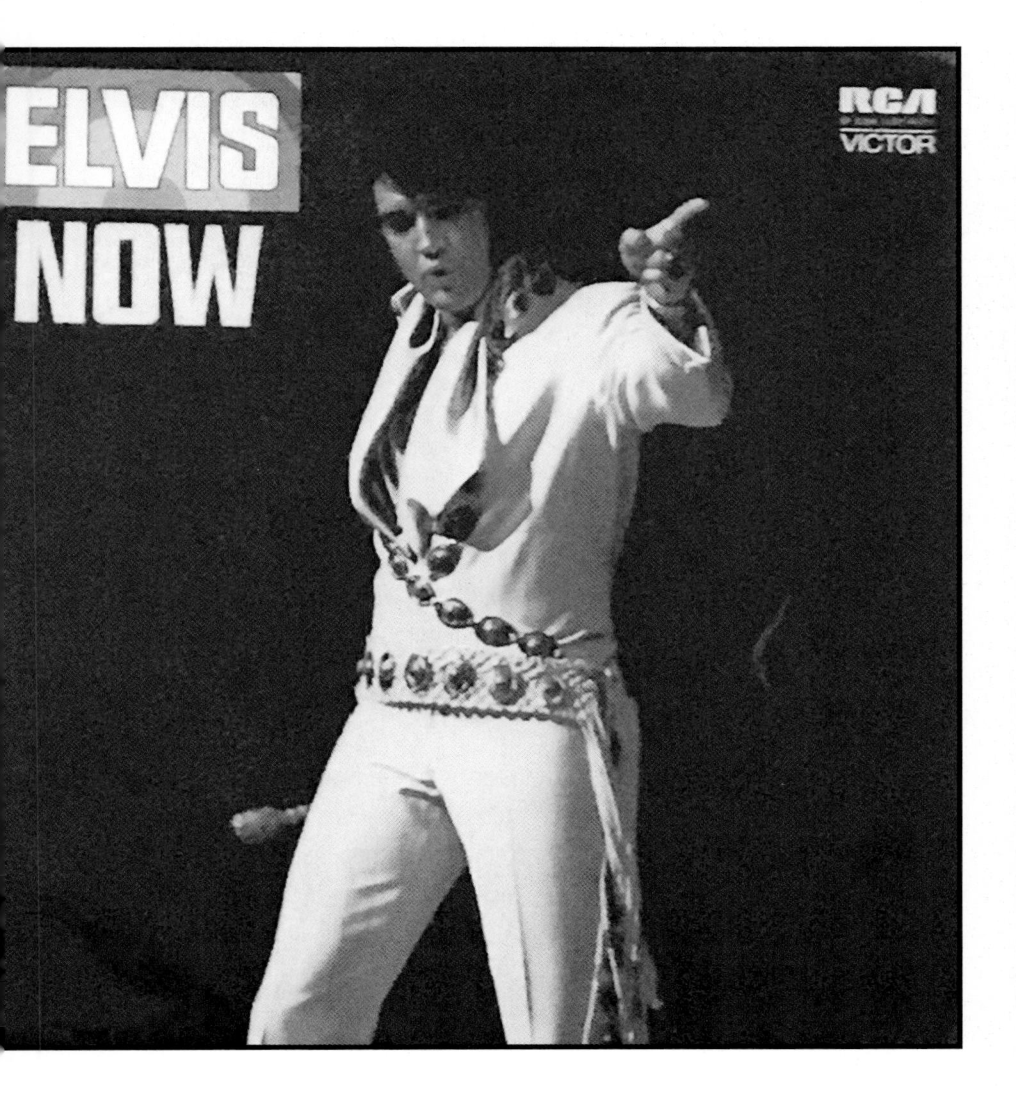

March 1971

AMAZING GRACE

So far in this book, we've looked at songs recorded by Elvis that were either written for him or that he covered after they were originally recorded by others in the 1940s, '50s, '60s or '70s. Next however, we feature one that has its origins back in the eighteenth century.

'Amazing Grace' is a Christian hymn published way back in 1779. It was written by John Newton, a poet and clergyman in the UK. He spent time in the Royal Navy before becoming involved in the Atlantic Slave Trade. Out at sea in 1748 he encountered an horrendous storm. The lashing rain and strong winds battered his vessel. At one stage, fearing for his life, Newton called out to God for mercy. It was that moment he started his spiritual conversion. Newton was ordained in the Church of England in 1764 and started to write hymns with poet William Cowper.

'Amazing Grace' was written to illustrate a sermon on New Year's Day of 1773. There are no records to say whether music was used in the earliest performances of the song. Some historians believe it would have been chanted. In America, 'Amazing Grace' became well known during the early nineteenth century as part of the Second Great Awakening. The most popular tune used during the song is called 'New Britain', although there are more than 20 different melodies which have been used over the years.

Elvis's version of 'Amazing Grace' features on the third and final gospel album to be released in his lifetime, *He Touched Me*. It is different from the 1960s releases, *His Hand in Mine* and *How Great Thou Art*, as it is more contemporary in its feel. It also uses different musicians to the previous two. Allmusic.com said "This is Elvis's contemporary gospel record, including material from Bill Gaither (the title song), Andraé Crouch ('I've Got Confidence') and Dallas Frazier ('He Is My Everything'). His vocal backgrounds come from the Imperials and J.D. Sumner & the Stamps, and the instrumental arrangements leave space for electric guitar and electric bass."

He Touched Me was certified gold on 27th March 1992 and platinum on 15th July 1999. It is spiritual and contemporary but still finds a special place for the traditional 'Amazing Grace', recorded on 15th March 1971.

EARLY MORNING RAIN

'Early Morning Rain' was written by Canadian, Gordon Lightfoot. Elvis recorded the track in the studio and on stage.

Its lyrics feature a man who thinks that luck has left him behind. He's watching the take off of a Boeing 707 plane, while also being far away from home. Some online sources say the song was inspired by Lightfoot seeing off a friend at Los Angeles airport. It was the first of his songs to become famous and went on to become the most covered. Judy Collins covered the track, recording it before Gordon Lightfoot released his version. Peter, Paul and Mary included the track in their *See What Tomorrow Brings* album from 1965. Bob Dylan featured the song on his 1970 *Self Portrait* LP and, more recently, Paul Weller's version reached number 40 in the UK charts in 2005.

Gordon Lightfoot has several celebrity fans including Bob Dylan who said that when he heard a Gordon Lightfoot song he wished "it would last forever". Lightfoot's other songs include 'For Lovin' Me', 'Steel Rail Blues' and 'Ribbon of Darkness'. Among the countless artists to record his songs are the Kingston Trio, Marty Robbins, George Hamilton IV and Jerry Lee Lewis.

Elvis's studio version of the song was recorded on 15th March 1971. It features on the 1972 release *Elvis Now*, which has ten tracks on it. The LP sees Elvis tackle a variety of genres, including pop, soul, country and gospel. When Elvis returned to the stage after the Aloha from Hawaii concert had finished and the audience had gone home, he performed further songs to be included in the American airing of the show.

One of those songs was 'Early Morning Rain'. The others were from the film *Blue Hawaii* including the title track 'Hawaiian Wedding Song', 'No More' and 'Ku-U-I-Po'.

Composer Gordon Lightfoot said in an archive interview that he learnt to play the guitar as a youngster by listening endlessly to Elvis's 'Heartbreak Hotel'. Lightfoot said: "I was really impressed with the recording [of 'Early Morning Rain']. It was probably the most important recording that I have by another artist. He did another one too. He did a rockabilly version of another one called 'For Lovin' Me.'"

Elvis returned to 'Early Morning Rain' for his final television special, *Elvis in Concert*, in 1977. This time though there was a packed out audience to enjoy the live version of the song.

THE FIRST TIME EVER I SAW YOUR FACE

Countless people have recorded this track including Peter, Paul and Mary in the 1960s. Johnny Cash did a version and there's even a Gregorian chant take. The most famous version belongs to Roberta Flack. Roberta Flack's version of 'The First Time Ever I Saw Your Face' became the breakout hit for her in 1972, although the song had first appeared on Flack's 1969 album *First Take*. Her rendition was much slower than the original and around twice the length.

Damien Barber and Mike Wilson sang 'The First Time Ever I Saw Your Face' in 2011 on their CD *The Old Songs*. At the time they said: "This is from the pen of Ewan MacColl and the singing of Peggy Seeger. If one analogy of a folk song is that of a beautifully smoothed pebble on a beach, picked up and rolled by the sea to perfection over time, then this gem has been rolled over every beach on the planet!"

More recently Sarah McQuaid sang 'The First Time Ever I Saw Your Face' in 2014 on her CD *Walking into White*. She said in her liner notes: "Ewan MacColl wrote this for Peggy Seeger, and it's been recorded by so many illustrious names that I feel a bit presumptuous for having had a go at it myself, but I couldn't resist. I think it's one of the most perfect love songs ever written."

Ewan MacColl wrote 'The First Time Ever I Saw Your Face' in 1957 for his then-lover, and later wife, Peggy Seeger. It is said that he wrote and taught it to her over the telephone when she needed a song for a play she was cast for. According to an article written in the UK-based newspaper the *Guardian*: "Ewan MacColl left school at 14, was a political activist at 15, founded a theatre troupe at 16, found himself on MI5's files at 17, and became the Godfather of British folk revival at 35 – Ewan MacColl's early CV was something extraordinary, evidence of a fearless, galvanic character whose influence is still causing ripples."

His daughter, Kirsty MacColl was an English singer and songwriter. She recorded several pop hits between the early 1980s and the 1990s; ironically, one of those was called 'There's a Guy Works Down the Chip Shop Swears He's Elvis'.

Ewan MacColl made no secret of the fact that he disliked all of the cover versions of the song. His daughter-in-law once wrote: "He hated all of them. He had a special section in his record collection for them, entitled 'The Chamber of Horrors'. He said that the Elvis version was like Romeo at the bottom of the Post Office Tower singing up to Juliet. And the other versions, he thought, were travesties: bludgeoning, histrionic, and lacking in grace." Oh dear!

MacColl's collection of cover versions must have been huge. Singers from Aaron Neville to We Five, via around 100 other notable artists, have recorded versions of the track. Many more are thought to exist. Among those many versions are Elvis's take on 'The First Time Ever I Saw Your Face'. It was the B-side of the monster hit 'An American Trilogy' released as a single in 1972.

Elvis recorded 'The First Time…' on 15th March 1971. He performed 12 takes before the master was selected. It has since made its way on to various Elvis compilation albums. Elvis also featured live versions of the song in his concerts as late as December 1976 when he sang it for his then-girlfriend, Ginger Alden. In fact, it was an earlier girlfriend, Joyce Bova, who persuaded Elvis to record the track in the first place.

MAY 1971

HELP ME MAKE IT THROUGH THE NIGHT

Next a song that saw its composer go from sweeping floors at a studio in Nashville to becoming a successful singer–songwriter.

'Help Me Make It through the Night' was a number-one country hit written by songwriter and actor Kris Kristofferson. According to songfacts.com, Kristofferson was sweeping floors and emptying ashtrays at Columbia Records in Nashville. This was before he started scoring big with songs like the aforementioned and 'Me and Bobby McGee' (a number-one hit and an enduring rock classic for the late Janis Joplin), 'Sunday Mornin' Comin' Down', 'For the Good Times' and 'Loving Her Was Easier (Than Anything I'll Ever Do Again)'.

Kristofferson was a Golden Gloves boxer and a Rhodes Scholar who spent time at Oxford University in England before becoming a commercial helicopter pilot. But his first love was country song writing. He turned down a teaching position at West Point to work as a janitor at Columbia, trying to break into the music business. But it took some persistence and theatrics. For example, he is believed to have landed a helicopter in Johnny Cash's yard to get the famous country singer's attention so he could hand over some demo tapes of his original songs.

It was Sammi Smith's classic cover of 'Help Me Make It through the Night' that launched Kristofferson into the big time, earning him a Grammy for Best Country Song in 1971. It also won Smith a Grammy for Best Country Vocal Performance – Female.

Other people to have covered the track include Jerry Lee Lewis, Joan Baez, Olivia Newton-John and Andy Williams. Elvis recorded the track during his May 1971 Nashville sessions and Kristofferson was delighted Presley recorded some of his songs. In Ken Sharp's excellent FTD book *Writing for the King*, Kristofferson said: "It's one of the highlights for me to have had Elvis cut my songs. When I was first dreaming of becoming a songwriter I never would have dreamed that Elvis would sing one of my songs but three of them and with so much soul. I feel a lot of gratitude for that."

The sessions also produced songs like 'Until It's Time for You to Go', 'We Can Make the Morning' and 'Fools Rush In'.

'Help Me Make It through the Night' was the opening track on the gold-selling *Elvis Now* album. The LP was released nine months after Elvis laid down his vocals for the song.

IT'S ONLY LOVE

Next a track from the man who wrote 'Suspicious Minds', Mark James. He co-wrote 'It's Only Love' with Steve Tyrell. The song was first released by B.J. Thomas in February 1969.

We've already looked at Mark James so let's learn more about the song's co-writer. At 19 years old, Steve Tyrell began producing with the likes of Burt Bacharach. He worked on several Dionne Warwick hits such as 'The Look of Love' and 'Alfie'. Together with B.J. Thomas, he worked on the Bacharach–David song 'Raindrops Keep Fallin' on My Head', which went on to win the 1969 Oscar for Best Original Song from the classic Paul Newman and Robert Redford movie, *Butch Cassidy and the Sundance Kid*.

More recently Tyrell's performance of 'The Way You Look Tonight' in *Father of the Bride*, starring Steve Martin, pushed him centre-stage as a vocalist, with live performances and a recording career of his own.

Elvis recorded 'It's Only Love' on 21st May 1971 at RCA's Studio B in Nashville. The released version was take 10. It first appeared on a single alongside 'The Sound of Your Cry' in 1971 and was then re-released the following year as a Gold Standard single. The single reached number 51 on Billboard's Hot 100, number 51 on Cash Box Top 100 and number 19 on Billboard's easy listening charts.

It finally appeared on an LP when it was released as part of the *Elvis Aron Presley* silver box set in August 1980. Paired with 'Beyond the Reef', 'It's Only Love' reached number three in the UK charts when it was released as a single in 1980 to promote the box set.

LOVE ME, LOVE THE LIFE I LEAD

Next a track from a 1973 album that was entitled *Elvis* but has since become known as the *Fool* album, after one of the tracks featured on it. Now we're looking at a different song from the LP called 'Love Me, Love the Life I Lead'. It was written by song-writing team Roger Greenaway and Tony Macaulay.

Soul band the Drifters covered the song for their album *The Drifters Now*, which came out in 1973. However, the Drifters weren't the first to record the song. The American group the Fantastics moved to the UK (as the Drifters did) to try their luck in a soul boom there. Their version of 'Love Me, Love the Life I Lead' was released in late 1971.

During the '70s, Roger Greenaway was one of the songwriters responsible for many hits for the Johnny Moore-led Drifters who by then were based in the UK. Greenaway, with co-composer Roger Cook were responsible for 'Kissin' in the Back Row of the Movies', 'Like Sister and Brother', 'Love Games' and 'There Goes My First Love'. In 2009, Roger Greenaway was inducted into the Songwriters Hall of Fame.

Meanwhile Tony Macauley has won the British Academy of Songwriters, Composers and Authors Award twice as Songwriter of the Year (1970 and 1977). He is a nine-time Ivor Novello Award-winning songwriter. In 2007, he became the only British person to win the Edwin Forrest Award for outstanding contribution to the American theatre.

Elvis recorded 'Love Me Love the Life I Lead' on 21st May 1971 at RCA Studio B in Nashville,Tennessee. After completing it he moved on to tackle 'The First Time Ever I Saw Your Face'. More than two years later, 'Love Me, Love the Life I Lead' made its way on to the *Fool* album. That came out in July 1973.

The album itself sold over one-million copies worldwide despite being released soon after the much more successful *Aloha from Hawaii* album.

MERRY CHRISTMAS BABY

Elvis had scored huge success in 1957 with his first Christmas album. Over the years since its first release, the album has been reissued in various formats and continues to be re-released to this day.

The original album spent four weeks at number one in the Billboard album charts, so it's no wonder that Elvis's record label was keen for its star artist to record another festive offering. *Elvis Sings the Wonderful World of Christmas* might not have enjoyed the lasting success of his first Christmas album, but it still sold really well across the globe. It was certified gold on 4th November 1977, platinum on 1st December 1977, double platinum on 20th May 1988 and triple platinum on 15th July 1999.

As well as featuring the traditional Christmas offerings 'O Come All Ye Faithful' and 'The First Noel', there was the country-tinged 'Winter Wonderland' and love songs like 'It Won't Seem Like Christmas Without You'. One of the standout tracks was 'Merry Christmas Baby', an all-out bluesy offering that was also released as the single from the album. The song was written by Lou Baxter and Johnny Moore and originally recorded in 1947 by Johnny Moore's Three Blazers. This was a different Johnny Moore to the one that led the Drifters through many of their hits. Over the years many artists have tackled the track including Chuck Berry, Bruce Springsteen and Christina Aguilera.

As is often the case, this Christmas album was recorded way ahead of December. Elvis laid down the tracks for 'The Wonderful World of Christmas' over a two-day period, of the 15th–16th May 1971. 'Merry Christmas Baby' won praise from the critics. In his book, *Elvis Presley: A Study in Music*, written in 1979, Robert Matthew-Walker said:

> In 'Merry Christmas Baby' we encounter not only the finest recorded performance of these sessions but one of the greatest Presley

> performances committed to disc. It is a Blues track and once again his natural feel for this difficult medium is apparent. The Blues is a simple harmonic structure. This simplicity means almost any singer can sing, but only a handful can perform, the Blues. It is clear that Presley was one of this handful. It is a tragedy he never recorded a Blues album.

True words from Robert Matthew-Walker: this really shows Elvis at his sexy bluesy best. Even at just over seven minutes in duration, you lose yourself in the track and want it just to keep going on and on.

Several Elvis 'blues' compilations have been released over the years and are well worth a listen. The songs are often gathered from as early as the Sun Records days (like 'When It Rains It Really Pours') from the *Elvis is Back* album ('Like a Baby' and 'Reconsider Baby') and latter-day tracks like 'Hi Heel Sneakers'.

Elvis grew up with hearing the blues first hand from the many talented musicians that hung out on Beale Street in Memphis. The blues definitely ran through Elvis's veins, so a total 'blues' concept album was a missed trick.

UNTIL IT'S TIME FOR YOU TO GO

This track was recorded in 1971 and appeared on an Elvis album a year later.

'Until It's Time for You to Go' was written by Buffy Sainte Marie. The singer–songwriter was inspired to write this song after falling in love with someone who could not be with her. Although it was never released as a single, it became one of her most popular songs. According to Sainte-Marie's official site, the lyrics to the song are about "honesty and freedom inside the heart".

Buffy Sainte-Marie has enjoyed a long career that has seen her enjoy great success on the folk circuit. However, she's also dabbled in the worlds of rock, soundtracks, country and even children's television scores. Her songs have tackled issues like war and justice, an example being 'Universal Soldier', and love songs, like 'Until It's Time for You to Go'. The singer–songwriter released *Power in the Blood* in 2015. It was recorded in Toronto with producers Michael Phillip Wojewoda, Jon Levine and Chris Birkett. The title tune was a cover of a track made famous by Alabama 3. Another cover was of the UK-based reggae band UB40's 'Sing Our Own Song' along with new material from Sainte-Marie.

Other people who have recorded 'Until It's Time for You to Go' include Shirley Bassey, Glen Campbell, Cher, Petula Clark and Bobby Darin.

Elvis recorded the track on 17th May 1971. It appeared on *Elvis Now*, released in 1972. The song was also the only single to be taken from the album. The B-Side was 'We Can Make the Morning'. The pairing reached number nine on the Adult Contemporary Chart in the US in March 1972 and number five on the UK Singles Chart in April 1972.

March 1972

A great collection of songs was recorded at this session including 'Always on My Mind' and 'Separate Ways'. The songs were mainly laid-back, country-style love songs, with one exception…

BURNING LOVE

Dennis Linde wrote 'Burning Love' for Elvis, who recorded the song at RCA's Hollywood studios on 28th March 1972. Elvis at first was reluctant to do the song. He was going through a period of unrest in his life. Priscilla had left him. The excitement Vegas had provided initially during 1969 and 1970 was beginning to become too much of a chore, just like the movie years had been.

Persuasion from his friends and musicians around him encouraged Elvis to leave behind the love songs he seemed to prefer at that time and turn to a faster song again. 'Burning Love' reached number two on the Billboard's Hot 100 chart, enjoying almost four months in the chart.

We've mentioned the novelty song 'My Ding a Ling' by Chuck Berry previously. That song was the guilty party that prevented Elvis from having a big number-one hit with 'Burning Love'. However, it reached number one on Cashbox's top 40 charts for the week of 11th November. The song reached number seven in the UK. In October 1972, the RIAA certified the record as a million seller.

In the movie *Elvis on Tour*, Elvis can be seen performing the track. He had difficulty remembering the words for 'Burning Love' so he often had the song sheet nearby. Elvis also performed the number during the *Aloha from Hawaii* show.

In a bizarre marketing twist, Elvis's record label released 'Burning Love' on a budget album called *Burning Love and Hits from His Movies, Volume 2*. The classic track was included in an album that also featured the far inferior 'I Love Only One Girl' from *Double Trouble* and 'Tender Feeling' from *Kissin' Cousins*. It did make an appearance on the full-priced *Aloha from Hawaii* show LP, almost a year after it had been a hit.

Later in the 1970s, 'Burning Love' was once again relegated to the budget albums shelf when it appeared on an album called *Double Dynamite*. RCA redeemed themselves by releasing a CD a few years back called *Burning Love* featuring tracks from the time like 'Never Been to Spain', 'You Gave Me a Mountain', 'I'm Leavin'', 'Always on My Mind' and 'Separate Ways' (the latter of which received a similar budget-album treatment by RCA).

The focus at that time seemed to be on capturing Elvis live on stage, as was done in the 'Madison Square Garden' and 'Aloha' shows, released just a few months apart and with some track duplication in the concerts.

Marty Lacker, from the Memphis Mafia, the circle of close Elvis friends, said Presley wasn't that keen on 'Burning Love'. Could Presley himself have played a part in keeping it off his main full-priced albums at the time? We'll never know, but we'd love to know your thoughts – you can get involved by visiting our Facebook page: https://www.facebook.com/elvispresleystoriesbehindhissongs.

In the meantime, there's no denying the song was a classic – and a million-selling classic at that!

RCA
ELVIS
BURNING LOVE
(Ardiente amor)
IT'S A MATTER OF TIME
(Es cuestión de tiempo)

FIVE

JULY 1973 – STAX STUDIOS IN MEMPHIS

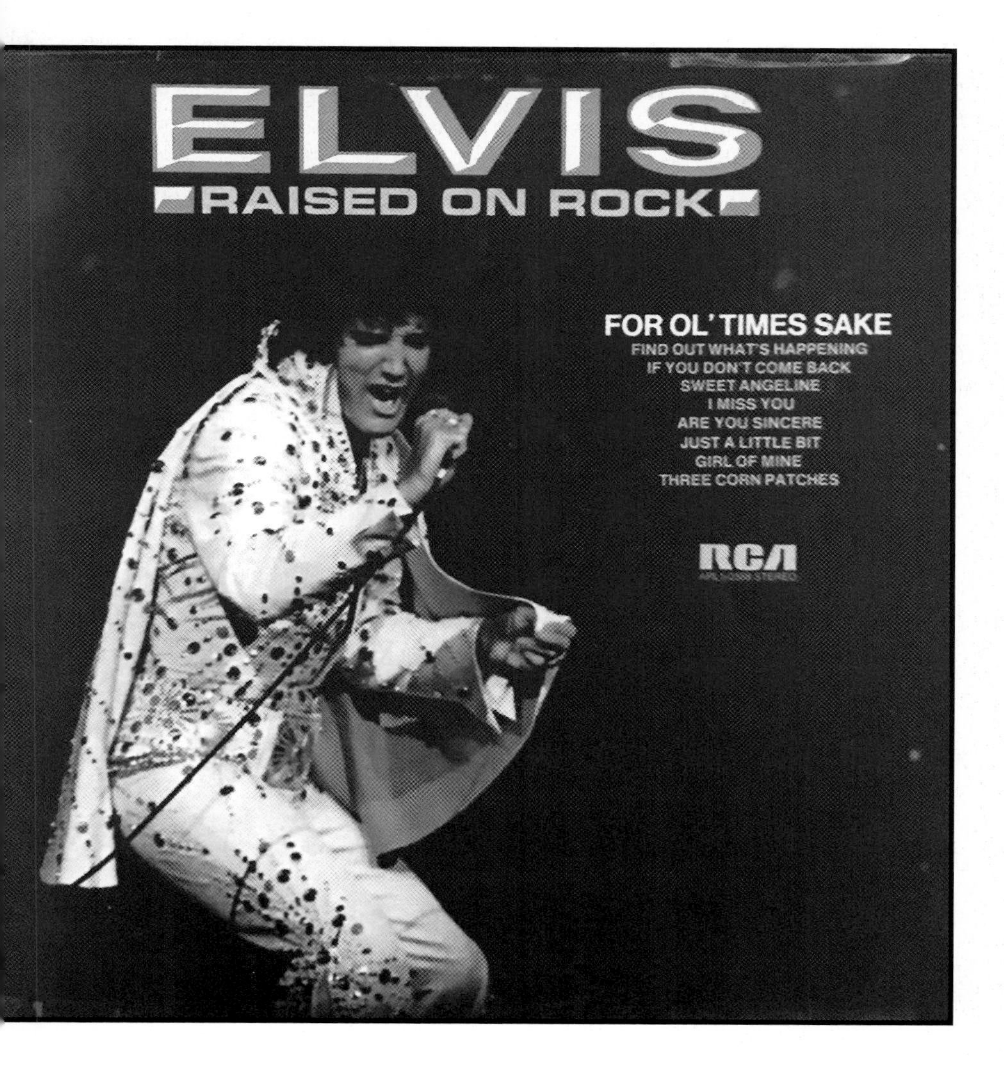

Elvis's first studio recordings for well over a year were also the first he made at the now-legendary Stax Studios in Memphis, which had produced countless soul hits in the 1960s.

The studio had originally been called Satellite when it started business in 1959. It was set up by Jim Stewart and his sister Estelle Axton. When they decided two years later that a name change was needed they took the first two letters from their surnames and so Stax was born. In just 15 years, the label saw hit after hit. The figures are impressive. According to the official website (www.staxrecords.com) "In 15 years, Stax placed more than 167 hit songs in the Top 100 on the pop charts, and a staggering 243 hits in the Top 100 R&B charts. It launched the careers of such legendary artists as Otis Redding, Sam & Dave, Rufus & Carla Thomas, Booker T & the MGs".

Elvis couldn't go back to American Studios where he had enjoyed immense success in 1969, as the label had shut its Memphis branch in 1973. Stax was recommended as a hit-making venue that had the advantage of being close to Elvis's home.

FIND OUT WHAT'S HAPPENING

This track was a top-20 hit in 1968 for Bobby Bare. It also made number five in Canada.

In the UK, the BBC recorded rocker Billy Fury doing a version of 'Find Out What's Happening' two years earlier in 1966. This wasn't released as a single, which is a shame as it would probably have been big for the star. However, at the time he was changing record labels, moving from Decca to Parlophone. That signalled the end of a seven-year run of success on the Decca label, which had netted him 26 hits. Thankfully the BBC studio recording survives. More recently, in 1993 an American country music band, Pearl River, recorded a version.

Robert Joseph 'Bobby' Bare is probably best known for the songs 'Detroit City' and '500 Miles Away from Home'. His earliest chart success came about due to a record company error. The young Bobby had recorded a demo of a song called 'The All American Boy'. The plan was that his friend Bill Parsons would record it for the label Fraternity Records. However, the label preferred Bobby's demo and so they released it. The record was a huge success reaching number two on the Billboard Hot 100. But there was a problem. The voice may have been Bobby's but the label clearly stated the artist as being 'Bill Parsons'. The mistake crossed the channel when the same song, with the wrong billing, peaked at number 22 in the UK singles chart in April 1959.

Undeterred, Bobby Bare continued. He didn't have to wait too long to have great success under his own name. The great Chet Atkins signed Bobby to RCA Victor at the start of the 1960s. The first single he released on the label was 'Shame on Me' in 1962. His second RCA Victor single, 'Detroit City', reached number six in the country charts while also climbing to number 16 in the Billboard Hot 100. That song earned Bare a Grammy Award for Best Country and Western Recording and the hit was soon followed by '500 Miles Away from Home'.

'Find Out What's Happening' was written by Jerry Crutchfield who, just like Bobby and Elvis, recorded for RCA Victor Records – in Jerry's case as part of the vocal group the Country Gentlemen. They later became known as the Escorts. Crutchfield also gained recognition as a producer, obtaining gold, platinum and multi-platinum status for albums he produced for people like Tanya Tucker and Lee Greenwood.

Elvis recorded his version of 'Find Out What's Happening' on 23rd July 1973 at the Stax recording studio in Memphis. The session marked the first time he'd recorded in Memphis since 1969.

GIRL OF MINE

The period 1972–4 was a busy one for Elvis when it came to sell-out crowds at huge concerts. He also found time to produce studio albums. These may not have been as strong as the albums recorded during 1969–71 but they sold well and had their own set of highlights. Next a track from the album *Raised on Rock/For Ol' Times Sake*.

The album was released 1st October 1973, having been recorded during a big session in Memphis. The venue this time was not American Sound Studio but

Stax studios. 'Girl of Mine' was written by Les Reed and Barry Mason. Elvis recorded his take on 24th July 1973.

Les Reed OBE was born in 1935 in Woking, England. As well as being a songwriter, arranger and musician, he's also found time to be an orchestra leader. Over the years he's written with many songwriters, mainly Barry Mason, Gordon Mills and Geoff Stephens. He's also composed hits with Johnny Worth, Roger Cook and Roger Greenaway. The website www.allmusic.com said: "Reed's sixty or more major hits have earned numerous gold discs, Ivor Novello awards and, in 1982, the British Academy Gold Badge of Merit. In the mid-1960s, it was unusual for a British singles chart not to list a Les Reed song."

His chief co-writer, Barry Mason, was also born in 1935, this time in Chorley, Lancashire in England. He wrote the bulk of his songs with Les Reed, earning many gold and platinum awards and five Ivor Novello awards.

Engelbert Humperdink recorded 'Girl of Mine'. It was listed as being recorded in 1972, but Les Reed himself believes it may have been earlier. According to an interview on www.songlink.com, Les Reed said:

> All of Tom Jones' early recordings were top favourites with Elvis and he contacted a local radio station in Memphis with the result they played 'Green Green Grass of Home' five times! Geoff Stephens and I wrote 'Sylvia' and 'This Is Our Dance' for Elvis which were both recorded. A little later Barry Mason and I wrote 'Girl of Mine' which I recorded with Engelbert and was subsequently done by Elvis. Other songs were in the pipeline but he became ill and didn't do them. 'Delilah' was a top favourite with him and he always used it to warm up before a performance.

Elvis's version of 'Girl of Mine' closes side one of his 1973 album *Raised on Rock/For Ol' Times Sake*. It was one of ten tracks to be featured on the album.

IF YOU DON'T COME BACK

Although the July 1973 Stax session wasn't as productive as RCA bosses had hoped, another track it did produce was 'If You Don't Come Back' – the first track tackled on 21st July 1973.

The song was written by two very familiar names from Elvis's earlier recordings: Jerry Leiber and Mike Stoller. The pair had written countless rock and roll classics for the young Elvis but fell out of favour with Colonel Parker. The controlling manager thought they were getting too close to his young star. Despite having written hit after hit, the pair would thus see none of their songs recorded by Elvis for many years.

In fact, during the 1960s and '70s, anything he did record by Leiber and Stoller had already been a big hit for someone – like 'Little Egypt', from the film *Roustabout*, which had already been huge for the Coasters and 'If You Don't Come Back', which scored well for soul band the Drifters. According to the website www.funky16corners.com:

> Written by Jerry Leiber and Mike Stoller, and recorded not long after they started working with The Drifters, 'If You Don't Come Back' has lyrical echoes of the kind of tunes the pair had been recording with The Coasters. Leiber and Stoller manage to take a song that would have worked in a more humorous setting with the Coasters, and tone it down a little, giving the Drifters record (with a lead vocal by Johnny Moore) a bit of an edge. It's one of the rougher, more soulful things the Drifters ever laid down, with a great guitar/horn riff repeated in the verse and some cool group harmonies in the chorus. The lyrics are brilliant.

According to the Rock & Roll Hall of Fame: "The Drifters served to link Fifties rhythm & blues with Sixties soul music. They epitomised the vocal group sound of New York City. Theirs was the sweet but streetwise sound of R&B suffused with gospel influences." The name 'Drifters' was chosen by Clyde McPhatter, who was the first lead singer of the band. The name turned out to be highly appropriate as more than 50 full-time members have 'drifted' in and out of the group since it was formed at the beginning of the 1950s. Ben E. King, Rudy Lewis and Johnny Moore were other well-known lead singers over the years.

However, leaving the Drifters was not always a great career move. Clyde McPhatter left for a solo career that started well, but was short lived chart-wise. Ben E. King enjoyed the most success with timeless tracks like 'Stand by Me' and 'Spanish Harlem'. Whoever was leading the band didn't matter as the high standard was maintained throughout the Drifters' recording career on Atlantic Records, which lasted from late 1953 to early 1966.

Johnny Moore, who had led the band for a short period in the '50s and again from 1964, returned to the band in the early '70s. During that decade they were chiefly based in the UK producing more middle-of-the-road soul tracks like 'Hello Happiness' – and a return to the movie theme with 'Kissin' in the Back Row of the Movies' around 10 years after the band had enjoyed success with 'Saturday Night at the Movies.'

There is still an official line up of the Drifters today; however, the band has no original members.

Back to 'If You Don't Come Back': in 1968 Gary Walker and the Rain issued a version. The band was formed after the Walker Brothers split.

Fast forward to 21st July 1973 and on the same night Elvis recorded 'If You Don't Come Back', he rehearsed 'It's Diff'rent Now' and laid down 'Three Corn Patches' and 'Take Good Care of Her'.

I'VE GOT A THING ABOUT YOU BABY

We've already mentioned the songwriter Tony Joe White as he wrote 'Polk Salad Annie', which Elvis introduced on his return to live performances. He also composed 'Rainy Night in Georgia', made popular by Brook Benton, and in the 1980s, 'Steamy Windows' and 'Undercover Agent for the Blues' for Tina Turner. He wrote our next song too, the studio track 'I've Got a Thing about You Baby'.

Elvis recorded 'I've Got a Thing about You Baby' during his Stax sessions on 22nd July 1973. The session saw Elvis joined by his trusted musicians including James Burton and Reggie Young on guitar. Tommy Cogbill stood in on bass and Ronnie Tutt took command behind the drums. That July, Elvis had just finished more gruelling touring and many have said his heart wasn't in it for this recording session. He turned up three hours late on the first night and later left without recording anything. He was late again the next night. In the book *Elvis Presley – A Life in Music*, Ernst Jorgensen said: "The sound of his voice on the session tapes makes it painfully evident that he had little interest in recording at all."

'I've Got a Thing about You Baby' is a great track. But compared to recordings Elvis made on stage earlier in 1973, you can tell his heart really isn't in it.

Ernst Jorgensen said the December sessions were more positive: "Elvis Presley's career had never seen a year of greater highs or lows than 1973. From the triumph of *Aloha from Hawaii* Elvis had gone into a tailspin of failure on all fronts: plunging record sales, divorce, problems with his health and his weight. Now, just days before Christmas, at the conclusion of a set of sessions forced on him by his record company, there once again was reason for hope. Felton Jarvis had recorded eighteen new songs in a week, and Elvis, Tom Parker, and RCA could have been forgiven for believing that another turnaround was still within reach."

Compared to the American Sound Studio recordings in Memphis in 1969 – which garnered countless hits rising high into the top 10 in various charts around the world – none of the five A-side Stax singles, issued between 1973 and 1975, reached Billboard's top 10. Only three of them made it into the top 20. 'Raised on Rock' didn't even make it into the top 40. 'I've Got a Thing about You Baby' did little better, stalling at number 39. It sold more in the UK but still only made number 33.

In 2016, the Royal Philharmonic Orchestra visited the song to give it a modern-day makeover. It starts with the bass-line used in the *Jailhouse Rock* soundtrack song 'Baby I Don't Care' and features prominent drums throughout the verses. It's a totally different track and worth comparing with the other to find your favourite version.

RAISED ON ROCK

It would be easy to look at the 1970s as being filled with Vegas shows, countless tours, jumpsuits and big ballads. However, Elvis could still rock out in the 1970s and there are many great examples where the King reclaimed his rock 'n' roll crown with high-energy offerings. Examples include 'Burning Love', 'Way Down', 'T-R-O-U-B-L-E' and 'Raised on Rock'.

'Raised on Rock' was written by Mark James, who was best known for writing 'Suspicious Minds', which helped cement Elvis's big comeback. Elvis was the first to record 'Raised on Rock', but it's since been covered by Johnny Winter in 1974, Doug Parkinson in 1975, Pratt and McClain a year later and, more recently, Tom Green recorded the track in 2009.

Elvis turned his attention to the song on 23rd July 1973. Between 11pm and 3.30am at Stax, Elvis laid down 'Raised on Rock' and 'For Ol' Times Sake'. Both songs shared the title of the album they were eventually issued on.

On www.allmusic.com, reviewer Thomas Ward said: "A self-consciously tough rock song, 'Raised on Rock' is not one of Presley's more successful songs of a difficult artistic period and as such was neither a hit nor artistic triumph at the time, and if anything, has aged less well than many of Elvis's other songs from the period. The song's lyrics are quite dreadful in places, and the song opens with the trite 'I remember as a child I used to hear/Music that they played Lord with a feel/Some call it folk, some call it soul/People let me tell you it was rock and roll'." The reviewer went on to say: "The song seems forced, as if it was a conscious attempt to 'contemporise' Presley to a mid-70s audience who listened to Led Zeppelin and other rock bands. It doesn't work, and is one of the weaker songs in Presley's canon."

Views are mixed on the songbase on www.elvisnews.com with Elvis Rimes saying: "This is a catchy number and well delivered. Always been a favourite of mine and I believe this to be a stand out track on the album." However, Cruiser621 says: "This song stinks to put it bluntly." And Derek D said: "Having played this track a few times of late, I believe, done correctly, there is a market here for a remix. Give the recording a heavier upbeat backing, could be interesting. The words to the song are okay, just the original backing seems a big let down."

Ernst Jorgensen's opinion in his book *A Life in Music* was: "The lyrics to 'Raised on Rock' (which had Elvis growing up on the music he himself had helped create) were downright silly."

10–16th December 1973 – Stax Studios, Memphis

GOOD TIME CHARLIE'S GOT THE BLUES

Composer Danny O'Keefe recorded 'Good Time Charlie's Got the Blues' on no less than three occasions. The first version was in 1967, either for the Jerden label or for Piccadilly, but it was not released; then came a version on the Cotillion label in 1971; finally, O'Keefe recorded a slower version in 1972.

In the meantime, a relatively unknown group called the Bards, from Moses Lake, Washington, recorded the number and released it in 1968 on the Parrot label and in 1969 on the Jerden label (Jerden 907). It was issued as a single, reaching number nine on the Billboard Hot 100 singles chart, number five on the adult contemporary chart and number 63 on the country chart.

O'Keefe's version stayed on the Billboard chart for 14 weeks and sold a million copies. In an interview with *Mojo* magazine in 2010, O'Keefe recalled the writing of 'Good Time Charlie's Got the Blues': "It was very simple and got to the heart of the matter. It was written in not much over an hour. I think I hoped that a country artist would cover the song, but it made reference to pills and those references were taboo for country singers then."

Other people to have recorded 'Good Time Charlie's Got the Blues' include Willie Nelson, Waylon Jennings and Jerry Lee Lewis.

Elvis recorded his version of 'Good Time Charlie's Got the Blues' on 13th December 1973. It was typical of the type of songs Elvis was recording at the time dealing with love and opportunities that had been lost. It's worth noting that Elvis did not sing the lines "I got my pills to ease the pain. Can't find a thing to ease my brain."

The song was the closing track on the *Good Times* album that was released in March 1974.

HELP ME

Time now for a song written by country and gospel singer–songwriter Larry Wayne Gatlin. 'Help Me' appeared on the *Promised Land* album. Elvis recorded his version of the song on 12th December 1973 as part of his Stax recording sessions.

Larry Gatlin formed a group with his brothers Steve and Rudy in the late 1970s. The trio enjoyed great success in the country music world. Combining a solo career and hits with his brothers, Gatlin performed on 33 Top 40 hits. The band's chart success continued through the 1980s, with their biggest hits being 'Broken Lady', 'Houston (Means I'm One Day Closer to You)' and 'Talkin' to the Moon'.

Larry Gatlin's early success came thanks to country singer Dottie West. She had spotted him in Las Vegas and thought he looked like Mickey Newbury. She recorded two of Gatlin's compositions, 'You're the Other Half of Me' and 'Once You Were Mine'. West also passed one of Gatlin's demo tapes around Nashville, Tennessee, and even arranged for him to relocate there, purchasing a plane ticket for him. Now that is having faith in someone's talents!

Larry Gatlin also wrote 'Bitter They Are, Harder They Fall', which Elvis also recorded. That song appeared on *From Elvis Presley Boulevard, Memphis, Tennessee* released in 1976 on RCA Records.

Elvis not only recorded Gatlin's song 'Help Me' in the studio, it was also one of the tracks he included in his live set when he performed live in Memphis in 1974. RCA were there to capture the song live.

IF THAT ISN'T LOVE

Next a song written by Dottie Rambo, who wrote more than 2,500 songs, including her most notable 'He Looked beyond My Fault and Saw My Need', 'We Shall Behold Him' and 'I Go to the Rock'. But the track we're going to look at is 'If That Isn't Love'.

Elvis recorded the track at Stax studios in Memphis on 16th December 1973. It was the first track he laid down that night, before moving on to 'Spanish Eyes' and 'She Wears My Ring'.

Rambo's songs have been recorded by a virtual who's who in the music world. Her biggest song featured the powerful vocals of the late Whitney Houston: this version of 'I Go to the Rock' appeared on the motion picture soundtrack for *The Preacher's Wife*. The recording garnered Rambo and Houston the 1998 GMA Dove Award for Traditional Gospel Song of the Year. Whitney Houston said: "It was a pleasure to record one of Dottie Rambo's songs, 'I Go to the Rock' for *The Preacher's Wife*. It was one of my favourites. What a sweet lady and gifted songwriter."

In 2002, Rambo re-entered the studio to record her first solo album in 18 years. The result was the award-winning hit *Stand by the River*. The title track, a duet with Dolly Parton, would go to the number-one spot of the Christian Country Radio Chart, as did its follow up, 'I'm Gonna Leave Here Shoutin''.

In an archive interview, Country legend Dolly Parton said: "Dottie Rambo is a special and precious person. I have always loved her and her writing. I think she is one of the most incredible writers of our time... or anybody's time."

Rambo died on 11th May 2008 as a result of injuries sustained in a bus accident along Interstate 44 just outside Mount Vernon, Missouri. She had just finished a performance at Calvary Life Church in Granite City, Illinois and was en route to a Mother's Day show in Texas when the 1997 Prévost bus she was travelling in ran off the road, struck a guard rail and hit an embankment. Rambo was pronounced dead at the scene.

Elvis's version of 'If That Isn't Love' would have sat comfortably on one of his gospel albums, but its release came on the *Good Times* album in 1974. The ten tracks came in at a rather short 29 minutes and 23 seconds. His next album, *Elvis Recorded Live on Stage in Memphis*, came in at a much better 42 minutes.

Back to Whitney Houston: in one of her later interviews, she recalled meeting Elvis. During her filmed interview with *Access Hollywood*, the award-winning pop diva recalled meeting the cultural icon as a child while her mother toured as one of Presley's backup singers. "It was one of those moments that I won't forget as a kid. It wasn't like, 'Hi Mr. Elvis, nice to meet you,' we didn't do that. We just sat back and looked at him. Amazing to look at."

Back in 1963 Whitney's mother, Cissy Houston joined three other singers to form the Sweet Inspirations. According to www.elvis.com.au, it was during Cissy Houston's soprano obbligato on 'Are You Lonesome Tonight?' that Elvis started laughing at the midnight show on 26th August 1969. Elvis changes the lyrics to be funny, and then cannot keep a straight face the rest of the song. He seems to be somewhat amused by the soprano performance by Cissy Houston who sings her part perfectly. It would become known as 'Are You Lonesome Tonight – The Laughing Version'.

I GOT A FEELIN' IN MY BODY

Dennis Linde was an American singer and songwriter who is probably best remembered in the Elvis world for writing the classic 1972 hit 'Burning Love'.

However, 'Burning Love' wasn't the only song Linde composed for Elvis. 'I Got a Feelin' In My Body' was recorded by Elvis at Stax on 10th December 1973. Recently it was remixed by Tommi Sunshine and Wuki at the request of Sony, Elvis's record label.

Linde wrote numerous country hit songs for the likes of Roger Miller and Roy Drusky. His songs were recorded by Tanya Tucker, Gary Morris, Don Williams, the Judds, Alan Jackson, Mark Chesnutt and Garth Brooks, among several other acts. Linde was elected to the Nashville Songwriters Hall of Fame in 2001 and selected as BMI's Songwriter of the Year in 1994.

It was the success of 'Burning Love' that launched Linde to the forefront of Nashville songwriters and gained him his first record deal, with Elektra. 'I Got a Feelin' in My Body' has an obvious gospel tinge with its references to Moses walking the children out of Egypt land and Daniel facing the lion.

Swedish musician Per-Erik Hallin sang and played piano with Elvis in 1973 and 1974. Elvis called him Pete. The first song 'Pete' worked on with Elvis was 'I Got a Feelin' in My Body'. In an interview with www.elvis.com.au, Per-Erik Hallin said about recording the song:

> It went well. I probably would have been more nervous today, I think, than I was then, I was so young. But it was really fun, because he recorded most of it right away, something most artists don't, not even then, when you record the rhythm track first and then the singer does the vocal overdub some time later. But this was more like a live performance, even the background chorus was recorded directly.

He continued:

> There were no rehearsals, but they were playing a demo again and again and again. And then, all the musicians wrote down what they heard, chords and such. And then they used numbers, it was the first time I've seen it. Instead of the name of the chords you wrote 1, 2, 3 and 4. They called it 'the Nashville number system'. Then suddenly it was time to make a recording and that was more like a 'jam', it was very relaxed and inspiring.

You can read the full interview with Per-Erik Hallin here: http://www.elvis.com.au/presley/interview-with-per-erik-pete-hallin-elvis-presley.shtml.

IF YOU TALK IN YOUR SLEEP

'If You Talk in Your Sleep' is our next track. It saw the light of day in 1975 on the *Promised Land* album. However, it had been recorded at the December 1973 recording sessions at Stax, which as we've already mentioned were much more productive than the July recording dates.

The song was written by Red West and Johnny Christopher. Robert Gene 'Red' West has had many careers. He's been an actor, a film stuntman and a songwriter. However, he's best known for being one of Elvis's oldest and closest friends. In an interview on the website www.elvis.com.au, Red West said the legend that he became friends with Elvis after saving him from a fight in school was totally true. He said:

> That is the real story. We had crew cuts, wore tee-shirts and blue jeans, Elvis had the long duck-tail, the long sideburns and he wore the loud clothes and naturally he was a target for all the bullies, and one day luckily I walked into the boys' bathroom at Humes High School and three guys were going to cut his hair just, you know, to make themselves look big or make them feel big or whatever, and I intervened and stopped it. I guess that stuck because a couple of years later after Elvis had his first record he came over and asked me if I would like to go with him, I think it was Grenada, Mississippi or somewhere, and I went and I was with him from then on, except for a couple of years in the Marine Corps. He was my good friend and I'll always remember him as that.

He may have been well known as a tough bodyguard for Elvis, but he could write some fantastic lyrics too. 'You'll Be Gone' with contributions from Elvis and Charlie Hodge and 'That's Someone You Never Forget' were a couple of the earliest tracks. Red also co-wrote 'If You Think I Don't Need You' with Joey Cooper for the motion picture *Viva Las Vegas*. He teamed up with Joey Cooper again on 'I'm A Fool', which Ricky Nelson recorded. Red West also co-wrote the song 'Separate Ways' for Elvis in 1972. It was the B-side release of the single 'Always on My Mind'.

Back to 'If You Talk in Your Sleep': the song was also covered by Little Milton who enjoyed a top-40 Billboard Soul Singles chart hit. Elvis's version was released as a single in North America on 10th May 1974, with the B-side 'Help Me'. It reached number six on the Billboard Country Singles chart in June 1974 and number 17 on the Billboard Pop Singles chart in August 1974.

In Las Vegas on 19th August 1974 Elvis departed from the conventional opening, not starting with 'Also Sprach Zarathustra' or 'See See Rider' but instead with 'Big Boss Man'. He also included many songs he had not performed live before – 'Down in the Alley', 'Good Time Charlie's Got the Blues', 'I'm Leavin'', 'Softly as I Leave You' and 'Promised Land' – making this probably the most unique concert Elvis gave in the 1970s. Elvis also performed a live version of 'If You Talk in Your Sleep' during the show.

Unfortunately, many of the songs were dropped soon after, returning to the tried and tested formula of previous concerts. However, some of the songs did remain during the Vegas season including 'Promised Land', 'Big Boss Man' and 'If You Talk in Your Sleep'.

The unique opening night was recorded by RCA and saw its release on the Follow that Dream CD, *Nevada Nights.*

IT'S MIDNIGHT

It's time for another track from the *Promised Land* album: 'It's Midnight'. The song had been the flipside of Elvis's hit single 'Promised Land', which had been issued a few months before the album in September 1974. 'It's Midnight' enjoyed its own chart success reaching number nine in the country charts. It had been recorded on 10th December 1973 as part of the Stax sessions.

The song was written by Billy Edd Wheeler and Jerry Chesnut. Wheeler's other hits include the Johnny Cash and June Carter classic 'Jackson' and Kenny Rogers' 'Coward of the County'. His songs have been performed by almost 200 artists including Nancy Sinatra, who starred with Elvis in the movie *Speedway*, Neil Young, Bobby Darin and Jefferson Airplane.

Other Jerry Chesnut songs recorded by Elvis include 'T-R-O-U-B-L-E', 'Love Coming Down' and 'Woman Without Love'. Chesnut is probably best remembered for 'A Good Year for the Roses' recorded by another Elvis, Elvis Costello (as well as by George Jones and Alan Jackson). He also wrote Faron Young's huge hit 'It's Four in the Morning'. Jerry Chesnut described Elvis as: "the superman of the music world". In an interview with www.elvis.com.au he said: "I guess I was expecting some supernatural feeling but the fact is… we shook hands, and in a voice kinda like a humble and shy teenage boy he asked 'How are you doin?' It amazes to me this day how very simple and sincere true greatness can really be!" Read the full interview here: http://www.elvis.com.au/presley/jerry-chesnut-remembers-elvis-presley.shtml.

LOVE SONG OF THE YEAR

We're staying at Stax but moving to the end of 1973 now for a song Elvis recorded called 'Love Song of the Year'. This was on 12th December 1973 and Elvis had already laid down 'Mr. Songman' and 'Thinking About You'. After 'Love Song of the Year', he would move on to 'Help Me', which we've already looked at.

'Love Song of the Year' was written by Chris Christian from Abilene, Texas. Over the years his songs have been recorded by a variety of chart stars including Hall and Oates, Olivia Newton John, the Pointer Sisters and the Carpenters. Christian has written more than 2,000 songs! He's also found time to be the founder and chief executive officer of his own music production and publishing companies, Home Sweet Home Records, YMC Records and LCS Music Group, Inc., as well as the largest motion-picture sound stage in the South, 'The Studios' at Las Colinas.

According to his own website, www.ccentertainment.com:

> His 30 years in the music industry have led albums that have received nine Grammy Award nominations as a music producer, artist and publisher, winning four Grammys. He has also been nominated for seven Gospel Music Association Dove Awards as an artist, music producer, publisher and songwriter, winning five Doves. Chris was also responsible for starting the career of Amy Grant, and has produced over 100 albums that have sold in excess of ten million copies.

Chris Christian was working with Wayne Newton in Las Vegas when he got a call from Elvis himself. In an archive interview, Christian said: "He called me over at the Sands and said 'I just recorded your song and I'm opening here tonight. It's going to be real busy but I'd love you to come over and listen to the acetate and see if you like it'." Christian said he was 'blown away' by the call and the fact Elvis had recorded one of his songs.

Christian has had a busy life in music but he has another passion too. In 2015, he became the vice chairman and managing partner for the WNBA's Dallas Wings.

Elvis's version of 'Love Song of the Year' appeared on the *Promised Land* album. It was released on 8th January 1975 – the day Elvis turned 40.

LOVING ARMS

Tom Jans was an American folk singer–songwriter and guitarist from San Jose, California. He takes his place in the Elvis world for composing the song 'Loving Arms' that Elvis recorded for his *Good Times* album.

The song was first performed by Kris Kristofferson and Rita Coolidge on their album *Full Moon*, the first of three duet albums by the couple, who had married just weeks before. Dobie Gray also recorded 'Loving Arms' as a single and as the title song to one of his albums. While Kristofferson's solo projects featured his own penned material, *Full Moon* included several covers like 'Loving Arms'. During the 1970s and 1980s, Rita Coolidge enjoyed success across the board. She could be regularly found on Billboard's pop, country, adult contemporary and jazz charts. Together with Kristofferson, Coolidge won two Grammy Awards.

Composer Tom Jans was raised near San Jose. His paternal grandmother had been involved in music, playing in the Rocky Mountain Five jazz group. When asked in an interview who were his influences, Jans said they were wide-ranging, from Hank Williams to flamenco (his mother was from Spain) to the Beatles. Jans sadly suffered serious injuries, especially to his kidneys, in a motorcycle accident in 1983. He died aged 36 of a suspected drug overdose the following year. His most famous song 'Loving Arms' was performed by Mentor Williams' brother Paul at Jans' funeral.

Tom Waits dedicated a song to Jans, whom he and his wife had befriended, 'Whistle Down the Wind (For Tom Jans)' from the album *Bone Machine*. In an interview, Waits said: "It was written about another friend, but it was the kind of song that Tom Jans would have written. He was there in spirit."

Elvis recorded 'Loving Arms' at Stax on 13th December1973.

Felton Jarvis revisited the song in 1980 for his *Guitar Man* project, which saw new backings being added to Elvis's original vocals, but more about that album in a future edition.

MY BOY

Next an album track and hit single for Elvis entitled 'My Boy'.

The music was composed by Jean-Pierre Bourtayre and Claude François, and the lyrics were translated from the original French version to English. The original title translates as 'Because I Love You My Child'. The lyrics were translated by Phil Coulter and Bill Martin.

The English lyricists of 'My Boy' have enjoyed further success. Bill Martin has been presented with three Ivor Novello awards, including one as Songwriter of the Year. His co-writer Phil Coulter has gained 23 platinum discs, 39 gold discs, 52 silver discs, two Grand Prix Eurovision awards and five Ivor Novello awards.

Actor Richard Harris had already enjoyed huge success with 'MacArthur Park', which mentioned that "cake out in the rain". It was certainly one of the more lyrically intriguing songs ever recorded.* Harris then turned his hand to 'My Boy', performing it as part of a music contest in 1971 run by Radio Luxembourg. It didn't win the contest, but Harris recorded the song and released it as a single later that year. The song reached number 41 on the Billboard pop chart and peaked at number 13 on the Billboard adult contemporary chart.

---

* In an interview with *Q* magazine, Jimmy Webb, who wrote 'MacArthur Park', said: "It's clearly about a love affair ending, and the person singing it is using the cake and the rain as a metaphor for that. OK, it may be far out there, and a bit incomprehensible, but I wrote the song at a time in the late 1960s when surrealistic lyrics were the order of the day."

Speaking on his website, www.philcoulter.com, the songwriter said:

> Richard Harris, who was a major movie star, had enjoyed a surprise hit with a brilliant and complex seven minute song called 'MCARTHUR PARK' [sic]. By any standards it was a pop classic, but Harris went back to making movies. Harris and I used to drink in the same pub in Chelsea, The Queens Elm, popular with emigre Irish. We became friends and I persuaded him to go back into the studios to record again. The result was a hit single and album called 'MY BOY'. On the back of that we toured the U.S. for eight weeks. I can't remember a lot about that tour, and the bits I can remember you don't want to hear about. Trust me. It was a real bonus and one of the biggest thrills of my life when two years later 'MY BOY' became an international smash hit for Elvis Presley.

Elvis recorded his version of 'My Boy' at Stax on 13th December 1973. It was one of the tracks featured on his 1974 album *Good Times*. RCA released two singles from the album: 'I've Got a Thing about You Baby' and 'My Boy'

Presley's version of the song reached number 20 on the Billboard pop chart and spent one week on top of the Billboard adult contemporary chart in April 1975. 'My Boy' also peaked at number 14 on the Billboard country chart. However, it enjoyed its biggest success in the UK, reaching number five.

Norbert Putnam was the bassist for the December sessions at Stax. In an interview with the *Houston Press*, Putnam talked about one song Elvis attempted, similar to 'My Boy', that proved to be too painful for Elvis to complete. Putnam said:

> It was a song called 'We Had It All' that Dobie Gray had previously done, about a chance, sad meeting between a divorced husband and wife, or at least ex-lovers. Presley decided on the spot he wanted to do it.
>
> Now Elvis was a very quick study, he could hear vocals and arrangements once or twice, grab the lyric sheet, and just kill it.
>
> But on this particular night, we did four, five, six takes, and he wasn't getting it. I'd never seen him have problems like that before.

According to Norbert Putnam, Elvis just threw the microphone on the ground and loudly proclaimed to the stunned assembled: "You can put that one out after I've been dead 20 years!" You can read the full interview with Norbert Putnam here: http://www.houstonpress.com/music/elviss-bassist-recalls-stax-sessions-one-song-the-king-couldnt-finish-6517720.

PROMISED LAND

During the '70s Elvis recorded lots of love songs and ballads, but on those occasions when he did a fast track he proved without a doubt that he could still rock out with the best of them. One of those tracks was 'Promised Land'.

According to www.songfacts.com, the track was written when its composer Chuck Berry was serving time in jail for transporting a girl across state lines for immoral purposes. He had to borrow an atlas of the US from the prison library to plot his hero's journey from Virginia to California. Chuck Berry was one of the original rock and roll legends. He was born on 18th October 1926, in St. Louis, Missouri. Sadly, the legendary star died at the age of 90 in March 2017.

When his death was announced, the tributes started to pour in. US singer–songwriter Bruce Springsteen said he was "the greatest pure rock 'n' roll writer who ever lived". Mick Jagger of the Rolling Stones said Berry "lit up our teenage years, and blew life into our dreams of being musicians and performers". The guitarist and songwriter died Saturday 18th March in the US state of Missouri after a seven-decade career. Seen as one of the fathers of rock 'n' roll, he influenced generations of succeeding musicians, most notably the Beatles, the Rolling Stones and the Beach Boys. Rocker Alice Cooper tweeted that Berry was "the genesis behind the great sound of rock 'n' roll". "All of us in rock have now lost our father," he said.

Berry was known for trademark four-bar guitar introductions and quickfire lyrics that reflected the rebelliousness of 1950s teenagers. His hits included 'Johnny B. Goode', 'Roll Over Beethoven' and 'Sweet Little Sixteen'. He received a lifetime achievement Grammy in 1984 and was among the first inductees to the Rock & Roll Hall of Fame in 1986. In a bizarre twist, he had scored one of his biggest ever hits in 1972 with a novelty song called 'My Ding-a-Ling'.

Early in 1955, Berry met blues legend Muddy Waters, who suggested Berry go and meet the bosses of Chess Records. Berry wrote and recorded a song called 'Maybellene' and took it to Chess. They must have loved what they heard as they offered Berry a contract on the spot. Within a few short months, 'Maybellene' had reached number one on the R&B charts and number five on the pop charts.

Looking at his other great tracks, there's always a mix of clever lyrics and distinctive sounds. Berry became one of the most influential figures in the history of rock music. He had countless high-profile fans. Beatle John Lennon said "If you tried to give Rock and Roll another name, you might call it Chuck Berry." Lifelong fan Keith Richards from the Rolling Stones said: "What interested me about Chuck Berry was the way he could step out of the rhythm part with such ease, throwing in a nice simple riff and then drop straight into the feel of it again." When he performed with Berry on stage, Richards said: "When you're working with Chuck, you've got to be prepared for anything, anytime. But I still can't dislike him. I love him and I love his family."

In 2016, Berry announced he would be releasing his first album in nearly four decades. He dedicated it to his wife of 68 years, Themetta 'Toddy'. The album, *Chuck*, was recorded in St Louis, Missouri. It came out in summer 2016 showing Berry still loving the blues and rock 'n' roll – it's a great album from a 90-years-young Chuck Berry.

Berry himself once said: "Describe Elvis Presley? He was the greatest who ever was, is or ever will be."

Elvis visited Berry's back catalogue a number of times. In both 1963 and 1964 he recorded 'Memphis Tennessee' with the plan of releasing it as a single. Sadly, it only appeared as an album track on 1965's *Elvis for Everyone* album.

Elvis included 'Johnny B Goode' on stage as well as a short take of 'Hail Hail Rock and Roll' – and of course, he recorded his powerful version of 'Promised Land' at Stax.

The December 1973 Stax Records sessions showed the singer once again reaching out to publishers other than those he owned for songs, and the repertory embraces material by Berry, Waylon Jennings and Larry Gatlin, among others.

On www.allmusic.com, the reviewer says: "Elvis sounds bold and confident in ways that make this album [*Promised Land*] a diverting, if not profoundly exciting experience."

Elvis recorded 'Promised Land' on 15th December 1973. On the same night he tackled 'Your Love's Been a Long Time Coming' and 'There's a Honky Tonk Angel'.

TALK ABOUT THE GOOD TIMES

'Talk About the Good Times' was written by a composer who had already seen his songs recorded with great success by Elvis: Jerry Reed.

Reed was a singer, guitarist and songwriter. He also found time to appear in several films, including the hugely successful *Smokey and the Bandit*. His hit songs include 'Guitar Man', 'U.S. Male' and 'A Thing Called Love', all of which were recorded by Elvis. Other tracks Jerry Reed wrote included 'Alabama Wild Man' and 'When You're Hot, You're Hot'. That track earned a Grammy Award for Best Male Country Vocal Performance. After signing with RCA in the mid-'60s, Reed began having hits of his own. He also started making regular appearances on primetime TV variety shows hosted by Johnny Cash and Glen Campbell.

Elvis's take on 'Talk About the Good Times' was recorded on 14th December 1973 at Stax Studios. We've previously mentioned that this was a more productive session than the July dates. In fact, on the 15th December Elvis laid down 'Promised Land', 'Your Love's Been a Long Time Coming' and 'There's a Honky Tonk Angel'. On the 16th December, Elvis recorded 'If That Isn't Love', 'Spanish Eyes' and 'She Wears My Ring'.

'Talk About the Good Times' came from the 1974 album *Good Times*. Critic Bruce Eder wrote about the album: "It wasn't necessarily what long-time fans or potential listeners among younger audiences were looking for, but the album has more than stood the test of time, even if it isn't his best work of this period."

Of the song, 'Talk About the Good Times', the website www.elvis.com.au says:

> It doesn't work as well as two of his other Jerry Reed covers, 'Guitar Man' and 'US Male'. Perhaps it's because Reed is not present in the studio to provide guitar accompaniment this time.
>
> The underlying song and its associated message are strong. Lyrics like "Most folks couldn't tell you who their neighbours are" and "All the guns are loaded, front doors are bolted", are even more relevant now than in the 1970s.

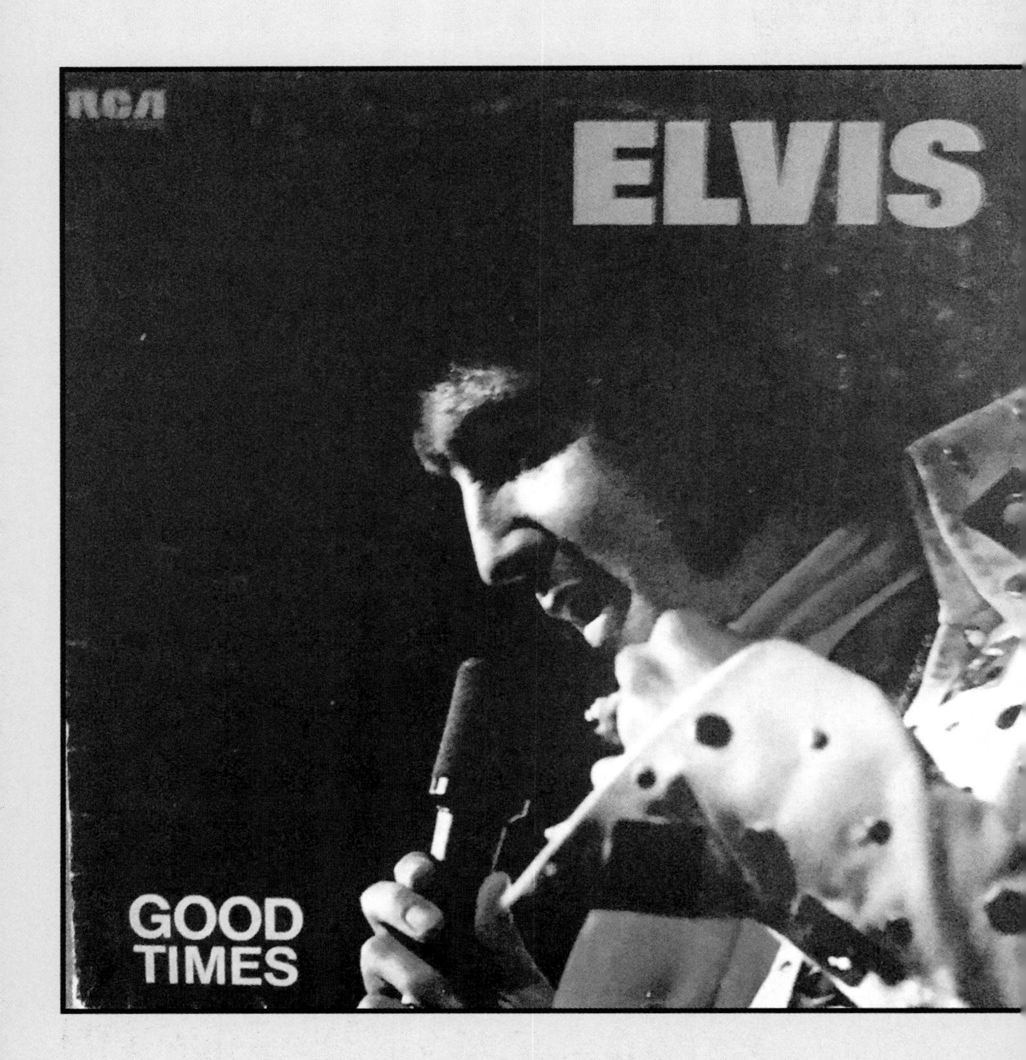
RCA
ELVIS
GOOD
TIMES

SIX

BACK TO THE '50s – THE SUN RISES AND A LEGEND BEGINS

We're turning the clock right back to start and looking at the 1954–6 period in the recording career of the man they called the King.

July 1954 – Sun Studios in Memphis

ELVIS'S FIRST SINGLE – THAT'S ALL RIGHT (MAMA) – SUN 209

This time we're going way back to the 1950s, more than 60 years ago, to a tiny studio in Memphis Tennessee where music history was made, a studio run by one man with a dream: to find a fresh and new sound for the teenage market (and to make his fortune). That man was Sam Phillips and the studio was the Memphis Recording Service, home of the Sun label. The young man who was to change music forever – a truck driver called Elvis Presley.

Where better to start than with 'That's All Right' (often known as 'That's All Right, Mama')? Although not strictly the beginning, it was certainly the start of the most amazing career in music for Elvis. Elvis had already visited the studio to make some private recordings, so he was already known to Sun's secretary, Marion Keisker. On the second occasion he visited the studio, Sam Phillips was there. That was in January 1954.

Sam may not have seen a global superstar in the making on that occasion, but he certainly saw enough from the visit to plant a seed in his head – though it would be a few more months before he would call Elvis into the studio. In the summer of 1954 Sam had a song called 'Without You' given to him by song publisher Red Wortham. Sam felt there was an air of vulnerability about the track but who could record it in the best way possible? The only person he could think of who might be able convey the needed vulnerability was the young Elvis.

The 19-year-old truck driver headed to the studios and did his best with the song, but he didn't sing it to Sam's satisfaction. However, Phillips wasn't ready to give up. He asked Elvis what songs he could sing. Presley opened his heart and performed virtually every song he knew. Elvis recalled that day with Memphis reporter Bob Johnson in 1956. He said: "I guess I must have sat there at least three hours. I sang everything I knew – pop stuff, spirituals, just a few words of anything I remembered."

Whatever else he did sing on that day must have impressed Phillips enough for him to call a good friend. That man was the late Scotty Moore. Scotty had been a session musician for a while and Sam thought he was the right man to listen to Elvis, to see whether he could have a singing career. Scotty never minced his words, so Sam knew whatever the guitarist said would be how he really felt. So Elvis went over to Scotty's house. Bill Black was also there. It became the first time the trio ever played together, even if it was behind closed doors.

According to Scotty Moore, the trio ran through Billy Eckstine's 'I Apologise', the Ink Spots' 'If I Didn't Care', Hank Snow and Eddy Arnold's latest hits and a Dean Martin-styled version of 'You Belong to Me'. Bill Black wasn't overly impressed at that initial meeting. However, Scotty must have sensed something. He said to Sam Phillips: "Well, you know, he didn't really knock me out, but the boy's got a good voice." That was enough for Sam. He set up what was to become a world-famous meeting. Watching the purse strings, he only booked in Scotty and Bill to accompany Elvis and not the rest of their band, the Starlight Wranglers.

Scotty Moore passed away in June 2016. But his amazing guitar work, which influenced some of today's most famous guitarists, could be heard on all Elvis's Sun recordings, his RCA material in the '50s and some of the big hits in the '60s. Keith Richards of the Rolling Stones famously said: "When I heard Heartbreak Hotel, I knew what I wanted to do in life. It was as plain as day. All I wanted to do in the world was to be able to play and sound like that. Everyone else wanted to be Elvis, I wanted to be Scotty Moore." Scotty Moore was inducted into the Rock & Roll Hall of Fame in 2000. In 2015 he was placed at number 29 in *Rolling Stone* magazine's 100 greatest guitarists list.

When the news of his death was announced, fellow musicians paid tribute, with Billy Idol tweeting: "Not many guitarists in R&R were as original and as inventive as Scotty Moore RIP." Country star Billy Ray Cyrus tweeted: "RIP Scotty Moore. You will be deeply missed. One thing's for sure… the King is rockin' in Heaven tonight!!"

The rockin' started on Monday 5th July 1954, when Elvis, Scotty and Bill stood together for the first time in the famous studio. Sam Phillips was at the recording desk in the control room. They ran through a number of false starts before they finally attempted 'Harbor Lights', which had already been a big hit for Bing Crosby in 1950. Then they tried Leon Payne's 'I Love You Because'. It had been a number-one country hit for its author in 1949 and a number-two hit for Ernest Tubb on the hillbilly charts in the same year. Later the song would become massive for Jim Reeves.

According to a historical article in the UK's *Independent* newspaper:

> Finally they decided to take a break. It was late, the boy was clearly discouraged, and everybody had to work the next day. Maybe, Sam thought, they ought to just give it up for the night, come back on Tuesday and try again. Scotty and Bill were sipping Cokes, not saying much of anything. Sam was doing something in the control room and, as Elvis explained it afterwards, "this song popped into my mind that I had heard years ago, and I started kidding around with."

That song was 'That's All Right'. It had been a hit for Arthur Big Boy Crudup. Presley would return to Crudup's catalogue a few more times during the '50s, but this was to be the most significant moment. In an archive interview, Scotty Moore said:

> All of a sudden Elvis just started singing this song, jumping around and acting the fool, and then Bill picked up his bass, and he started acting the fool, too, and I started playing with them. Sam, I think, had the door to the control booth open. I don't know, he was either editing tape or doing something. And he stuck his head out and said, "What are you doing?" And we said, "We don't know". "Well, back up," he said, "try to find a place to start, and do it again."

According to Peter Guralnick, in his book *Sam Phillips: The Man Who Invented Rock N Roll*:

> The first time Sam played it back for them, "We couldn't believe it was us," said Bill. "It just sounded sort of raw and ragged," said Scotty.

"We thought it was exciting, but what was it? It was just so completely different. But it just really flipped Sam."

'That's All Right' was to become the first single by Elvis Presley – and one of the songs that music critics argue over: was it really the first rock and roll record? Or did that honour belong to 'Rocket 88' by Jackie Brenston, recorded in March 1951? The latter featured a 19-year-old Ike Turner and was also recorded at Sun. No wonder Sam Phillips became known as the Father of Rock 'n' Roll.

Before the debut Elvis single was released, Sam Phillips gave a copy to respected local DJ Dewey Phillips who presented the *Red Hot and Blue* show on WHBQ. Dewey and Sam were good friends and would remain so until Dewey's death at the end of the 1960s. Dewey was the only one the Sun label owner trusted to give an honest opinion about 'That's All Right'.

Dewey loved it.

The next night he played it over and over again on the air, as the phones lit up and he called in the nineteen-year-old singer himself for an interview. "He said, 'Mr. Phillips, I don't know nothing about being interviewed.' I told him, 'Just don't say nothing dirty.'"

Already starting to whip up a storm, 'That's All Right' was released on 19th July 1954 with the catalogue number Sun 209. It would soon change, but for now the label credited Elvis, Scotty and Bill. Today the Sun single that started it all for Elvis is known as the 'Holy Grail of Rock 'n' Roll' among Elvis fans and collectors. Copies occasionally show up online and at auctions. Expect to pay several hundred pounds for the privilege of owning a genuine piece of music history.

BLUE MOON OF KENTUCKY

After equally wowing and scaring each other with what they had stumbled across on the 5th July 1954, Elvis, Scotty, Bill and Sam Phillips were back in the very same room at Sun the next day to record the flipside.

In the book *The Blue Moon Boys – The Story of Elvis Presley's Band* written by Ken Burke and Dan Griffin, Scotty Moore said:

> We all of us knew we needed something... and things seemed hopeless after a while. Bill Black is the one who came up with 'Blue Moon of Kentucky'... We're taking a little break and he starts beating on the bass and singing 'Blue Moon of Kentucky', mocking Bill Monroe, singing the high falsetto voice. Elvis joins in with him, starts playing and singing along with him.

Bill Monroe wrote 'Blue Moon of Kentucky' in 1946, and recorded the first version of the song playing mandolin and backed by his band the Blue Grass Boys. Monroe, who died in 1996, was one of the most famous bluegrass musicians of all time (the name bluegrass is derived from his backing band – the Blue Grass Boys). Kentucky is his home state and in this song he is heartbroken over a girl who left him, but wishes her well.

In 1938, Bill Monroe and his brother Charlie had broken up their successful duet act, the Monroe Brothers. That same year Bill formed his own band, the Blue Grass Boys. According to a biography on the website www.doodah.net: "In 1939 Bill Monroe joined the Grand Ole Opry and was a member until his death in 1996. For more than half a century, being a Blue Grass Boy was the crowning achievement of many musicians' careers; for others, a stepping stone to establishing their own bands."

Elvis with Scotty and Bill took what was already becoming a bluegrass classic and transformed 'Blue Moon of Kentucky' into a whole different affair. The song unintentionally provided the un-named backing band with a title... with disc jockeys introducing them as Elvis Presley and his Blue Moon Boys.

Among those to have covered the song is Al Kooper, who recorded it on his debut solo album, *I Stand Alone*. Ex-Beatle Paul McCartney did a version and Elvis's one-time Sun-label pal Carl Perkins did a cover too. Patsy Cline, Charlie Feathers, George Jones, Sonny James, Benny Martin, Rick Nelson, Jerry Reed, Jeannie C. Riley and Ricky Skaggs have all recorded 'Blue Moon of Kentucky'.

In the 7th August 1954 issue of *Billboard* magazine, Elvis was reviewed in the column 'Review Spotlight on... TALENT' where it was written: "Presley is a potent new chanter who can sock over a tune for either the country or the r. & b. markets. On this new disk he comes thru with a solid performance on an r. & b.-type tune and then on the flip side does another fine job with a country ditty. A strong new talent." Towards the end of the same year, the *Billboard* announced Elvis had been voted number eight on the disk jockeys' Most Promising list. Higher up the list were Maxine and Jim Edward Brown who later became part of the Browns, who would go on to enjoy a massive hit with 'The Three Bells' that told the story of a little Jimmy Brown, from his birth, to his marriage and through to his death.

So Elvis was at number eight. Maxine and Jim Edward were at number four and the number-one spot for the most-promising list of 1954 was taken by a Tommy Collins who was signed to Capitol. According to the website www.rocky-52.net, Tommy Collins released the jaunty 'You Better Not Do That', which became a huge hit in early 1954, spending seven weeks at number two on the country charts. Since the song was a success, Collins continued to pursue a light-hearted, near-novelty direction with his subsequent hits, and the formula initially worked.

Between the fall of 1954 and the spring of 1955, he had three top-10 hits – 'Whatcha Gonna Do Now', 'Untied' and 'It Tickles' – and in the fall of 1955 released the double A-sided single 'I Guess I'm Crazy' and 'You Oughta See Pickles Now', which both reached the Top 15. In addition to these hit singles, Faron Young had a huge hit with Collins' 'If You Ain't Lovin', which was one of many songs that Collins wrote but didn't record that became hits. So he enjoyed great success and rightly earned his place in the most-promising list. But his career was nowhere near the global success enjoyed by the number-eight entry, Elvis Presley.

But then Elvis wasn't yet the King of Rock and Roll. In 1954, the press were calling Elvis a "young hillbilly singing star".

MY HAPPINESS

However, before Elvis started to excite the listeners locally and a little more further afield with his Sun releases, he actually paid to make a private recording. 'My Happiness' was recorded by the young Elvis in 1953, at Sun. It was one of the only times Elvis paid to sing a song! He was charged $3.25. Elvis also recorded 'That's When Your Heartaches Begin', which he re-recorded later in the same decade after being signed to RCA. 'My Happiness' has been called the Holy Grail of Elvis Presley music – the very first song recorded by the man who would be the King.

There's some debate over the exact date when Elvis recorded 'My Happiness'. Most online sources quote 18th July 1953 as the date when Presley first went to the Memphis Recording Service and unwittingly started on a journey that would change his life and the lives of many others. The ballad was recorded on an acetate disc. Marion Keisker recorded the young Elvis on that day, which gained her an important place in rock 'n' roll history.

Although she didn't know it at the time, the conversation she had with the teenager would also go on to become famous. Marion asked Elvis: "What kind of singer are you?" He said, "I sing all kinds." Marion then asked, "Who do you sound like?" Elvis replied, "I don't sound like nobody." How right he was. That was in July 1953 – a year later Elvis released 'That's All Right' on Sun Records and the rest, as they say, is history.

The Presley family didn't own a record player at the time and Elvis couldn't afford duplicate copies so he left the studio master acetate of 'My Happiness' at the Memphis home of Ed Leek, a high-school classmate. Leek kept the record in a safe for six decades. After he and his wife died, their niece Lorisa Hilburn inherited it.

Hilburn, of Rockledge, Florida, contacted Graceland and it was offered for auction. In January 2015, the acetate of 'My Happiness' was sold at auction for $300,000. At the time it was reported the buyer was an undisclosed Internet buyer. However, we've since learned it was Jack White (who played Presley in the 2007 comedy *Walk Hard*). Soon after the purchase, White organised for the Country Music Hall of Fame and Museum to have its music archivist,

Alan Stoker, carefully make a digital copy of the fragile disc. (Stoker has his own Presley connection as the son of Gordon Stoker, part of the legendary Jordanaires, a quartet that backed Elvis on numerous hits from 1956 onwards.) A limited-edition vinyl facsimile of the acetate was then sold as part of the worldwide Record Store Day. Copies now sell on sites like eBay for upwards of £40.

The first known recording of 'My Happiness' was in December 1947 by the Marlin Sisters. However, the song first became a hit in May 1948 as recorded by Jon and Sondra Steele, with rival versions by the Pied Pipers and Ella Fitzgerald entering the charts. According to the website www.sunrecords.com:

> In 1953 Elvis is working at Parker Machinists Shop right after graduation. That summer he drops by The Memphis Recording Service, home of the Sun label and makes a demo acetate of 'My Happiness' and 'That's When Your Heartaches Begin' for a cost of about $4.00. (The studio came to be known as Sun Studio though never officially named that until the 1980s.) The studio owner isn't in, so his assistant, Marion Keisker handles the session.

The website continues:

> Elvis wants to see what his voice sounds like on a record and he has aspirations to become a professional singer. He takes the acetate home, and reportedly gives it to his mother as a much-belated extra birthday present. By the fall, he is working at Precision Tool Company, and soon changes jobs again, going to work for Crown Electric Company. At Crown, he does various jobs, including driving a delivery truck. He also goes to night school and studies to be an electrician.

HARBOR LIGHTS

The magic was obvious – 'That's All Right' came out of nowhere. It was like a huge bolt of lightning had hit the tiny Sun studio and all those inside. The effect of this metaphorical lightning was a charge of musical electricity. If you listen to the songs that Elvis attempted before 'That's All Right', it is easy to appreciate how unexpected the explosion of that song really was.

Elvis at heart was a ballad singer and a gospel performer, and yet he was moments away from a rock 'n' roll breakthrough. Before that, 'Harbor Lights' was the first song put on tape at the session. Sam Phillips considered the recording to be unworthy of release. It was 22 years later, in 1976, that RCA released the master (take 2) on the LP *Elvis – A Legendary Performer, Volume 2*. Phillips felt at the time that Elvis's voice was high and thin on this recording. He was probably still finding his confidence, which was just around the corner when he tackled 'That's All Right' – that great event was just moments away, although listening to 'Harbor Lights', you'd never believe rock 'n' roll history was within touching distance.

According to elvisblog.net: "Sam Phillips filed the tape away as nothing more than a warm-up effort, where the boys got used to working together. When RCA bought Elvis's contract and his entire Sun catalogue of 19 songs, they apparently saw little value in Harbor Lights. It remained unreleased for the next twenty years." The blog goes on to say: "The instrumentation is sparse and at a surprisingly low volume. Even Elvis's chorus of whistling in the middle did nothing to enhance this generally weak ballad." Elvis then attempted 'I Love You Because' – but more on that elsewhere…

'Harbor Lights' was written by Jimmy Kennedy and Hugh Williams in 1937. It soon became popular thanks to recordings made by Frances Longford and Claude Thornhill & His Orchestra. The song then lay redundant until enjoying a new lease of life in 1950 when it was recorded by Bing Crosby. The most successful cover was by Sammy Kaye, who enjoyed a number-one hit with the song. Ten years later it was back in the charts thanks to the Platters who peaked at number eight on the Billboard charts with their recording.

ELVIS'S SECOND SUN SINGLE – GOOD ROCKIN' TONIGHT – SUN 210

It was back in June 1947 that composer Roy Brown recorded his version of 'Good Rockin' Tonight'. In the same year, a 12-year-old sang on stage backed by Mississippi Slim – that boy would go on to record 'Good Rockin' Tonight' and become known globally by his first name: Elvis.

Before he recorded 'Good Rockin' Tonight', Brown had offered the song around to established artists of the day. Wynonie Harris turned it down. Blues singer and guitarist Cecil Gant was then approached to record the track. However, after hearing Brown sing it, Gant contacted the president of DeLuxe Records, Jules Braun. Brown was instructed to sing the song down the phone. Braun asked him to sing it again. When Brown handed the phone back to Gant after that second performance, Jules Braun said: "Give him fifty dollars and don't let him out of your sight." Five weeks later, Brown recorded the song for DeLuxe Records. When the song started to gain interest, Wynonie Harris decided it had been a mistake to turn down the song and quickly recorded an energetic version of 'Good Rockin' Tonight'.

Brown's original recording reached number 13 of the Billboard R&B chart and then number 11 when it was re-released, but it was Harris's version that became a number-one R&B hit and remained on the chart for six months.

Although he enjoyed more success in the 1950s, the following decade proved to be very slow for Roy Brown. There were a few sessions for little-known labels like Mobile and DRA. Then the mighty Chess brought Brown into the studio to cut four tracks in 1963 – but then decided not to release them. Bizarrely, Brown became an encyclopaedia salesman, travelling from door to door, winning customers with signed photos of himself as a blues star of yesteryear. Brown once recalled: "I sold a lot of encyclopaedias that way".

Further recordings were made towards the end of the '60s and Brown made a successful appearance at the Monterey Festival with '50s star Johnny Otis; but this work, he said, was less lucrative than selling encyclopaedias!

In September 1954, 'Good Rockin' Tonight' became the second Sun Records release by Elvis, along with 'I Don't Care if the Sun Don't Shine' on the flip side.

Presley and his bandmates hewed closer to the original Roy Brown version. Fellow Sun label artist, Carl Perkins, featured the track on his 1958 album *Whole Lotta Shakin'*. Eleven years after Elvis recorded the track, Link Wray did a version, in 1965. Paul McCartney also recorded the song for the *Unplugged (The Official Bootleg)* album.

Other people to have recorded this rock 'n' roll classic include Ricky Nelson in 1958, Montrose in 1973, Bruce Springsteen in 1978, Gene Summers in 1981, Lonnie Lee in 1993 – and Buddy Holly, Pat Boone, Jerry Lee Lewis, James Brown and the Doors.

I DON'T CARE IF THE SUN DON'T SHINE

Next a song written by a man who is credited with writing lyrics and music for more than one thousand songs. The composer is Mac David and the song 'I Don't Care if the Sun Don't Shine', which would be the flipside of 'Good Rockin' Tonight', Elvis's second single on the legendary Sun label. Mac's younger brother, Hal David, enjoyed great success when he teamed up with Burt Bacharach. Mac David was well known for his work on films like *Cinderella* and *Alice in Wonderland*, both from the famous Disney studios. In fact, he had originally written 'I Don't Care if the Sun Don't Shine' for the 1949 animated film *Cinderella*; however, it wasn't included.

One year later the track was a hit for Patti Page, whose version reached number eight in the Billboard Charts in 1950 and became her first top-10 hit. Another famous version, recorded before Elvis tackled the track, was by Dean Martin in his pre-rat-pack days. This version came from the 1953 film *Scared Stiff* starring Martin and Jerry Lewis. The comedy pairing first appeared on television in 1948 on the first-ever broadcast of *Toast of the Town* on CBS. This later became known as *The Ed Sullivan Show*.

Following further TV success, Martin and Lewis were signed to Paramount to make a series of films. Their first was *My Friend Irma* in 1949. They made 16 films up to and including 1956, ending with *Hollywood or Bust*. All the movies were produced by Hal B. Wallis, who would later produce many of Elvis's movies. After Martin and Lewis split, both enjoyed hugely successful solo careers in movies and on TV. According to Lewis, the two did not talk for twenty years, on which Lewis commented: "the stupidity of that, I cannot expound on. The ignorance of that is something I hope I'll always forget."

In 1976, Martin made a surprise appearance on Lewis's annual Labor Day telethon for the Muscular Dystrophy Association, orchestrated by mutual friend Frank Sinatra. According to Lewis, the two spoke "every day after that".

Elvis recorded 'I Don't Care if the Sun Don't Shine' on 10th September 1954, at Sun Records. Marion Keisker added a verse to Elvis's version and Buddy Cunningham provided the beat in the song, not on drums but an old record box which was empty. He's never been officially credited on the session.

When Elvis signed with RCA Records in November 1955, RCA reissued all five of his Sun singles. On the strength of its appearance on the EP *Any Way You Want Me*, 'I Don't Care if the Sun Don't Shine' reached number 74 on Billboard's Top 100 chart in October 1956, staying on the chart for six weeks.

ELVIS'S THIRD SUN SINGLE – MILKCOW BLUES BOOGIE – SUN 215

Elvis recorded our next track late in 1954, still basking in the glory of his first real success with 'That's All Right'. In the fall of 1954, Elvis, Scotty and Bill tackled an interesting track that was already more than 20 years old: 'Milkcow Blues Boogie' (although its original title was just 'Milk Cow Blues').

It was written by Kokomo Arnold who was a blues singer and slide guitarist. After running a bootlegging operation in Chicago during Prohibition, he moved down south and recorded under the name of 'Gitfiddle Jim' for the Victor label. He moved back to Chicago and made 88 recordings for the Decca label. Arnold's song 'Milk Cow Blues' was first recorded in 1930 by Sleepy John Estes then Robert Johnson took the track and re-named it 'Milkcow's Calf Blues'. It was one of the songs Johnson recorded at his last recording session in 1937. It was released in the same year by Vocalion Records. Next Johnnie Lee Wills recorded a version in 1941. He was the young brother of Bob Wills, who was known as the King of Western Swing. Funnily enough, Bob Wills also recorded a version of the song with a vocal by Tommy Duncan.

Elvis recorded a rockabilly-style re-named version of the song. By now it was called 'Milkcow Blues Boogie'. Elvis appeared to tip his hat to the Wills version of the track when he recorded his version at Sun.

After Elvis, Eddie Cochran recorded the track. Mike Seeger, Bob Crosby, Ricky Nelson, George Lewis, the Kinks, the Chocolate Watchband, We Five, Mungo Jerry, Commander Cody and his Lost Planet Airmen, Aerosmith, Jerry Lee Lewis, Glen Campbell, Willie Nelson and even more artists all recorded versions after Elvis laid down his take at Sun. Scotty Moore, who played guitar on Elvis's Sun Records version, also recorded his own take of the track in the 1960s.

In January 1955, Elvis's version of 'Milkcow Blues Boogie' was released as the B-side to 'You're a Heartbreaker'. It finally appeared on a long-playing release in 1959 on the RCA release *A Date With Elvis*, one of the albums released to keep the fans happy while their 'King' was doing his National Service in Germany.

YOU'RE A HEARTBREAKER

'Milkcow Blues Boogie' would be released on a Sun Single with the catalogue number Sun 215. It was the last single to be released on Sun during that first magical year of 1954, coming out in December.

The song was backed by a track written by Jack Sallee and featured tongue-twisting lyrics that would appeal to love-lorn teens of the mid-1950s. This is not a coincidence. The song was written for Elvis at the request of Sam Phillips who was looking for new material for his hot property. Here's an example:

> You're a heartbreaker,
> You're a love faker,
> A heartbreaker playing with fire.
> You're a tear snatcher,
> You're a quarrel patcher,
> But you can't break my heart anymore.

The lyrics were never going to set the world on fire, but they served a purpose and the song is popular among fans.

It was, however, the poorest seller of the Sun singles at the time. It lacked an explosive solo from Scotty Moore, but it drives along quite nicely. It is more country than rock 'n' roll, but it is Elvis at Sun, so it's hard to find too much fault in it. Although the song did not reach the national charts, it did receive some important recognition. The track was the first Elvis track to have a song sheet issued. That sheet is a pretty rare find these days. Another first for this track is that it was the first original song Elvis recorded. Sallee had been a Theatre Manager in Covington, Tennessee.

The single 'You're a Heartbreaker' and 'Milkcow Blues Boogie' would be released on both a 45 rpm and a 78rpm single on the now-legendary yellow Sun label. If you can find one, expect to pay upwards of £500 for a 45 rpm original version. RCA Victor would re-release this single and others soon after buying Elvis's contract. 'You're a Heartbreaker' also appeared on the 1959 long-playing album *For LP Fans Only*, another one of the releases that kept Elvis in the hearts and minds of his legions of fans while he was carrying out his National Service in Germany.

Billy Swan, who scored a massive hit with 'I Can Help' (also recorded by Elvis), performed a Sun Medley in 1999 that featured 'You're a Heartbreaker'. The song was also covered by Tom Green in 2004.

ELVIS'S FOURTH SUN SINGLE – BABY LET'S PLAY HOUSE – SUN 217

Elvis Presley's fourth single for Sun Records, recorded on 5th February 1955, was 'Baby Let's Play House'. It was released on Sun with 'I'm Left, You're Right, She's Gone'. As well as being released as a Sun single, 'Baby Let's Play House' made EP and LP appearances. The song enjoyed national success having a ten-week residency on Billboard's country chart and peaking at number 10.

Sam Phillips said the song also marked the first time drums were used on a Presley single. 'Baby Let's Play House' was written and originally recorded by

Arthur Gunter, a popular R&B singer at the time. Elvis took the track and made the definitive version by adding the "babe, babe, b, baby" phrasing throughout the song. Elvis also studied Gunter's original lyrics and made a few changes, where "you may have religion" became "you may drive a pink Cadillac". Soon after, Elvis would be forever associated with that car, after purchasing one for his beloved mother, Gladys, even though she couldn't drive.

The song's composer Arthur Gunter was born in Nashville, Tennessee. He entered music as a child when he formed a gospel group with his brothers and cousins. They became known as the Gunter Brothers Quartet. In the early 1950s, Gunter started recording for Excello Records. It was in November 1954 that Gunter recorded his recently penned song 'Baby Let's Play House'. It was recorded for the Excello. The track enjoyed national success, peaking at number 12 in the US Billboard R&B chart. It was to become even better known once Elvis got his hands on the track.

In an archive interview Gunter said: "Elvis got that number and made it famous. But I didn't get a chance to shake his hand." He did benefit from the royalties from that early Elvis recording. Gunter stayed on the books at Excello Records until 1961. Gunter gave a few performances during the '60s and sadly died of pneumonia in 1976. He was only 49 years old.

Several stars have recorded versions of 'Baby Let's Play House' including Buddy Holly in America and Vince Taylor in the UK. Many others were to follow and then in 1994 – on *It's Now or Never*, the tribute to Elvis CD – Michael Hutchence from INXS joined with NRBQ to do their version of the song.

Elvis added 'Baby Let's Play House' to his live sets as he zig-zagged across America in 1955. He also sang the track on his second appearance on the Dorsey Brother's Stage Show on 4th February 1956.

The song is a plea from the singer to his girlfriend to return to him because he wants to 'play house' with her, a slang term for an unmarried couple living or sleeping together. The suggestive lyrics added to the controversy already surrounding Elvis and his gyrations. The teenagers weren't complaining – they had found their hero in Elvis Presley.

I'M LEFT, YOU'RE RIGHT, SHE'S GONE

While the singer is clearly enjoying his life in 'Good Rockin' Tonight', there's an air of heartbreak in 'I'm Left, You're Right, She's Gone', which was paired with the previous song as Elvis's fourth single. In the song, Elvis is admitting to his friend that he was right all along about the girl who had stolen his, Elvis's, heart. Allmusic.com critic Thomas Ward says that in the hands of anyone else, this song would be "unlistenable" with lyrics he described as "banal". However, Ward says Elvis transforms the track into one of his "most fun" recordings of that period.

Jerry Lee Lewis, Carl Mann and Charlie Feathers are among the many that have since covered the song.

It was written by Bill Taylor and Stan Kesler. Kesler also wrote 'Playing for Keeps', which Elvis would record at RCA several months later. He also wrote 'Thrill of Your Love' that Elvis covered for the excellent *Elvis is Back* album, on his return from the army in 1960. Kesler was also a member of the band, the Snearly Ranch Boys, the Memphis group that also featured co-writer Bill Taylor. Taylor was a trumpet player and a record-company owner. Bill Taylor would go on to form a song-writing partnership with Thomas LaVerne, writing songs like 'I Am What I Am' for Jerry Lee Lewis.

The title has often confused people as throughout the track Elvis sings "You're right, I'm left, she's gone" leading many to ponder if somewhere along the line the title got mixed up. Although at one stage in the track Elvis does sing:

> Well, I thought I knew just what she'd do
> I guess I'm not so smart
> Oh, you tried to tell me all along she'd only break my heart
> I'm left, you're right, she's gone…

A bluesy, much slower song does exist that was given the title 'My Baby's Gone' and was also recorded at Sun. Some online sources say it was this version that was originally sent out to local DJs in Memphis. However, it was the faster version that saw the light of day first.

ELVIS'S FIFTH SUN SINGLE – MYSTERY TRAIN – SUN 223

Next a Sun Records classic from 1955. 'Mystery Train' was originally the B-side to 'I Forgot to Remember to Forget'. But the sheer strength of the song proved it would be more than a filler track. *Rolling Stone* magazine described 'Mystery Train' as "a mesmerizing fusion of country and rock that's since become an enduring classic in both fields and eventually landed at number 77 on *Rolling Stone*'s list of the 500 Greatest Songs of All Time. Much of the song's lasting appeal comes courtesy of the almost otherworldly tone that Moore pulled from his trusted Gibson ES-295. "'Mystery Train' became like a signature thing for me".

It has certainly become one of the best known 'train blues' songs of all time. 'Mystery Train' was originally recorded by Junior Parker in 1953. Junior Parker mixed with the best from an early age. He learned his initial licks from Sonny Boy Williamson and toured with the legendary Howlin' Wolf while he was just a teenager. In the same year that Elvis paid to make a private recording at Sun, Junior Parker and his band the Blue Flames arrived to record at the famous Memphis studios. Success soon followed with their first hit at Sun called 'Feelin' Good'. Later that year, Junior cut 'Love My Baby' and a rather laid-back version of 'Mystery Train' for Sun. Hayden Thompson was to revive 'Love Me Baby' while of course Elvis breathed even more excitement into 'Mystery Train'.

According to allmusic.com: "Parker was exceptionally versatile –- whether delivering 'Mother-in-Law Blues' and 'Sweet Home Chicago' in faithful down-home fashion, courting the teenage market with 'Barefoot Rock,' or tastefully howling Harold Burrage's 'Crying for My Baby' (another hit for him in 1965) in front of a punchy horn section, Parker was the consummate modern blues artist, with one foot planted in Southern blues and the other in uptown R&B." The success lasted until the mid-1960s – but towards the end he found himself doing covers of Beatles tracks to make some money. Unfortunately, he succumbed to a brain tumour in 1971 just before he reached his fortieth birthday. Junior Parker's impact has never been forgotten and in 2001 he was inducted into the Blues Hall of Fame.

RCA Victor re-released Elvis's version of Mystery Train in December 1955 after acquiring it as part of the label's new contract with Presley. This issue of the song peaked at number 11 on the national Billboard Country Chart. It was the first recording to make Elvis Presley a nationally known country music star.

Bill Black, who was part of Elvis's early band at Sun, continuing on into the RCA years before branching out on his own and with his combo, was a big fan of 'Mystery Train'. Apparently, when a friend visited his home in Memphis, Black pointed to a framed 78 rpm Sun record of 'Mystery Train' on the wall, and said: "Now THERE was a record."

I FORGOT TO REMEMBER TO FORGET

Next, a song Elvis initially didn't want to tackle. Recorded with just Presley on rhythm guitar, Scotty Moore on lead guitar and Bill Black on bass, Elvis felt it was too country. Then a drummer was added to the session, changing the feel of the track, and he was happy. We're talking about 'I Forgot to Remember to Forget'. The drummer wasn't DJ Fontana, but a Johnny Bernero. It was only discovered in the 1970s that the drummer on Elvis's later Sun recordings (including 'Mystery Train', 'I Forgot to Remember to Forget', 'Trying to Get to You' and 'When It Rains It Really Pours') was Bernero and not Fontana.

Bernero dropped out of Sun at an early stage and so, over the years, his contribution became temporarily forgotten. During the day the young drummer worked for the Memphis Light Gas and Water Company, which was near the Sun studios. Bernero got to know Sam Phillips. It wasn't long before the talented drummer was playing on sessions for the likes of Billy Riley, Warren Smith and Elvis. Bernero wasn't satisfied with the small session fees he received and persuaded Phillips to let him record his own songs. Unfortunately, these didn't surface until the late 1980s when 'Rockin' at the Woodchopper's Ball' and 'Bernero's Boogie' were finally released.

'I Forgot to Remember to Forget' was written by Charlie Feathers and Stan Kesler. The latter had already written Presley's 'I'm Left, You're Right, She's Gone' when he had the idea for this tune. In an archive interview Stan Kesler said: "At that time, I was on the kick of catchy titles. When I began to think about that phrase, it just expanded into 'I Forgot to Remember to Forget Her'. From there, I started working on it, and it all fell together."

'I Forgot to Remember to Forget' was recorded at Sun Studio on 11th July 1955 by Elvis, Scotty, Bill, and Johnny Bernero and released on 20th August 1955, along with 'Mystery Train'. What a great A- and B-side pairing that single was! It was re-released by RCA Victor in December 1955 as the label tested the market with their new signing.

'Heartbreak Hotel' may have been *the* national breakthrough US number-one hit but 'I Forgot to Remember to Forget' reached the top of the country charts on 25th February 1956.

Among those who covered the track after Elvis were the Beatles, who performed the song once for their BBC radio show, *From Us to You*, on 1st May 1964, with George Harrison on lead vocals. Jerry Lee Lewis recorded the song in 1957 and again in the 1960s. Composer Charlie Feathers recorded it, as did Johnny Cash who covered the song in 1959 on the Sun LP *Greatest!* Other artists to record the song include Elvis sound-a-like Ral Donner, French rock and roll star Johnny Hallyday, Wanda Jackson, Chris Isaak and Bob Dylan.

Other Sun Highlights...

BLUE MOON

At a time when Elvis was putting in electrifying studio performances with 'That's All Right' and 'Blue Moon of Kentucky', 'Blue Moon' seems like a bit of an oddity. It's set apart from the other songs recorded at Sun and features Elvis in falsetto during the song – something that is indeed very rare in Elvis recordings!

According to elvis-history-blog.com: "As a teenager in Memphis, Elvis probably heard multiple recordings of the song on the radio. He obviously liked the pop ballad, as, according to biographer Peter Guralnick, Elvis was already singing the song when he first hooked up with Sun Records in 1954. In fact, Guralnick believes that Elvis, Scotty Moore, and Bill Black tried to record it in July 1954 as a possible flip slide to 'That's All Right'."

'Blue Moon' was written by Richard Rodgers and Lorenz Hart in 1934. It was a hit twice in 1949 with successful recordings in the US by Billy Eckstine and Mel Tormé. In 1961, 'Blue Moon' became an international number-one hit for the doo-wop group the Marcels on the Billboard Hot 100 chart and in the UK Singles chart. It was the group's first hit and sold more than 2.5 million copies. They also recorded the theme song 'The Greatest Love' for the motion picture *The Interns* and appeared with Chubby Checker in the film *Twist Around the Clock*.

Over the years, 'Blue Moon' has been covered by various artists including versions by Billie Holiday and Rod Stewart. Fast and slow versions of 'Blue Moon' were used in the 1981 horror-comedy film *An American Werewolf in London*. Elvis's recording session for 'Blue Moon' took place on 19th August 1954 with Elvis, Scotty and Bill, and Sam Phillips in the control booth. Peter Guralnick said of the session: "On August 19 they spent hours doing take after take of 'Blue Moon,' in an eerie, clippity-clop version that resembled a cross between Slim Whitman's 'Indian Love Call' and some of the falsetto flights of the r&b 'bird' groups (the Orioles, the Ravens, the Larks). After it was all over, Sam wasn't satisfied that they had anything worth releasing, but he never uttered a word of demurral for fear of discouraging the unfettered freshness and enthusiasm of the singer."

Music historian Colin Escott said of 'Blue Moon': "Elvis skips the bridge and the final verse that contains the happy ending, neatly transforming the 32-bar pop classic into an eerie 16-bar blues. Hart's original lyrics describe a man whose longing for love is finally rewarded. Elvis used only the following two opening stanzas, repeating and separating them with falsetto moans." It is a strangely haunting listen. If you have never heard the track, give it a spin. It's not one you will forget in a hurry!

I'LL NEVER LET YOU GO

We stay at Sun and go to 10th September 1954. Elvis and his band had already laid down 'Tomorrow Night', which would finally see the light of day some ten years later with added overdubs. After 'Tomorrow Night', Elvis tackled 'I'll Never Let You Go (Little Darlin')' that had originally been recorded by Jimmy Wakely for the Decca label back in 1943.

Jimmy Wakely was one of the last singing cowboys. As well as releasing singles in the 1930s, '40s and '50s, he appeared in several Western movies, appeared on radio and TV shows and even had his own series of comic books. Wakely was a shrewd business man too, owning two music publishing companies later in life. Like many of his peers he performed countless times on the *Grand Ole Opry*, making his final appearance just before he died in 1982 at the age of 68. Wakely was inducted into the Nashville Songwriters Hall of Fame in 1971.

After Elvis recorded his version of 'I'll Never Let You Go', he and the band recorded 'Satisfied'. Sadly that recording is thought to have been lost forever. (Check your attics just in case.) After all, the long-lost recording of 'I'm a Roustabout', likewise thought to have been gone forever, was found in the songwriter's attic almost 50 years after Elvis recorded and then discarded the song... so you never know.

Elvis's version of 'I'll Never Let You Go' takes the reverse approach to 'Milkcow Blues Boogie'. The latter starts slow then breaks out into a sweat as it speeds up. However, most of 'I'll Never Let You Go' is taken at a slow dreamy pace, before all of a sudden, a bolt of lightning seems to hit the little Memphis studio and the band go all rock 'n' roll for the final section of the track.

JUST BECAUSE

On 10th September 1954, Elvis and his band were back at Sun recording 'Just Because'. Even then, the track was already an oldie, having first been recorded by Nelstone's Hawaiians way back in 1929. Four years later, the Shelton Brothers recorded a version.

RCA Victor were to release Elvis's version of 'Just Because' on his legendary debut album in 1956. However, they had previously released the song by Nelstone's Hawaiians and also a version by the Lonestar Cowboys. All those versions happened before Elvis even stepped up to the mic to record his take on 'Just Because'.

Although the song was recorded during Elvis's short but essential time at Sun, Sam Phillips didn't release it. The song was included as part of the package that came when RCA signed Elvis towards the end of 1955. 'Just Because' did appear on Elvis's awesome debut LP. Although Elvis had recording sessions on 10th and 11th January at the RCA Victor recording studios in Nashville, Tennessee, and on 30th and 31st January at the RCA Victor studios in New York, additional material was still needed to flesh out the LP. Songs were pulled from the recording sessions at Sun Studio on 5th July, 19th August and 10th September of 1954, and on 11th July 1955.

Even so, the album's running time was only 28 minutes. Nowadays albums are incredibly important, either as a physical release on CD or as an MP3 download. The importance of the long-playing album really started in the mid-'60s, with the Beatles' *Revolver* and *Rubber Soul*, and then its essential role was sealed by the great Brian Wilson when the Beach Boys released *Pet Sounds* in 1966. Ever since, concept albums have been a great love for many artists.

Back in 1956 it was viewed as another way to promote whichever artist was hot property, so sometimes the tracks on the early rock and roll albums were a bit hit or miss. However, with Elvis's 1956 debut album, the material was mainly top-notch stuff. The cover itself would grab the attention of rock 'n' roll hungry teenagers all over the world. Its now-iconic cover photo captures the young Elvis in action at the Fort Homer Hesterly Armory in Tampa, Florida, on 31st July 1955. The sleeve also boasts the famous eye-catching green and pink lettering spelling out the name Elvis Presley. Then you get home and remove the shiny black vinyl from the sleeve – put the needle on the record and Elvis blasts out of your speakers with his energy packed cover of 'Blue Suede Shoes' – what an opener!

Side one of Elvis's debut album ends with 'Just Because'. The LP was released in March 1956, so Elvis's take on 'Just Because' was making its debut here despite being already a year and a half old. With the track's energy from start to finish, it certainly didn't sound out of place amongst the RCA material recorded in early 1956. It sounds strange, but it seems to work and gives Elvis's cover a unique edge. It is definitely one to check out. Keep in mind that Elvis was only 19 at the time and already experimenting with the sound of his songs.

LITTLE MAMA

Many treats came out in 2012 with the release by the RCA/BMG collectors' label, Follow That Dream (FTD) Records, of the limited-edition box set, *A Boy from Tupelo*. The CDs featured all the material recorded by Presley from 1953 to 1955, including all of the alternate takes and all of the recordings that had been missing from previous releases, with the exception of 'Satisfied' (stated by Jørgensen himself, in the book which was released with the CD, to be lost).

The collection saw the first-time-ever release of 'Little Mama', which Elvis performed at the *Louisiana Hayride* in March 1955. The previous year, DJ Frank Page had been the first to introduce Elvis live on the *Louisiana Hayride*. In his book *Something in the Water*, Frank remembered the first night Elvis appeared at the *Hayride* which was on 16th October 1954. He said:

> I remember talking to Elvis backstage that night. I was interested in how he was being received wherever he appeared because a decision would have to be made right away whether or not to put him back on the show. He said he had been working a few clubs in the Memphis area and that, frankly, he didn't go over big with an older audience, that it was teenagers who dug what he was doing. I could understand that. He was a good-looking boy, dressed conservatively. Elvis had brooded for several weeks about the rejection he encountered at the Grand Ol' Opry and had just about decided to give up singing when he got this chance to appear on the Hayride. Had we turned him down, he might have given it up. He told me that Jim Denny, who ran the talent office at the Opry, told him he'd better stick to truck driving, that he'd never make it as a

> singer. I told Elvis not to pay any attention to that kind of advice, to give it a try and make up his own mind without listening to anyone else.
>
> We booked Elvis back on the show and on November 6, 1954 signed him to a year's contract at union scale. Scale was $15.00 per sideman, double scale for the leader. That meant $15.00 each for Scotty and Bill and $30.00 for Elvis. It was evident to all at this time that Elvis had arrived and was where he should be. Soon, the young people began showing up in droves, riding the trolley or dropped off by parents, squealing and eventually swooning when that became 'the thing'.

One of the song's composers was Ahmet Ertegun, best known as the founder and president of Atlantic Records, and for discovering or championing artists like Aretha Franklin and Ray Charles.

Louisiana Hayride was a radio and later television country music show broadcast from the Shreveport Municipal Memorial Auditorium in Shreveport, Louisiana. During its heyday from 1948 to 1960, it helped to launch the careers of some of the greatest names in American country and western music. Elvis Presley performed on the radio version of the programme in 1954 and made his first television appearance on the TV version on 3rd March 1955.

At the time of writing, it's not known if the *A Boy from Tupelo* box set will be re-released as a cheaper set, as many of Elvis's box sets have been in recent years.

However, a live version of 'Little Mama' is available on the *Greatest Live hits of the 50s*, which came out in October 2012 and is still available online. The company behind that release, the Memphis Recording Service, has previously released the expanded edition of *Blue Hawaii* and *Such a Night – Elvis Pearl Harbour Concert* from 1961. They've also recently brought out recordings from all of Elvis's early TV appearances up to and including the *Frank Sinatra and Elvis Timex Special* from 1960.

TRYING TO GET TO YOU

Next a song www.allmusic.com described as "arguably the finest songs of all the Sun sessions".

'Trying to Get to You' is a song that Elvis Presley made his own due to his hugely committed vocal and the simple carefree abandon with which he performed it. As a song, it is perhaps the most finely crafted of all the material Presley performed between 1954 and 1955. It was recorded at Sun's studios in Memphis on 11th July 1955 – and what a session that was, as Elvis also tackled the great 'Mystery Train' on the same day. Listening to those tracks, you can see how in just one year the band had become more polished, the sound was better than ever, and yet this was still pure and raw rock and roll music. It's clear Elvis's confidence had also grown considerably in that one year.

'Tryin' to Get to You' was composed by Rose Marie McCoy and Charles Singleton. McCoy wrote songs for Big Maybelle, Louis Jordan and Nappy Brown. It was in 1954 that she joined together with songwriter Charles Singleton, which led to greater success. Their first hit, 'It Hurts Me to My Heart', was recorded in 1954 by Faye Adams. Their collaboration lasted about eight years. They also penned Elvis Presley's 'I Beg of You', Ruth Brown's 'Mambo Baby' and Nappy Brown's 'Little by Little'. McCoy and Singleton's songs also made their way into successful recording sessions for Nat King Cole, Eartha Kitt, Little Willie John, the Clovers, Big Joe Turner, Eddy Arnold and even a young soul singer called Aretha Franklin.

Elvis wasn't the first to record 'Tryin' to Get to You'; that honour went to a Washington DC based band, the Eagles, in 1954. This was a completely different band to the rock group who bought us such classics as 'Hotel California' and 'Take It Easy' during the 1970s.

Presley recorded five versions of 'Trying to Get to You'. The first were on 23rd March 1955 and again on 11th July 1955. Later in his career he would return to the song during live sets, including the *'68 Comeback Special*, recorded for NBC TV, for the 1974 album, *As Recorded Live on Stage in Memphis*, and the 1977 swansong *Elvis in Concert*.

On the original Sun Records version, Presley swapped his usual rhythm guitar for the piano. Because his piano playing was not up to the expected standards, producer Sam Phillips erased it from the master take. However, once Elvis was signed to RCA the piano started to reappear. You can hear it starting to come through on Elvis's self-titled 1956 LP.

'Trying to Get to You' was also released by the Teen Kings, whose lead singer was none other than a young Roy Orbison in April 1956. The star of the TV show *The Adventures of Ozzie and Harriet*, Ricky Nelson, also recorded the track. But these were more laid back than the electrifying version a 20-year-old Elvis performed at the tiny Sun studio in Memphis.

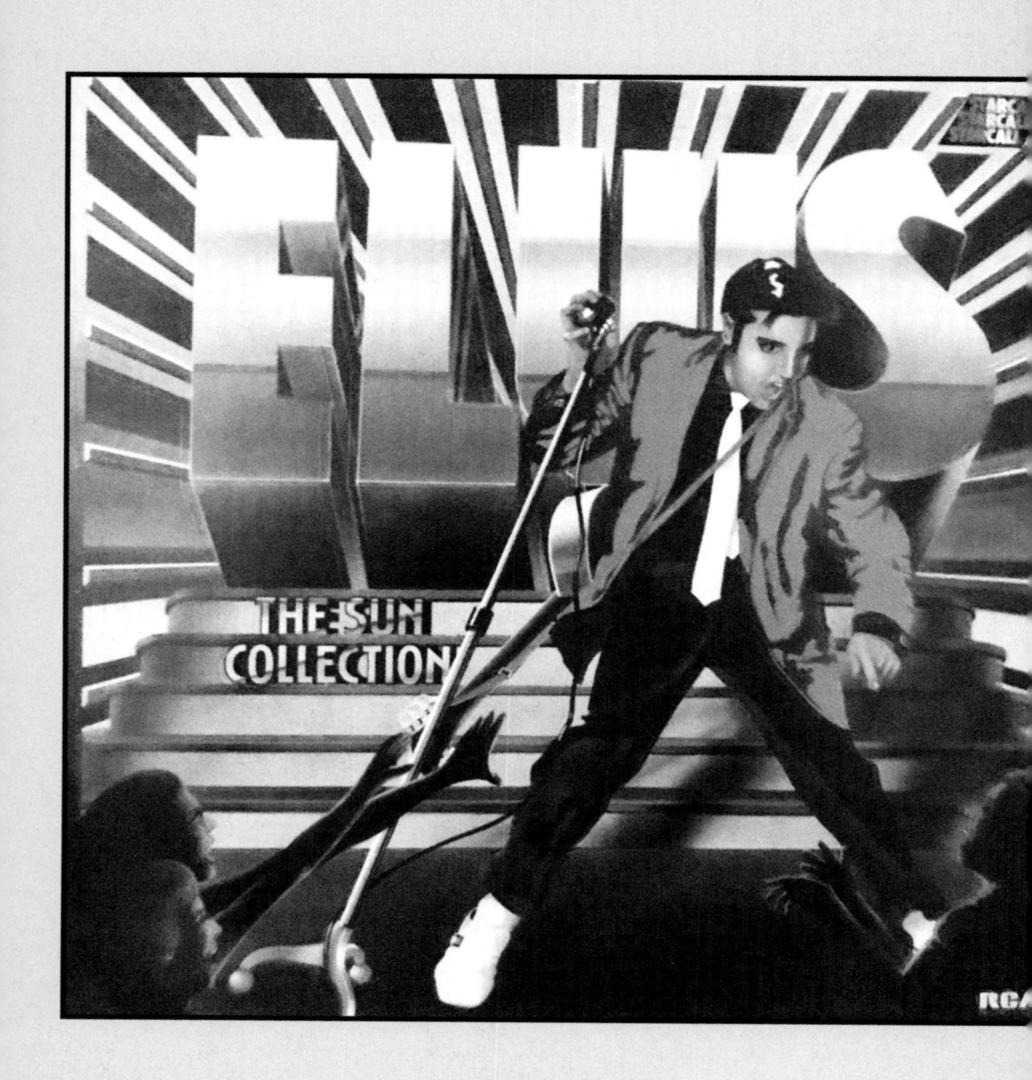
THE SUN
COLLECTION
RCA

SEVEN

ELVIS IN 1956 – THE KING OF THE WHOLE WIDE WORLD

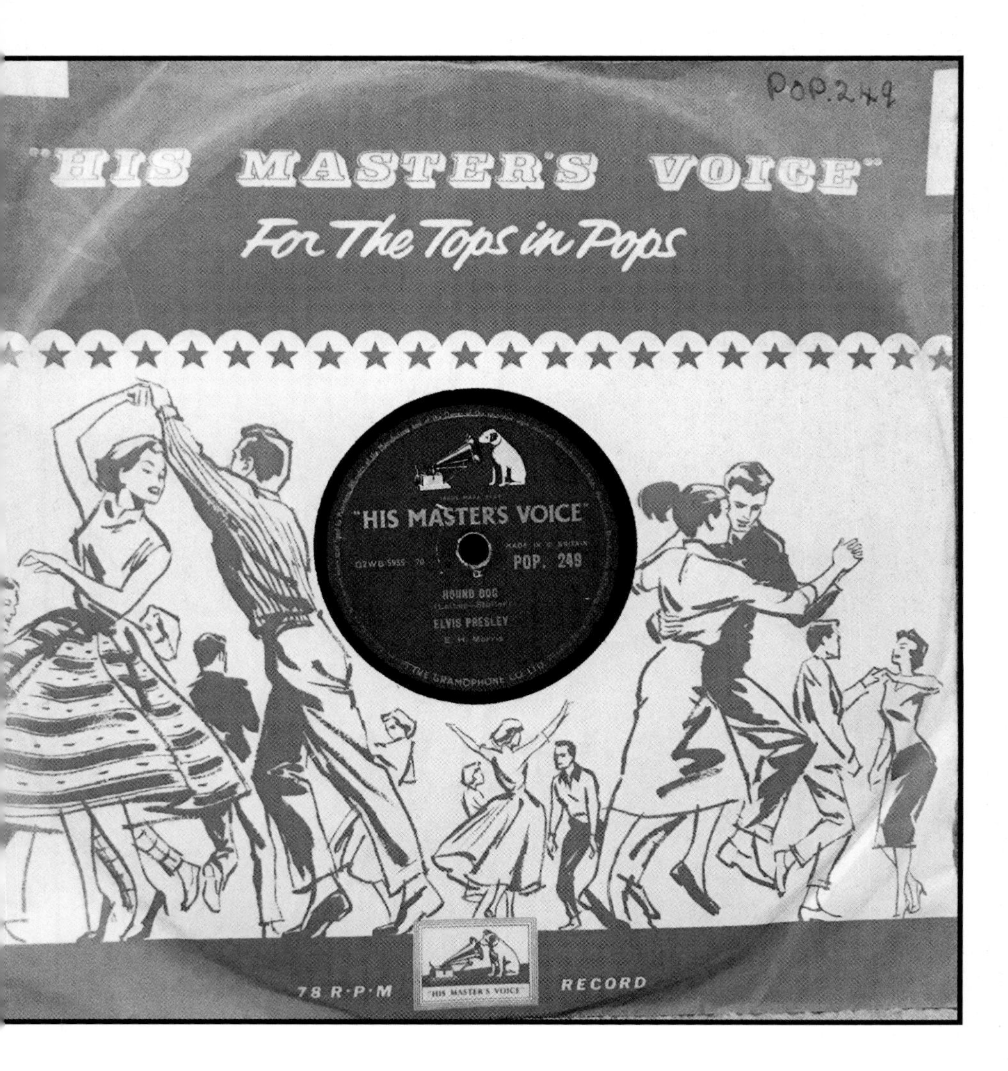

This was the year Elvis exploded on to US televisions nationwide and blasted out of record players globally. Having signed Elvis to RCA records at the end of 1955, the company quickly booked their new star in for a recording session in January 1956. According to the *Memphis Press-Scimitar* article from Tuesday, 22nd November 1955:

> Elvis Presley, 20, Memphis recording star and entertainer who zoomed into bigtime and the big money almost overnight, has been released from his contract with Sun Record Co. of Memphis and will record exclusively for RCA-Victor, it was announced by Sam C. Phillips, Sun president.
>
> Phillips and RCA officials did not reveal terms, but said the money involved is probably the highest ever paid for a contract release for a country-western recording artist. "I feel Elvis is one of the most talented youngsters today," Phillips said, "and by releasing his contract to RCA-Victor we will give him the opportunity of entering the largest organization of its kind in the world, so his talents can be given the fullest opportunity."

It was a huge deal for the time. Sam Phillips sold Elvis's contract to RCA Victor for $35,000, plus $5,000 in back royalties he owed Elvis. It was the largest amount paid for a single performer up to that time.

To the public it looked like RCA had the greatest confidence in their new star. But behind the scenes they were extremely nervous. When Carl Perkins scored big with 'Blue Suede Shoes' in early 1956, there was even talk in the management corridors that they had signed the wrong artist! Their fears were soon to disappear as Elvis went on to enjoy a hugely successful career with the label, scoring countless gold records with the company.

Highlights from 10th and 11th January 1956

HEARTBREAK HOTEL – RCA STUDIO, NASHVILLE

The words "I walk a lonely street" had apparently jumped out at songwriter Tommy Durden. For years, Durden would say that he'd read a newspaper article that told the sad story of a man who killed himself in a hotel, leaving a short suicide note of just those five words. The chilling sentence stayed with Durden, who took the newspaper article around to a friend's house. That friend was Mae Boren Axton, who had already enjoyed some success as a songwriter earlier in the 1950s, and together they wrote a song based on that headline.

Well, that was what we were told for the last 60 years.

In 2016, new evidence emerged to suggest that this might not be the actual story behind the song. Axton died in 1997, Durden in 1999. To the end, they credited the broken-hearted man in that elusive newspaper article as their inspiration. However, according to the July 2016 edition of *Rolling Stone*:

> The tale really began in November 1953, when a 25-year-old man named Alvin Krolik walked into Chicago's Albany Park police station and confessed to a string of armed robberies at Windy City hotels, restaurants and liquor stores. A former Marine Corps judo instructor, Krolik claimed to be an accomplished artist and budding author whose heartbreak over his failed marriage – to nightclub accordionist Agnes Sampson – sent him into a criminal spiral.

Krolik claimed he was done with crime and had even penned a memoir to save others from his fate. "I have to get this thing off my mind," he told police. "I'm tired of the panderers and streetwalkers I've been living with." In wire stories that ran in newspapers from the Northeast to Texas and California, reporters further captured Krolik's regrets and his heartache over the split with Agnes: "I still love her madly."

Then, stories quoted a passage from Krolik's 'unpublished autobiography', said to be in the hands of a New York publisher: "If you stand on a corner with a pack of cigarettes or a bottle and have nothing to do in life, I suggest you sit down and think. This is the story of a person who *walked a lonely street*. I hope this will help someone in the future."

News coverage in several cities highlighted the evocative metaphor Krolik had chosen to represent his life – a sad walk down a lonely Street – in headlines and subheads.

So after all these years it seems Krolik *may* be the inspiration behind 'Heartbreak Hotel'. But with both songwriters no longer with us, we will never know for certain.

In 1955, Mae landed a part-time job working as the public relations secretary for Elvis's manager, Colonel Tom Parker. Soon after, she met the young rising star himself. One of the first things she recalled saying to Elvis was "you need a million-seller and I'm going to write it for you."

As Axton and Durden discussed how they could turn the newspaper article into a song, Axton suggested that there be a 'heartbreak hotel' at the end of the lonely street. That was how it started and in no time at all Axton and Durden had written about a dark desolate hotel where "the desk clerk's dressed in black" while "broken hearted lovers cry away their gloom."

Knowing they had written something special, Mae Axton took the song along to Elvis. She recalled in an archive interview Elvis's reaction to the song. He said: "Hot dog, Mae, play it again." Elvis told Mae it reminded him a little of Roy Brown's 'Hard Luck Blues'. You can hear that track here: https://www.youtube.com/watch?v=4a9JVDKDIm4.

Elvis was signed to RCA Records at the end of 1955 and, on 10th January 1956, just two days after Elvis turned 21, the young singer found himself in the RCA recording studios. A different studio, a different producer – Sam Phillips had sold his star, so now Steve Sholes was producing with engineer Bob Ferris. There were still some familiar faces there – Scotty Moore, Bill Black and D.J. Fontana were back in the studio with the young star, but the RCA sound was filled out with the likes of Floyd Cramer on piano, guitarist Chet Atkins and the Jordinaires. These musicians and backing vocalists would become a mainstay in Elvis's recording career well into the 1960s.

There was an echo to the song, which added to the overall darkness of the track along with Elvis's heart-wrenching singing. Elvis never lost faith in the track; however, initially others were not impressed. Former producer Sam Phillips described the song as a "morbid mess". Producer Steve Sholes – who had overseen the signing of Elvis to RCA was – a very worried man. In an archive interview he said: "The bosses all told me it didn't sound like anything, it didn't sound like his other records, and I'd better not release it. I [had] better go back and record it again."

However, Elvis stuck with the song and knew in his heart it would be the one that would launch him into the big time, and high up the main charts.

The single was released on 27th January 1956. Over the next few months, Elvis would promote the song on three of his six appearances on the *Dorsey Brothers Stage Show*. (There's more about that show to come.)

On 3rd April 1956, it was on the play list when Elvis appeared with Uncle Miltie on the *Milton Berle Show*. All the TV exposure and the no-doubt-endless playing on various radio stations led to Elvis's dream coming true. The former Memphis truck driver had his first American number-one pop single. It also topped the country chart and went top five on the R&B chart.

I GOT A WOMAN

Lots of people have covered our next track including Elvis; however, the original belongs to the great Ray Charles. Charles' version of 'I Got a Woman' was released as a single in December 1954 on the Atlantic label with the flipside 'Come Back Baby'. Both songs would later appear on his 1957 album, *Ray Charles*.

The song's origins are based on a gospel song called 'It Must Be Jesus', by the Southern Tones. The story goes that Ray Charles heard this version on the radio while touring with his band in the summer of 1954. He and band member Renald Richard penned 'I Got a Woman' turning it into a gospel frenetic-paced track with secular lyrics. The music itself sends a nod towards jazz and R&B. It became Charles' first big hit, soaring to number one in the Billboard R&B chart during January 1955.

The *New York Times* 2004 obituary said: "Charles could belt like a blues shouter and croon like a pop singer, and he used the flaws and breaks in his voice to illuminate emotional paradoxes. Even in his early years he sounded like a voice of experience, someone who had seen all the hopes and follies of humanity."

Charles became an architect of soul music but his immense talent meant that he could tackle most music categories. The same *New York Times* article said: "By singing any song he prized – from 'Hallelujah I Love Her So' to 'I Can't Stop Loving You' to 'Georgia on My Mind' to 'America the Beautiful' – Mr. Charles claimed all of American music as his birth-right." Joe Levy, the music editor of *Rolling Stone*, said, "The hit records Charles made for Atlantic in the mid-50s mapped out everything that would happen to rock 'n' roll and soul music in the years that followed."

Countless versions of 'I Got a Woman' have been recorded since Ray Charles laid down the track at Atlantic. In 1962, the Philadelphia jazz organist Jimmy McGriff recorded an instrumental version of this song that charted at number 20 in the US. Known for his unique organ sound and gospel influence, McGriff was a popular performer on the R&B club circuit until his retirement in 2007. Ricky Nelson had a minor hit with the track in 1963 and the song has also been covered by many other artists, including the Beatles and Bill Wyman's Rhythm Kings. Jo Stafford did a version that was specially rewritten and recorded as 'I Got a Sweetie'. Bobby Darin, Ace Cannon, Adam Faith and Booker T. & the M.G.'s all did versions.

On his first national TV appearance in 1956, Elvis wore a black shirt, white tie, dress pants with a shiny stripe, and a tweed jacket. He sang 'I Got a Woman' and a medley of 'Shake, Rattle and Roll' and 'Flip, Flop & Fly' on the *Dorsey Brothers Stage Show*. Elvis had recorded the track just a few days previously on 10th January 1956, to be included on his first album *Elvis Presley*.

Elvis would return to the song on his return to live performances. During the '70s, he often paired 'I Got a Woman' with the track 'Amen'.

I WAS THE ONE

Next we head to 11th January 1956 where between 4.00pm and 7.00pm at RCA's Studios in Nashville Elvis laid down the takes for 'I Was the One'. Produced by Steve Sholes, 'I Was the One' became the B-side of 'Heartbreak Hotel'.

The song was written by Aaron Schroeder, Bill Peppers, Claude Demetrius and Hal Blair. Aaron Schroeder wrote seventeen songs for Elvis Presley including five that reached number one: 'A Big Hunk O' Love', 'Good Luck Charm', 'I Got Stung', 'Stuck on You' and 'It's Now or Never'. Schroeder was founder and president of Musicor Records (1960–5), a front runner of the independent labels to be distributed by a major company worldwide. He discovered, managed and directed the career of Gene Pitney and produced the Academy Award nominee for Best Song, 'Town Without Pity'.

Songwriter and publisher, William 'Bill' Peppers had a few hit songs before he died at just 40. Another song he wrote, 'My Lips Are Sealed', was recorded by Jim Reeves.

Claude Demetrius had worked very closely with Louis Jordan in the 1940s. Some of Demetrius's best-known compositions from that era were co-written with Jordan's wife, Fleecie Moore, including the song 'Ain't That Just Like a Woman'. In 1956, Demetrius began writing for Gladys Music, Inc, newly formed by Jean and Julian Aberbach. The company owned the exclusive publishing rights to the music of Elvis Presley. In 1957, he composed 'Mean Woman Blues' for Presley's 1957 motion picture soundtrack, *Loving You*.

Demetrius co-wrote 'Santa, Bring My Baby Back (To Me)' with Aaron Schroeder, which appeared on the 1957 *Elvis' Christmas Album*. But it was in 1958 when Demetrius scored his biggest success of all with his composition of 'Hard Headed Woman'. The song became the first rock and roll single to earn the RIAA designation, 'gold record'. It was written for Presley's 1958 movie *King Creole*. 'Hard Headed Woman' was released as a single, rising up the charts and only stopping when it hit the top.

The fourth writer of 'I Was the One' was Hal Blair. He also wrote 'Ninety Miles an Hour Down a Dead End Street', first recorded by Hank Snow. One of Blair's biggest hits was 'Please Help Me I'm Falling', first recorded by Hank Locklin and later covered by Dolly Parton, Gladys Knight, John Fogerty and Eddy Arnold.

Among those who covered 'I Was the One' was Jamie Coe, who drew the interest of several record companies over the years without ever quite achieving the big breakthrough his talents merited, even though some of his material was produced by the great Bobby Darin. Later, Jimmie Dale Gilmore covered 'I Was the One'. Swedish band Streaplers also recorded a cover in 1978.

Elvis performed 'I Was the One' on his final appearance on the *Louisana Hayride* on 16th December 1956. Earlier in the year he performed the track on the *Dorsey Brothers Stage Show*.

MONEY HONEY

On the same day Elvis recorded 'Heartbreak Hotel' – 10th January 1956 – he laid down two other songs. One of those was 'Money Honey'.

The track had been a huge hit for the Drifters, with Clyde McPhatter leading the group at that time. McPhatter sings about wanting a girl who can support him, but she's not having it. It was written by Jesse Stone, who we mentioned previously. As well as being a songwriter he was also a producer for Atlantic Records. In his book *The Genius of Clyde McPhatter*, Nick Tosches said: "If there is one voice through which the glories of R&B ran their course in the 1950s, it very well may be Clyde McPhatter's." On the website www.rockhall.com – dedicated to the Rock & Roll Hall of Fame – it says of McPhatter:

> Clyde McPhatter possessed a unique vocal instrument, a lively high tenor that captured the promise of the teenage Fifties. McPhatter was one of the first singers to cross over from the church to the pop and R&B charts. He was a Baptist minister's son who was born in North Carolina and spent his teen years up north, in New Jersey and New York. He made the crossing from sacred to secular at age 18, when he was invited to join singer Billy Ward's vocal group, the Dominoes, after

turning heads with his performance of Lonnie Johnson's 'Tomorrow Night' in an amateur show at Harlem's Apollo Theatre. McPhatter was initially billed as 'Clyde Ward,' and it was claimed that he was Billy's brother.

McPhatter's radiant, gospel-trained tenor exploded onto the R&B scene in the early Fifties on 'Do Something for Me,' 'Have Mercy Baby,' 'The Bells' and other of the Dominoes' dozen R&B hits. On 'Have Mercy Baby,' which topped the R&B charts for ten weeks in 1952, McPhatter worked himself to the brink of tears. By recasting gospel's fervid emotionality – a style known as 'sanctified' singing – in a rhythm & blues setting, he presaged what would come to be known as soul music.

Chafing under Ward's discipline, McPhatter left the Dominoes in 1953 and was quickly offered a recording contract and star billing with his own group – the Drifters. He left the band when Uncle Sam came calling for a stint in the army. After his time in the forces, McPhatter returned to the studio, not with the Drifters, but as a solo artist.

In 1958, McPhatter scored the biggest hit of his career, 'A Lover's Question', a doo-wop/R&B classic that captured the beauty of his amazing voice. He enjoyed a dozen more R&B and pop hits with songs like 'Treasure of Love' and 'Without Love (There Is Nothing)'. His contract with Atlantic ended in 1959, but more success was to follow with other labels, including Mercury where he enjoyed success with another huge hit 'Lover Please'. However, a move to the Amy label failed to see any significant chart success with the songs released. According to his biography on www.rockhall.com, a disillusioned McPhatter moved to England, where he was still revered in 1966.

He returned to the States in 1970, marking the event with an album entitled *Welcome Home*. It was to be his last recording. McPhatter's career had been in steady decline due to mounting personal problems, including debilitating alcoholism. Sadly, he died in his sleep of a heart attack at the age of just 39 years old.

'Money Honey' was the closing track on Elvis's debut album, *Elvis Presley*. It was released in the UK as *Elvis Presley Rock 'n' Roll*.

The recording sessions took place on 10th and 11th January 1956 at the RCA Victor recording studios in Nashville, Tennessee, and on 30th and 31st January 1956 at the RCA Victor studios in New York.

Highlights from 30th and 31st January 1956 – RCA Studios, New York City

Just under three weeks after completing his essential first recording session for his new label, Elvis was back behind the microphone. This time the setting was RCA's New York studio.

Just like the first session in Nashville, this New York recording date heralded some classic material from the King of Rock 'n' Roll.

BLUE SUEDE SHOES

'Blue Suede Shoes' was written by Elvis's Sun-record-label friend Carl Perkins. According to the Rockabilly Hall of Fame, 'Blue Suede Shoes' has been called the first true rock 'n' roll hit, in the sense that it was an all-market hit, meaning it sold well in the pop, country and R&B charts. 'Blue Suede Shoes' was the first record to borrow from all three categories and become a hit on all three charts.

It all started the year before, in 1955, when Johnny Cash suggested to Carl Perkins he write a song based on a saying he had heard previously. That line was "don't step on my blue suede shoes". Funnily enough, just a few nights later Perkins was singing in Jackson when he also saw a dancer trying to stop people from stepping on his new blue suede shoes. The following morning, at 3am, Carl Perkins started to write the lyrics to 'Blue Suede Shoes'. Apparently the initial lyrics were written on an empty potato bag – how very rock and roll!

Just a few weeks later, Perkins had worked up the song and felt ready for it to be heard for the first time. He went to Sam Phillips at Sun where three takes were put down on tape. The original line was "three to get ready now go boy go". It was Sam Phillips himself who recommended Perkins change the words to "go cat go!"

On 1st January 1956, 'Blue Suede Shoes' was released, backed with 'Honey, Don't' that had been recorded at the same session. Billboard said at the time that the song had a "strong R&B styled backing. Fine for the jukes." Carl Perkins' original version of 'Blue Suede Shoes' appeared on Billboard's Hot 100 at the beginning of March 1956. Just when it was looking like Perkins was going to be a major star, disaster struck. As Carl and his band were heading to New York to promote 'Blue Suede Shoes' on the national *Perry Como Show*, their eight-seat Chrysler crashed into a poultry truck in Delaware. Sadly, farmer Thomas Phillips was killed. Jay Perkins suffered a fractured neck and Carl received a broken shoulder, cracked skull and lacerations Unfortunately, Jay was diagnosed with a brain tumour and died in 1958, an event that contributed to Perkins hitting an artistic slump and developing a serious drinking problem.

While Perkins was recovering, 'Blue Suede Shoes' continued to climb the charts. In April 1956, it finally topped most of America's charts. Although it spent almost five months on Billboard's country and pop charts, it was excluded from the number-one position by 'Heartbreak Hotel'. By early May, both Perkins and Sun Records had logged their first million-seller. In the same month Perkins was able to appear on the *Perry Como Show* to honour the booking that should have happened in March.

While Perkins' original is pure rockabilly, Elvis's take on his friend's song is rock 'n' roll. Elvis had recorded his version of 'Blue Suede Shoes' in January 1956. But both he and Steve Sholes, RCA's A&R man who had been responsible for signing Elvis to the label, agreed not to release Elvis's version of 'Blue Suede Shoes' as a single while Carl's was still rising up the various charts.

Elvis's version first appeared on a four-track extended play released in March 1956 and then appeared as the opening track on Presley's debut album. Elvis introduced his version of 'Blue Suede Shoes' to a national television audience when he performed it along with 'Heartbreak Hotel' on the *Dorsey Brothers Stage Show*.

Elvis returned to the song in 1960 for the movie *G.I. Blues*. Presley mimed to his 1956 version of 'Blue Suede Shoes' when he did a screen test in Hollywood.

It was this test, one of three, that proved to be the successful one, leading Elvis into the first of 33 movies in Tinseltown.

Carl Perkins recorded 'Blue Suede Shoes' first, followed by Elvis and then Eddie Cochran. The great Buddy Holly also recorded a version. In the 1960s Bill Haley, the Dave Clark Five and the Beatles all recorded versions of 'Blue Suede Shoes'. The song continued to be covered into the 1970s. Albert King did a take for the LP *Blues for Elvis – King Does the King's Things*. Black Sabbath featured it on their *Black Mass* EP in 1970. Jerry Lee Lewis included 'Blue Suede Shoes' in his live set at the 1973 London Rock and Roll Show. Johnny Rivers reached number 38 in the US charts with a version in 1973. And although Johnny Cash is not known to have recorded a studio version of the song he inspired, he did perform it in a duet with Perkins on TV.

As well as being recorded and performed live by a number of artists, 'Blue Suede Shoes' has also made it into other songs, including Chuck Berry's 'Roll Over Beethoven' ("I'm giving you the warning, don't you step on my blue suede shoes").

The song inspired so many covers over the years but the most famous cover of all has to be Elvis's version of 'Blue Suede Shoes'.

I'M GONNA SIT RIGHT DOWN AND CRY OVER YOU

After recording 'Blue Suede Shoes', 'My Baby Left Me', 'One Sided Love Affair' and 'So Glad You're Mine' on 30th January 1956 at RCA Studios in New York, Elvis and the band were back again the next day to record 'I'm Gonna Sit Right Down and Cry (Over You)' as well as a cover of the Little Richard classic 'Tutti Frutti'.

'I'm Gonna Sit Right Down…' was written in 1953 by Joe Thomas and Howard Biggs. Howard Biggs established a song-writing partnership with Joe Thomas and they co-wrote the songs 'Got You on My Mind', a number-one R&B hit for John Greer in 1952, later recorded by Big Joe Turner, Jerry Lee Lewis, Eric Clapton and others. Biggs also wrote 'If I Could Have Your Love Again' with singer Brook Benton. He later led the Howard Biggs Orchestra, which backed leading jazz and R&B vocalists including Dinah Washington, Dakota Staton, Marie Knight and Johnny Hartman.

'I'm Gonna Sit Right Down and Cry (Over You)' was originally recorded by Roy Hamilton in 1954. According to well-respected Elvis biographer Peter Guralnick, Hamilton was a major influence on the young Elvis. The pair would meet at American Sound Studios in 1969.

'I'm Gonna Sit Right Down and Cry (Over You)' has become something of a minor pop standard, largely due to being recorded by Elvis and the Beatles (whose version appears on their *Live at the BBC* album). The fab four had also included the song in sets at the Star Club in Hamburg, Germany, just a short while before they hit the big time and became a globally known band.

Other people who have recorded 'I'm Gonna Sit Right Down and Cry (Over You)' include the Swinging Blue Jeans, Shakin' Stevens and Del Shannon.

Elvis's version of 'I'm Gonna Sit Right Down and Cry (Over You)' was the third track on side two of his now-legendary debut album in 1956.

LAWDY MISS CLAWDY

Next a classic track from the pen of singer–songwriter Lloyd Price – 'Lawdy Miss Clawdy'. Price recorded his version of the song before Elvis even set foot in a studio, but Presley would cover the track in the '50s and '60s (during the *'68 Comeback Special*), and then live in concert during the 1970s. It features in the movies *Elvis on Tour* and *Elvis Recorded Live on Stage in Memphis*, and he was still singing it during some of his 1976 and 1977 tours.

Elvis first recorded the song on 3rd February 1956 at the RCA Studios in New York. He also tackled 'Shake Rattle and Roll' on the same day. The next day Elvis was back on the *Dorsey Brothers Stage Show* for his second appearance performing 'Baby Let's Play House' and 'Tutti Frutti'.

Lloyd Price's version became one of the biggest selling R&B records of 1952 and crossed over to other audiences. Lloyd Price was still at school when he started working for a New Orleans radio station called WBOK. Working at the same station was DJ James 'Okey Dokey' Smith and one of his catch phrases was 'Lawdy Miss Clawdy'. Price recorded the original version on 13th March 1952 at Cosimo Matassa's J&M Studios in New Orleans. It was produced by Dave Bartholomew who worked closely with Fats Domino for many years. Bartholomew was not happy with the first takes of the song. But as legend has it, Fats Domino arrived at the studio and was persuaded by Barthlomew to be a part of the session. Not bad when a hit maker like Fats Domino appears on your first-ever recording. Funnily enough, Fats would go on to record his own version of the song in 1974.

Price's version was released on Specialty Records in April 1952. It entered Billboard's R&B chart taking up residence in that chart for 26 weeks. For seven of those weeks it was at number one. 'Lawdy Miss Clawdy' was named the R&B Record of the Year for 1952 in both *Billboard* and *Cashbox* magazines. In 1995, it was added to the Rock & Roll Hall of Fame's list of the 500 Songs that Shaped Rock and Roll.

Back in the 1950s, when you had a successful song, it was not unusual for other artists either to cover the track or to try to write a follow up that sounded very similar. Nowadays, there are court cases when songs sound like they have copied other tracks – and these can cost millions. However, back in the 1950s it seemed to be a common practice. In 1953, singer Tommy Ridgley, a friend of Price's who had nearly recorded 'Lawdy Miss Clawdy' first, recorded a follow-up 'Oh, Lawdy, My Baby'. In 1958, Price's former valet, Larry Williams, reworked the song to become 'Dizzy Miss Lizzy'. In 1956, Little Richard recorded a version of 'Lawdy Miss Clawdy'. The Four Lovers and Johnny Devlin both did versions in the same year. In 1964, 'Lawdy Miss Clawdy' was recorded by Johnny Rivers and in the UK by the Swinging Blue Jeans. During the remainder of the 1960s, it was recorded by the Hollies, the Animals, the Buckinghams, Joe Cocker and the Beatles for their film *Let It Be*. 'Lawdy Miss Clawdy' was also covered by the Nashville Teens, Ronnie Hawkins, Commander Cody and His Lost Planet Airmen, Conway Twitty, Ronnie McDowell, Carl Perkins, Travis Tritt, Steve Young and many more.

Lloyd Price enjoyed several other hits including 'Personality', 'Stagger Lee' and 'I'm Gonna Get Married'. He was inducted into the Rock & Roll Hall of Fame in 1998.

Elvis's version was included in the 1959 album *For LP Fans Only*. Interestingly it was the first album in recording history to exclude the performer's name from the outside jacket. Even the LP's title was not prominent: it appeared in a box with the RCA logo. The front cover featured a smiling Elvis in a red shirt. By then, it didn't even need his first name on the front. His face was recognisable around the globe. The back cover photo was of Private Presley in his Army dress uniform.

For LP Fans Only reached number 19 on Billboard's top LPs chart and had an eight-week stay on the chart. Track two on side one of that LP was 'Lawdy Miss Clawdy'. It had previously been released as a single in the US and the UK back in 1956.

MY BABY LEFT ME

After making his first appearance on National TV on the *Dorsey Brothers Stage Show*, Elvis stayed in New York. Around 11am on Monday 30th January 1956, Elvis and his band headed for the RCA Studio, where they recorded for seven hours that day, then three hours on 31st January with a further lengthy session on 3rd February 1956. These New York sessions yielded 'Blue Suede Shoes' and seven other tunes: 'My Baby Left Me', 'One-Sided Love Affair', 'So Glad You're Mine', 'I'm Gonna Sit Right Down and Cry Over You', 'Tutti Fruitti', 'Lawdy Miss Clawdy' and 'Shake, Rattle and Roll'.

'My Baby Left Me' had first been released by RCA back in 1950, when its composer Arthur Crudup laid down the original version. Elvis's version was to appear on the B-side of his 1956 single 'I Want You, I Need You, I Love You'. Wanda Jackson, who often shared the same bill as Elvis Presley, did a version, then in 1970 Creedence Clearwater Revival included the song on their 1970 album, *Cosmo's Factory*. Former Beatle John Lennon did a version although it was incorrectly titled 'Since My Baby Left Me'. Straight after Elvis died in

August 1977, British Glam Rock band Slade covered the song and released it as a tribute to Elvis.

Elvis's own version of 'My Baby Left Me' also appeared on the 1956 extended play releases *Elvis Presley* and *The Real Elvis*. It would finally make an appearance on an LP during Elvis's time in the army – when it featured on the release *For LP Fans Only* in 1959.

TUTTI FRUTTI

Next a rock and roll classic that Elvis covered on his first album.

'Tutti Frutti' was a massive hit for the legendary Little Richard. Little Richard or, to give him his real name, Richard Penniman wrote some of his greatest tunes while he was working as a dishwasher. While working those long hot hours at the Greyhound bus station in Macon Georgia, he conjured up some of the best rock and roll tunes ever, including 'Tutti Frutti'. In an archive interview with *Rolling Stone* magazine, Little Richard said:

> I couldn't talk back to my boss man. He would bring all these pots back for me to wash, and one day I said, "I've got to do something to stop this man bringing back all these pots to me to wash," and I said, "Awap bop a lup bop a wop bam boom, take 'em out!" and that's what I meant at the time. And so I wrote 'Tutti Frutti' in the kitchen, I wrote 'Good Golly Miss Molly' in the kitchen, I wrote 'Long Tall Sally' in that kitchen.

Richard says that "Awap bop a lup bop a wop bam boom" was his catch phrase, something he would reply to folks who asked him how he was doing.

Success didn't come overnight for Little Richard. Back in 1952 he had signed a contract with RCA Records but everything they released was a failure. In 1953 he was back in the studio, this time at Peacock Records, where he worked with the Johnny Otis Trio. His break came when the singer Lloyd Price played a show in Macon, Georgia, and Richard, who was selling drinks at the gig, went to the dressing room and played Price 'Tutti Frutti' on the piano. Price loved it and soon after Richard had a record contract with Specialty Records. That was when those unforgettable hits were launched on an unsuspecting audience.

In 2010, the US Library of Congress National Recording Registry added the recording to its registry, stating that the hit, with its original a cappella introduction, heralded a new era in music

OK so Pat Boone may have recorded it… but it was nothing compared to Little Richard's version. Elvis couldn't top Little Richard's original but it's still many leagues above Pat Boone's.

Elvis Presley recorded the song for inclusion on his first RCA album, *Elvis Presley*. Elvis's cut of 'Tutti Frutti' was also released as an EP and as a single where it was listed by *Billboard* magazine as being in the top 20 for sales.

Elvis was one of many to have recorded the track. According to author Mark Lewisohn in *The Complete Beatles Chronicles*, "The Beatles performed 'Tutti Frutti' live from at least 1960 through 1962 (in Hamburg and Liverpool and elsewhere). Reportedly the lead vocal was always by Paul McCartney." Little Richard would later re-record the song in 1964 for Vee Jay Records' *Little Richard's Greatest Hits* and again in 1978 for a K-tel compilation titled *Little Richard Live*.

The Swinging Blue Jeans included a cover on their debut album *Blue Jeans A' Swinging* in 1964. It was one of two Little Richard covers on this album. Queen played 'Tutti Frutti' at every show of the Magic Tour in 1986 and the song is featured on the live album *Live at Wembley '86* (later retitled *Live at Wembley Stadium*).

Elvis's version was recorded on 31st January 1956 and came in at just under two minutes long. It was the opening track on side two of his classic debut album.

Elvis in TV Land – 1956

SHAKE, RATTLE AND ROLL/FLIP, FLOP AND FLY – ELVIS'S DEBUT ON THE DORSEY BROTHERS STAGE SHOW

1956 was an unforgettable year for Elvis Presley. Although he was to achieve so many things in his career, 1956 will always be the one music critics turn to when they want a year that defines the greatness of Elvis.

He made his first recording sessions at RCA and enjoyed the first of many number-one national hits. Elvis also made his first movie later in the year. Just after his first recording sessions with RCA, Elvis appeared for the first time on a national TV show called the *Dorsey Brothers Stage Show*. It was neither Tommy or Jimmy Dorsey who introduced the young star's debut. That honour went to Cleveland DJ Bill Randle.

In hindsight, Bill was the perfect person to introduce Elvis's appearance. *Time* magazine named Bill Randle the top DJ in America. His popularity and huge listening audience allowed him to bolster the careers of a number of young musicians, including the Four Lads, Bobby Darin and Fats Domino. Nicknamed the Pied Piper of Cleveland, a 1955 musical documentary film was made about him titled *The Pied Piper of Cleveland: A Day in the Life of a Famous Disc Jockey*. The film includes a Cleveland concert at Brooklyn High School on 20th October 1955 featuring Pat Boone and Bill Haley & His Comets with Elvis Presley as the opening act. It is the first film footage of a Presley performance.

According to an interview on www.americanmusicpreservation.com, Bill Randle said that Elvis wanted an upbeat number for his debut on the *Dorsey Brothers Stage Show* so he held off singing 'Heartbreak Hotel' until his 11th February appearance on *Stage Show*. He sang the song again on the 17th March and 24th March telecasts.

For his national television debut on 28th January, Elvis sang two songs in a medley: 'Shake, Rattle and Roll' and 'Flip, Flop and Fly'. Elvis also sang the Ray Charles song 'I Got a Woman' on that first TV appearance.

'Shake, Rattle and Roll' was written by Jesse Stone under his assumed song-writing name Charles E. Calhoun. He co-wrote 'Flip, Flop and Fly' with Lou Willie Turner. 'Shake, Rattle and Roll' was originally recorded by Big Joe Turner and was a huge hit for Bill Haley & His Comets.

In early 1954, Ahmet Ertegun of Atlantic Records suggested to Stone he write an up-tempo track for Big Joe Turner. Stone accepted the challenge playing around with a variety of phrases before coming up with "shake, rattle and roll". He may have made the phrase famous amongst rock and roll loving teenagers, but the saying had been around for several years. In fact as far back as 1919, Al Bernard recorded a song about gambling with dice with the same title. The phrase is also heard in 'Roll the Bones' by the Excelsior Quartette in 1922.

'Flip, Flop and Fly' was also a hit for Big Joe Turner. It's easy to see how the medley worked so well for Elvis in 1956 as the tunes are very similar. Some music historians have suggested that leftover verses from outtakes of 'Shake, Rattle and Roll' were then recycled into 'Flip, Flop and Fly'.

In his 2005 biography, *Tommy Dorsey: Livin' in a Big Way*, author Peter J. Levinson painted a pro-Dorsey picture of Elvis's appearances on *Stage Show*. Levinson explained that the brothers' concern about the programme's low ratings, especially in the south, led to them seeking out Presley and booking him. The author provides the following account from Tino Barzie, Tommy Dorsey's band manager:

> I started looking around for new acts – like some country-and-western people. Somebody turned me on to an act handled by Tom Parker. I asked, "What's his name?" "It's Elvis Presley." I said, "Elvis? What kind of name is that?" I tracked Presley down in New Orleans and spoke to Tom Parker. I told him we'd like to use Elvis on several shows. He was thrilled to death. I booked Elvis for the following Saturday. I bought him for four shows for a total of five thousand dollars.

The price of having Elvis Presley on an American TV show would soon sky-rocket.

HEARTBREAK HOTEL – MILTON BERLE SHOW

Elvis Presley's appearances on *Stage Show* made other TV producers sit up and take notice. Ed Sullivan said he would never have Elvis on his show, but he was soon to eat his words and pay vast sums to have the star on his programme. That was still weeks away. The next stop for Elvis in TV land was a big step up to one of the most popular shows of the day, hosted by Milton Berle. On 3rd April 1956, the *Milton Berle Show* broadcast live from the deck of the USS Hancock on NBC while docked at the Naval Air Base in San Diego, California.

As well as starring Elvis, Scotty, Bill and D.J. Fontana, the show also featured the Harry James Orchestra, Arnold Stang and Esther Williams. Elvis and his band performed a 13-second 'Shake, Rattle and Roll' in the beginning of the show, 'Heartbreak Hotel' and 'Blue Suede Shoes'. Elvis also performed a comedy sketch in which Milton Berle acted as Elvis's twin brother Melvin.

While thousands laughed at the comedy sketch, you can't help but wonder how Elvis felt about it. Elvis's own twin brother, Jesse Garon, had been still born and Elvis would often think about his twin. Larry Geller became Elvis's hairdresser and spiritual adviser from the mid-1960s. On his blog on the website www.elvispresleybiography.net, he said:

> When it came to Jesse Garon, he told me that as a child he would talk about him to anyone who would listen. "I have a brother!" he announced proudly, telling everyone how close they were, and how they talked together all the time. At night as he lay in his bed, in the dark and silence of his room, he would have special conversations with Jesse, and later tell people what his brother had said to him.

Larry said:

> I knew Elvis had a stillborn twin brother; my own younger twin sisters had told me after they read a story about him in a movie magazine. It was only after we met, in April of 1964, that I came to realize how deeply Elvis had been affected by this unfulfilled relationship.

One day Elvis told his hairdresser:

> I'll tell ya Larry, being a twin has always been a mystery for me. I mean, we were in our mother's womb together, so why was he born dead and not me? He never even got his chance to live. Think about it, why me? Why was I the one that was chosen? An' I've always wondered what would've been if he had lived, I really have. These kinds of questions tear my head up. There's got to be reasons for all this.

Two weeks after Elvis performed 'Heartbreak Hotel' on-board the USS Hancock it became his first number one. The exposure it received from the nationally viewed Milton Berle Show no doubt helped immensely.

As the host of NBC's *Texaco Star Theater* from 1948 until 1955 Milton Berle was the first major American television star and became known to millions of viewers as 'Uncle Miltie' and 'Mr. Television'. By the time Elvis was exploding onto the scene, Berle's star was starting to fade. In fact, Berle knew that NBC had already decided to cancel his show before Presley appeared. Berle later appeared in the *Kraft Music Hall* series from 1958 to 1959, but NBC was finding increasingly fewer showcases for its one-time superstar. By 1960, he was reduced to hosting a bowling program, *Jackpot Bowling*, delivering his quips and interviewing celebrities between the efforts of that week's bowling contestants. After the TV work dried up, Berle enjoyed great success in Las Vegas, playing to packed showrooms at Caesars Palace, the Sands, the Desert Inn and other casino hotels. As 'Mr. Television', Berle was one of the first seven people to be inducted into the Television Academy Hall of Fame in 1984.

Berle was responsible for Elvis's most controversial TV appearance later in 1956. We'll look at that next.

HOUND DOG – FROM THE MILTON BERLE SHOW

1956 was a year of immense success for Elvis. In the eyes of his countless teenage fans across the world, he could do no wrong. However, he had to handle the huge amount of criticism from the newspaper critics of the day.

By the summer of 1956 the Elvis controversy was about to hit its peak. It all happened on the *Milton Berle Show*. It was Elvis's second appearance on the show, having previously performed on board the USS Hancock. Presley's second appearance in the studio with Uncle Miltie was on 5th June 1956. For the first time, he appeared without his guitar and it was this appearance that led to screaming critics the next day.

"Mr. Presley has no discernible singing ability… For the ear, he is an unutterable bore," wrote critic Jack Gould in the next day's *New York Times*. "His one specialty is an accented movement of the body that heretofore has been primarily identified with the repertoire of the blonde bombshells of the burlesque runway. The gyration never had anything to do with the world of popular music and still doesn't." In the *New York Daily News*, Ben Gross described Presley's performance as "tinged with the kind of animalism that should be confined to dives and bordellos," while the *New York Journal-American*'s Jack O'Brien said that Elvis "makes up for vocal shortcomings with the weirdest and plainly suggestive animation short of an aborigine's mating dance." Meanwhile, the Catholic weekly *America* got right to the point in its headline: 'Beware of Elvis Presley'.

The press had a new name for the rising star, a name Elvis hated from the beginning – 'Elvis the Pelvis'.

The reason for this massive backlash? One song – 'Hound Dog'. It all started in relative calm, until midway through Elvis suddenly ad-libbed and instructed the shocked band to change the tempo.

He slowed it right down to a sexy bluesy number, gyrating his hips in rhythm with the slowed down beat – he was loving it, laughing between the lines, the audience went crazy. The band looked shocked at first by this impromptu change in the song, but they were used to Elvis springing surprises after several months on the road, and they soon settled in and started to enjoy this history-making moment.

Uncle Miltie loved it. Overnight ratings showed that Elvis's controversial appearance had allowed Milton Berle's show to beat out time-slot competitor Phil Silvers for the first time in several months. Straight after the song there was some great banter between Elvis and Uncle Miltie. You can hear the exchange on the audio version of this series.

"I wanna ask you something, Elvis," the deadpan comedian said. "If I did that thing the way you did it, do you think I could get all the girls?"

Presley replied, "Well, it might not help you get girls. But at your age, it would keep the blood circulating."

"At my age," sniffed a mock-offended Berle. "You make me feel like a used car."

It is one of Presley's most controversial performances but it also showed him at his absolute best. A few days after the show aired, letters starting arriving for Uncle Miltie. But these weren't fan letters, but what Berle called 'pan letters'. About ten days after the show, Berle called Colonel Tom Parker to tell him that based on the "hundreds of thousands of 'pan' letters" he had received following the show, "you have a star on your hands". Elvis had well and truly arrived.

Elvis certainly was becoming a major star. By the end of 1956, he had sold 10 million singles and 800,000 albums in just 12 months. And he was appearing on *The Ed Sullivan Show*, signed for three dates at the eye-popping price of $50,000.

I WANT YOU, I NEED YOU, I LOVE YOU – STEVE ALLEN SHOW

Earlier we looked at the exciting but highly controversial appearance by Elvis on the *Milton Berle Show*, singing 'Hound Dog'. The backlash from critics and parents made TV executives nervous – they knew they wanted Elvis because of the massive viewing figures he guaranteed. But they didn't want the controversy and countless complaints by mail.

The Steve Allen Show aired 1st July and, besides 'Hound Dog', Elvis sang 'I Want You, I Need You, I Love You'. This time though the young rocker was presented wearing formal attire. His body movements were subdued. Moreover, he sang 'Hound Dog' to a live basset hound – a move which angered Elvis fans at the time.

Stories over the years have made out that Steve Allen set out to demean Elvis. However, in interviews over the years, Allen has denied this strongly. Almost

40 years after the appearance, Steve Allen insisted he meant no disrespect, that Elvis was in on the gag from the beginning and that Elvis thought it was hilarious. Fans over the years have disagreed. There's been plenty of debate in magazines and online forum where many fans believe Elvis's appearance on *The Steve Allen Show* was a deliberate attempt to humiliate Elvis and ridicule rock 'n' roll music.

Later on that same night, a tired Elvis appeared on Hy Gardner's live TV interview show. "I don't feel like I'm doing anything wrong", he told Gardner. "I don't see how any type of music would have any bad influence on people. How would rock 'n' roll music make anyone rebel against their parents?"

Steve Allen had started life in radio, but is best remembered for his many television shows. He was no stranger to TV when, in June 1956, NBC offered Allen a new, prime-time, Sunday-night variety hour, *The Steve Allen Show*, aimed at dethroning CBS's top-rated *The Ed Sullivan Show*. One of the earliest guests was Elvis Presley, so understandably Allen didn't want to rock the boat too much, but still wanted Presley on his show.

In his book *HiHo Steverino*, Allen said: "For his own part, Elvis had a terrific time with us and lent himself willingly to our brand of craziness. He was an easy-going, likeable, and accommodating performer. He quickly become the biggest star in the country; but when I ran into him from time-to-time over the years it was clear that he had never let his enormous success go to his head."

However, Elvis has been quoted as saying: "it was the most ridiculous appearance I ever did and I regret ever doing it". He apparently said he would never do *The Steve Allen Show* again. Two very different accounts there!

The appearance may have been embarrassing for Elvis but it did him no damage at all. Straight after the performance, Ed Sullivan himself called Colonel Tom Parker saying he wanted Elvis on his show. Sullivan broke what had until that moment been a $7,500 price ceiling on star guests, offering the Colonel $10,000 per shot. The Colonel went straight back to Allen asking if he was able to match it then they would stay with him and turn down Sullivan. Allen said he told Parker to go with Sullivan. Maybe Allen was satisfied he'd done everything he wanted with the young singer.

When you look at the amazing appearances Elvis made on *The Ed Sullivan Show*, it seems pretty obvious that Allen made a huge mistake by not having the singer back. Then again, Elvis may never have gone back on the show anyway, if archive accounts are to be believed.

It may only have been one appearance, but for a variety of reasons, Elvis's spot on *The Steve Allen Show* has been preserved forever and is a part of the Elvis in '56 story.

As for the song, Elvis recorded the studio version of 'I Want You, I Need You, I Love You' on 11th April 1956 at RCA's Studio B in Nashville with an impressive line-up of musicians including both Scotty Moore and Chet Atkins on guitar; old faithfuls Bill Black and D.J. Fontana could be found in their usual places of bass and drums respectively.

Reviewing the song for www.allmusic.com, music critic Bill Janovitz said that 'I Want You, I Need You, I Love You' was: "effervescent rock & roll balladry bursting with potential and the knowledge that this was brand new and exciting music – neither the country & western that Nashville was used to, nor the Memphis blues."

The song was written by Maurice Mysels and Ira Kosloff. The ballad was backed with the rockin' 'My Baby Left Me' which had been recorded at Elvis's second recording session for RCA at the end of January 1956.

The song, another US number one, continued an unbelievable year for Elvis, which saw him spend roughly half of 1956 at number one in the charts with classic hits like 'Heartbreak Hotel' and 'Hound Dog' along with 'Don't Be Cruel' and 'I Want You, I Need You, I Love You'.

Studio Highlights – 2nd July 1956 – RCA New York

ANYWAY YOU WANT ME

Our next track was recorded on the very same one-day session that produced 'Hound Dog' and 'Don't Be Cruel'. 'Anyway You Want Me' showed Elvis in tender mood. It changed the way some of those in the studio that day saw Elvis, like Jordanaire Gordon Stoker, who said in an archive interview for Peter Guralnick's excellent biography *Last Train to Memphis: The Rise of Elvis Presley*:

> I wasn't all that impressed with him, as a singer. I mean, I kind of got a kick out of 'Don't Be Cruel'... but then with 'Anyway You Want Me,' all of a sudden I took a different attitude, the feeling that he had on that particular sound made the hair on my arm come up. I said to the guys, 'Hey men, this guy can sing!'

The song was written by Cliff Owens with Aaron Schroeder, the latter of whom also co-wrote 'Good Luck Charm' and 'Big Hunk o' Love' for Elvis. Schroeder was one of the key figures around the Brill Building in the 1950s and 1960s. He was a songwriter who preferred to collaborate with others, especially in improving the commerciality of a promising song. Several of his 300 published compositions were recorded by Elvis Presley, including the multi-million seller 'It's Now or Never'. According to rock and roll writer Spencer Leigh: "Besides writing rock 'n' roll songs, Schroeder maintained his contact with more traditional singers. In 1958, Frank Sinatra had a hit with 'French Foreign Legion' and Perry Como with 'Mandolins in the Moonlight'. Nat 'King' Cole recorded two of Schroeder's songs, 'Sweet Bird of Youth' (1959) and 'Time and the River' (1960)."

The lyric of 'Anyway You Want Me' was a real pledge of undying love that would have tugged on the heart strings of teenagers in 1950s America. With lines like: "I'll be as strong as a mountain/Or weak as a willow tree/Anyway you want me/ Well, that's how I will be" how could Elvis fail to win the hearts of teenage girls?

It became the B-side of the single 'Love Me Tender' – a real romantic 45 – appealing to Elvis's legions of female fans. It also took the heat off the controversial star by showing a more romantic and gentle side to the wild rockin' figure who had worried the parents earlier in 1956.

An instrumental version of 'Anyway You Want Me' was released by the Rockin' Rebels. However, the definitive version belongs to Elvis.

DON'T BE CRUEL

Here's a song that was paired with 'Hound Dog' when released as a single. It is the only single in history to have both sides reach number one in the US.

We're turning the spotlight on 'Don't Be Cruel'. The song's composer was Otis Blackwell, who would also pen Elvis's first UK number one, 'All Shook Up', as well as writing 'One Broken Heart for Sale' and co-writing 'Return to Sender' for Elvis. Blackwell also composed 'Fever', which was made famous by Peggy Lee and covered by Elvis on his 1960 album *Elvis is Back*. He also featured it in the *Aloha from Hawaii* show in January 1973.

We've already mentioned how Elvis took command of his recording sessions in 1956, deciding what he would record and which take would be released. Some songs had many takes before Elvis was satisfied. However, 'Don't Be Cruel' took around 20 minutes to perfect and record.

Blackwell was initially against giving up a percentage of his writer's fee, something Tom Parker, Elvis's manager, had insisted on. However, he soon realised that some of the fee on an Elvis song was going to be better than a full fee on someone else's version, so he agreed and watched the money start to roll in. In an archive interview, Freddy Bienstock, Elvis's Music Publisher, gave his reasons why Elvis received co-writing credit for songs like 'Don't Be Cruel'. He said:

> In the early days Elvis would show dissatisfaction with some lines and he would make alterations, so it wasn't just what is known as a 'cut-in'. His name did not appear after the first year. But if Elvis liked the song, the writers would be offered a guarantee of a million records and they would surrender a third of their royalties to Elvis.

The single was released in July 1956, but it did not appear on an album until the March 1958 release of *Elvis's Golden Records*.

Over the years 'Don't Be Cruel' has been covered by many artists including Bill Black, who appeared on Elvis's original. Black released as instrumental version in 1960 and just missed out on a US top-ten hit. In 1988, Cheap Trick reached number four in the US charts with their version.

Presley performed 'Don't Be Cruel' during all three of his appearances on *The Ed Sullivan Show* in September 1956 and January 1957. But we'll look at those performances elsewhere.

'Don't Be Cruel' went on to become Presley's biggest-selling single recorded in 1956, with sales over six million by 1961. It became a regular feature of his live sets until his death in 1977 and was often coupled with 'Jailhouse Rock' or '(Let Me Be Your) Teddy Bear' during performances from 1969. The 1956 studio version of 'Don't Be Cruel' was inducted into the Grammy Hall of Fame in 2002. In 2004, it was listed at number 197 in *Rolling Stone*'s list of 500 Greatest Songs of All Time.

HOUND DOG

Now for an absolute Elvis classic written by Jerry Leiber and Mike Stoller when they were teenagers.

However, they didn't write it for Elvis. It was blues singer Big Mama Thornton who recorded the original version. It was the first song that Leiber and Stoller produced. In a 2009 interview for *Mojo* magazine, Mike Stoller said: "Johnny Otis was supposed to run the session. We had rehearsed and he'd played drums. When we got in the studio [it was] his regular drummer. It wasn't happening. I said, 'Johnny, you've got to play the drums, do what you did in rehearsal.' So he said, 'Who's going to run the session.' I said, 'We will.'" Big Mama Thornton's version of 'Hound Dog' became a number-one R&B hit and her biggest success.

She might not have made her fortune as a singer, but she became a huge influence on many singers who went on to enjoy greater success including Elvis and Janis Joplin. Thornton's performances were characterised by her deep, powerful voice and strong sense of self. In an archive interview, Big Mama Thornton said: "My singing comes from my experience... My own experience. I never had no one teach me nothin'. I never went to school for music or nothin'.

I taught myself to sing and to blow harmonica and even to play drums by watchin' other people! I can't read music, but I know what I'm singing! I don't sing like nobody but myself."

Thornton originally recorded her song 'Ball 'n' Chain' for Bay-Tone Records in the early 1960s. The label didn't release the song; however, they must have seen some potential in the track as they held on to the copyright. Sadly, when Janis Joplin enjoyed success with the song later in the 1960s, Big Mama Thornton missed out on lucrative publishing royalties. In addition to 'Ball 'n' Chain' and 'They Call Me Big Mama', Thornton wrote twenty other blues songs. Her 'Ball 'n' Chain' is included in the Rock & Roll Hall of Fame list of the 500 Songs that Shaped Rock and Roll.

Thornton was found dead at age 57 by medical personnel in a Los Angeles boarding house on 25th July 1984 of heart and liver complications due to her long-standing alcohol abuse. Her weight dropped from 350 to 95 pounds (159 to 43 kg) within a short period of time, so she lost a total of 255 pounds (116 kg) because of her critical condition.

Thornton was nominated for the Blues Music Awards six times. In 1984, she was inducted into the Blues Hall of Fame.

'Hound Dog' became a huge number-one hit for Elvis Presley in 1956. He made his band record 31 takes of the song, over several hours, until he was satisfied with the right version. In the end, Presley chose version 28, declaring: "This is the one."

It wasn't Big Mama Thornton's version of 'Hound Dog' that persuaded Elvis to start performing it. He first heard the song in a jokey version by a Las Vegas band called Freddie Bell & the Bellboys in 1956.

Initially Mike Stoller was not impressed with Elvis's version of the song: "It just sounded terribly nervous, too fast, too white. But you know, after it sold seven or eight million records it started to sound better. I should also say that the other things we did with Elvis I liked very much."

Thanks to the success of Elvis's 'Hound Dog', Leiber and Stoller were hired to write many more songs for Elvis in the 1950s, including the memorable score for Elvis's third movie *Jailhouse Rock*.

According to songfacts.com, 'Hound Dog', released as a single with 'Don't Be Cruel', was the only single to have both sides reach number one in the US. The single was at the top of the US charts for 11 weeks, a US record that was not broken until 1992 by 'End of the Road' by Boyz II Men. Songfacts.com also states:

> Presley's guitarist Scotty Moore played on a P-90-equipped Gibson L-5 plugged into a Ray Butts amp. There are two guitar solos in the song, and at the beginning of the second one, Moore made some sounds that guitarists have been unable to replicate since. Moore claimed that he didn't even know how he did it, making it one of the great guitar mysteries in rock.

According to www.neatorama.com:

> In the weeks between laying down the track and its release hardly an interview went by without Elvis being asked when 'Hound Dog' would come out. Elvis's manager, Colonel Tom Parker, joked with RCA executives that the song was going to be so big that the company would have to change its symbol from the Victor Dog to a 'Hound Dog'.

Elvis performed 'Hound Dog' on *The Milton Berle Show*, the controversial appearance mentioned above, and to a Basset Hound on Steve Allen's show. The day after his appearance on Allen's show, Presley recorded the studio version of 'Hound Dog'.

Later, both 'Hound Dog' and 'Don't Be Cruel' were awarded platinum status. On top of all these titles, 'Hound Dog' was also voted the number-one most-played song on juke boxes on 1st September 1956. In 2004, *Rolling Stone* magazine placed Elvis's 'Hound Dog' at number 19 in its list of the 500 Greatest Songs of All Time. The song was inducted into the Grammy Hall of Fame in 1988.

LOVE ME

Let's look at another track written by the chart-topping composers that were Jerry Leiber and Mike Stoller.

The songwriters wrote the track as a bit of a parody; however, Elvis made it sound quite sincere in the original version he did. In later versions, during his concerts in the '70s, it didn't have the same air of sincerity but nonetheless it remained a fan favourite to the end.

Elvis was by no means the first to record the song, even though Leiber and Stoller had and would continue to write tracks aimed at Presley until Colonel Parker virtually blacklisted them (when the paranoid manager felt the duo were getting too close to his star.) 'Love Me' was first recorded by the R&B duo Willy and Ruth in 1954. That original version was featured in a Review Spotlight by *Billboard* during the summer of '54.

The original version was quickly followed the same year with cover versions by Georgia Gibbs, Connie Russell, Billy Eckstine, Kay Brown, the Four Escorts, the Billy Williams Quartet, the Woodside Sisters and the DeMarco Sisters, and in January 1955 by Jimmie Rodgers Snow. Most of these records were well reviewed in the music press at the time, but none became a big hit. The song's popularity would soon soar once Elvis turned his attention to it at a recording session on 1st September 1956.

Elvis recorded the song for his second album, *Elvis*, which was issued on 19th October. As well as being a highlight on the album, 'Love Me' was also released as part of an extended play single called *Elvis Volume One*. The EP climbed high in the charts peaking at number two in the Billboard Hot 100.

'Love Me' was not released as a solo single at the time. It was said that this was to avoid confusion with Presley's huge hit 'Love Me Tender'. However, this didn't stop Elvis from featuring the song on his second appearance on *The Ed Sullivan Show* on 28th October 1956. Elvis included this song in the *'68 Comeback Special* with the NBC network, and often performed it in concerts in the seventies, including his last tour in June 1977.

Robert Plant said in *Rolling Stone*'s '100 Greatest Singers of all Time' issue:

> When I met Elvis with Zeppelin, after one of his concerts in the early '70s, I sized him up. He wasn't quite as tall as me, but he had a singer's build, and he was driven. At that meeting, Jimmy Page joked with Elvis that we never sound checked – but if we did, all I wanted to do was sing Elvis songs.
>
> Elvis thought that was funny and asked me, "Which songs do you sing?" I told him I liked the ones with all the moods, like that great country song 'Love Me' – "Treat me like a fool/Treat me mean and cruel/But love me." So when we were leaving, after a most illuminating and funny 90 minutes with the guy, I was walking down the corridor.
>
> He swung 'round the door frame, looking quite pleased with himself, and started singing that song: "Treat me like a fool." I turned around and did Elvis right back at him. We stood there, singing to each other.

Wow. What a moment that must have been. Sadly, we don't have this short impromptu version of the song – if only someone could have recorded it!

The original version by the young Elvis from 1st September 1956 proved he was not only the King of Rock 'n' Roll, he could conquer the tender love songs too.

OLD SHEP

Time for a weepy now. 'Old Shep' was written by Red Foley and Arthur Williams in 1933, about a dog Foley owned as a child. Foley must have really loved the dog to write that song; and in turn, he then loved the track so much he recorded it on three separate occasions: 1935, 1941 and again in 1946.

A version of the song by Clinton Ford appeared in the UK singles chart in October 1959, spending one week at number 27.

Foley himself first recorded the song in the year Elvis was born. Then between the second and third recording, Elvis himself sang the song in public for the first time. It was on 3rd October 1945 that a 10-year-old shy Elvis sang 'Old Shep' as part of a singing contest at the Mississippi–Alabama Fair and Dairy Show. Accounts vary on where Elvis came in the competition. The majority say Elvis finished in fifth place, winning $5 and a free ticket to the fair rides.

Did something stir in the youngster on that day, something small, that made him think maybe he could make money from singing? After all, it was only eight short years later that Elvis went to the Sun studios to pay for his first private recording – and 11 years and a month after he sang 'Old Shep' he would sign to RCA for a substantial fee for the time.

Elvis returned to 'Old Shep' again in 1951 when he chose the song for another talent show, at Humes High School in Memphis where he was a student. This time he won an encore and female admiration for his performance on that day.

The song 'Old Shep' made the *Rolling Stone* magazine's top ten in the forty saddest country songs of all time feature.

The song's composer Red Foley enjoyed great success. For more than two decades, Foley was one of the biggest stars of country music, selling more than 25 million records. His 1951 hit, 'Peace in the Valley' (also recorded by Elvis) was among the first million-selling gospel records. A Grand Ole Opry veteran until his death, Foley also hosted the first popular country music series on network television, Ozark Jubilee, from 1955 to 1960. He is a member of the Country Music Hall of Fame, which called him "one of the most versatile and moving performers of all time" and "a giant influence during the formative years of contemporary Country music."

'Old Shep' has also shown up in the strangest of places. In the forever-popular British TV sitcom *Only Fools and Horses*, 'Old Shep' is Del Boy's favourite song about a dog. In the 1982 Christmas special 'Diamonds Are for Heather', Del gets a local band to sing 'Old Shep'. At the end of the episode, after being dumped by Heather, he pays some Christmas carol singers to sing the song to cheer himself up. In a later episode, 'Modern Men', Del has 'Old Shep' as the 'on hold' music on his mobile phone, plus it plays on the radio in Sid's café in 'The Long Legs of the Law'.

On 2nd September 1956, at Radio Recorders, Elvis finally professionally recorded several takes of 'Old Shep', all featuring him on piano. It was take five that became the master and was released by RCA. Strangely though, in the UK there was a mistake and an alternate take appeared on the first pressing of the British LP, *Elvis Presley Nº. 2*.

PARALYZED

A track now from Elvis's second LP. 'Paralyzed' was mainly written by hit maker Otis Blackwell, with Elvis receiving song-writing credit for his contributions to the finished song.

Blackwell penned some legendary rock and roll tracks including Little Willie John's 'Fever', Jerry Lee Lewis's 'Great Balls of Fire' and 'Breathless', Elvis Presley's 'Don't Be Cruel', 'All Shook Up' and 'Return to Sender' (with Winfield Scott), and Jimmy Jones' 'Handy Man'. During an appearance on *Late Night with David Letterman*, Blackwell said he'd never met Presley in person. He was a prolific songwriter composing more than a thousand songs, garnering worldwide sales of close to 200 million records.

In 1962, Colonel Tom Parker asked Otis to appear in the Presley movie *Girls! Girls! Girls!*, for which he had written 'Return To Sender', but Blackwell had a superstition about meeting Elvis. He once said that he didn't want to affect his success by meeting Elvis. Otis Blackwell was inducted into the Nashville Songwriters Hall of Fame in 1986 and in 1991 into the National Academy of Popular Music's Songwriters Hall of Fame.

'Paralyzed' reached number 59 on the Billboard pop singles chart in 1956 as part of an EP by RCA Victor in the U.S. called *Elvis Volume 1*. In the UK, 'Paralyzed' reached number eight in August 1957 during a successful 10-week chart run.

Elvis Presley also performed the song on the informal but wonderful 1956 Million Dollar Quartet sessions. The released version of the song was recorded at Radio Recorders, Hollywood, California, produced by Steve Sholes and engineered by Thorne Nogar. The sessions saw Elvis with familiar faces including Scotty Moore, Bill Black, D.J. Fontana and, providing back-up vocals, the Jordanaires.

This vocal quartet was formed as a gospel group in 1948 and became well known in the southern gospel realm. What made the Jordanaires stand out from other quartets of that time was how they would bring spirituals (such as 'Dry Bones') to a predominantly white audience. While continuing to turn out gospel albums of their own, the group become better known for the signature background harmonies they provided on dozens of secular records.

But how did their paths cross with Elvis? One Sunday afternoon in 1955, the Jordanaires played a show in Memphis with Eddy Arnold to publicise their new syndicated TV series, *Eddy Arnold Time*. (For the programme, the group used the name the 'Gordonaires'.) They sang 'Peace in the Valley' and when the show was over, Elvis Presley, an emerging singer, talked with them and said: "If I ever get a recording contract with a major company, I want you guys to back me up." Elvis, ever loyal to people he respected, was true to his word. Gordon Stoker was the first Jordanaire to sing with Elvis, at his first January sessions.

However, Elvis soon made it clear he wanted Stoker and the other Jordanaires as a permanent fixture on his studio recordings and TV appearances. Ironically, the Jordanaires would back Elvis on his version of 'Peace in the Valley' under two years after the then-unknown Presley had heard them singing it on Eddy Arnold's show. More on that song later.

The line-up consisting of Gordon Stoker, first tenor and manager, Neal Matthews, second tenor and lead, Hoyt Hawkins, baritone, and Ray Walker, bass, would be the group's most stable line-up, lasting throughout the 1960s and 1970s. In January 1978, the group performed a medley of Presley's songs on the NBC TV special, *Nashville Remembers Elvis on His Birthday*. The Jordanaires' story ended with the death of Gordon Stoker at the age of 88 on 27th March 2013. His son confirmed that the Jordanaires were formally dissolved, in accordance with his father's wishes.

But what a legacy they left behind.

READY TEDDY

"Ready, set, go-man-go" it's time for a song from the pens of John Marascalco and Robert Blackwell, which became a huge success for Little Richard in 1956. Elvis recorded his version in the same year – we're talking 'Ready Teddy'.

Little Richard released the song as the flip side to 'Rip It Up'. According to www.songfacts.com, "Kids didn't tell their parents, but the song is about a girl who wants sex: a 'ready teddy'." Little Richard claims that he had a big part in writing this song, but didn't have enough business sense to claim a credit. In a 1970 interview with *Rolling Stone*, he said: "They brought me the words and I made up the melody, and at the time I didn't have sense enough to claim so much money, because I really made them hits. I didn't get the money, but I still have the freedom."

The mid 1950s were a hugely successful time for Little Richard. However, he stunned teenagers around the globe in 1957 when he announced he was leaving the music business to pursue a life as a minister. As a child, he wanted to be part of the church, so as an adult he enrolled in Oakwood Theological College in Huntsville, Alabama. During his studies there, the British Invasion took over the musical landscape and Little Richard returned to rock 'n' roll. The teenagers welcomed him with open arms. In 1970, he earned a BA in Theological Studies at Oakwood and became an ordained minister in the Seventh Day Adventist Church. However, the call of rock 'n' roll meant many comebacks and successful tours running into this century.

Countless huge names have recorded their own versions of 'Ready Teddy'. Buddy Holly and Gene Vincent both recorded the track. It was one of the earliest recordings by a young group of lads who would soon become global stars – the Beatles.

Elvis recorded his version of 'Ready Teddy' on 3rd September 1956, on the third consecutive day of recording sessions for his second album, *Elvis*. He also sang it in front of some 60-million television viewers during his first appearance on *The Ed Sullivan Show* at CBS.

TOO MUCH

Next, a song that was Elvis's fifth regular single release for RCA. It followed 'Love Me Tender' and preceded 'All Shook Up', two massive number-one hits for Elvis. However, over the years the song has been somewhat neglected. One of the reasons could be that in a period when Elvis could do no wrong, and was scoring number one after number one, 'Too Much' was deemed a bit of a failure. Of course, it wasn't at all; however, the one thing it didn't do was provide Elvis with another number one on the main charts from *Billboard*. (Although all was not lost: it did make number one in the lesser recognised chart provided by Cashbox.) The single peaked at number two on the Billboard Hot 100.

It was written by Bernard Weinman and Lee Rosenberg and was first recorded in 1954 by Bernard Hardison on Republic Records. Elvis recorded 'Too Much' in September 1956 and it gained national exposure when it was performed on *The Ed Sullivan Show* on 6th January 1957. If you watch the footage of the show, Elvis does get a bit lost with the lyrics, but thankfully the Jordanaires went with the flow and Elvis got away with it.

One person who did make a mistake and wasn't allowed to forget it was Scotty Moore. In the BBC Radio series, *The Elvis Presley Story*, Scotty recalled how it came about:

> I don't remember now exactly what I had nailed down for the solo instrumental part. It was in an odd key... well, for most guitar players, I would say. When my instrumental part came, I absolutely just got lost. I didn't know where I was at. But from the experience we had already gained in these months behind us, in playing on stage, you go ahead, you just keep on going, and this is what I did. And this was the take that was released.

In *Elvis Presley: A Life in Music: The Complete Recording Sessions* by Ernst Jorgensen, the author said of 'Too Much': "It wasn't much of a song, but it did have a nice drive and the kind of rhythm that teenagers like." Apparently, the musicians had difficulty keeping this rhythm going all the way through for a complete take. Elvis's time was limited as he needed to return to work on the film *Love Me Tender*, so the official release of 'Too Much' was a splice of two takes.

WHEN MY BLUE MOON TURNS TO GOLD AGAIN

Next a song written by Wiley Walker and Gene Sullivan in 1940. The duo had both enjoyed solo careers before their successful partnership started in 1939. Sullivan had been a professional boxer, before turning to country music in 1932. They first recorded 'When My Blue Moon Turns to Gold Again' in 1941. This version achieved some local success but it would be the 1956 pop version by Elvis that finally launched the song. Other people to cover it include Eddy Arnold, Bill Monroe and Clarence Brown.

In 1946, Walker and Sullivan registered their only chart entry, 'Make Room in Your Heart for a Friend', which became a number-two US country hit. Later, Sullivan enjoyed a solo top-10 success in 1957 with his comedy number 'Please Pass the Biscuits'. In an archive interview, Gene Sullivan said:

> The 1940 recording session that Wiley Walker and I did for Columbia records was a mistake. We didn't know anything about original songs.
>
> We just recorded songs that we liked to sing. The Columbia A&R man, Art Satherley, trashed most of the tunes we recorded and we had to learn six new songs in one day.
>
> He finally sat us down and told us that we were going to have to come up with original songs if we wanted to stay in the recording business. That was all new to us because we had never done that. So I started to try to write songs.
>
> During that time, I was moving my family and everything we owned in our car from Lubbock Texas to Oklahoma City for a new job. I drove all night across Texas looking right into a bright full moon.
>
> The moon was so bright that I could even turn off the car headlights and still see the road. And that's where I got the idea for 'When My Blue Moon Turns to Gold Again'. And I wrote that song on that trip.

Elvis recorded his version of the song on 2nd September 1956 at Radio Recorders in Hollywood. He tackled the song after 'Paralyzed' and before 'Long Tall Sally'. Elvis also sang 'When My Blue Moon Turns to Gold Again' on his third and final appearance on *The Ed Sullivan Show*, where TV executives demanded Elvis should be filmed from the waist up.

On the evening of 6th January 1957, Elvis Presley took to *The Ed Sullivan Show* stage and performed great tracks like 'Hound Dog', 'Don't Be Cruel', 'Too Much' and one of Elvis's gospel favourites, 'Peace in the Valley'. Before slowing it down for 'Peace in the Valley', Elvis sang 'When My Blue Moon Turns to Gold Again'.

The studio version was the third track on side one of Presley's second album, *Elvis*.

1956 – Back into TV Land

LOVE ME TENDER – ED SULLIVAN SHOW – 9TH SEPTEMBER 1956

This was Elvis's crowning moment on '50s television. He had already appeared on *The Dorsey Brothers Stage Show*, then with Uncle Miltie on *The Milton Berle Show*, but throughout the King of television Ed Sullivan had been adamant he would *never* have Elvis Presley on his hugely popular show. However, after seeing the ratings go through the roof everywhere he appeared, Sullivan began to soften in his approach. Maybe he should have this youngster on his show…

After seeing the reaction on Steve Allen's show, a rival to his own programme, Sullivan was straight onto the phone to Elvis's manager. Steve Allen has said the call was made soon after the final credits had run on his show. Sullivan could have picked up Elvis for just $5,000 earlier in the year. This caution cost him in a big way.

As he spoke to Colonel Parker, he found himself agreeing to pay the unprecedented sum of $50,000 for what were to become three legendary appearances.

Let's bust a couple of myths – Elvis wasn't filmed only from the waist upward until his third appearance on Sullivan's show. And it wasn't even Sullivan who got the chance to introduce his most expensive act to date. That honour went to British actor, Charles Laughton. Sullivan wasn't backstage sulking about the amount he'd had to shell out. Unfortunately, he'd been in a car accident and had to watch the Presley debut from his hospital bed.

Elvis wasn't even in the New York studio for his debut performance but in a Hollywood studio with his trusted band – Scotty Moore, D.J. Fontana and Bill Black. The first song Elvis ever sang on *The Ed Sullivan Show* was 'Don't Be Cruel'. He would then sing 'Love Me Tender', the song that was the reason he was in Hollywood, filming his first-ever film, which shared its name with the song.

Nationwide disc jockeys apparently taped the performance so they could play the song, as it hadn't yet been released. This practice, along with the television appearance itself, helped to increase pre-orders for 'Love Me Tender' and thus to make it a guaranteed gold disc before its release. RCA brought forward the release date of the song due to sheer demand.

Viewers of all ages got to see Elvis in full, live from Hollywood, although items in the next day's press suggested directors were nervous. As soon as Elvis looked like he was about to cut loose, cameras zoomed in for a close up so as not to offend anyone.

Although Sullivan wasn't there to do the honours of introducing Elvis on his debut appearance, he was clearly delighted with the reaction to the young star. The 9th September edition of the show, starring Elvis and presented by Charles Laughton, enjoyed a TV audience reach of 82.6 per cent.

Parker was soon to price his young star out of the TV market with his fees. However, he did credit *The Ed Sullivan Show* for the success it gained for 'Love Me Tender'.

In 2006, the History Channel selected the 9th September appearance by Elvis as one of the '10 days that unexpectedly changed America'.

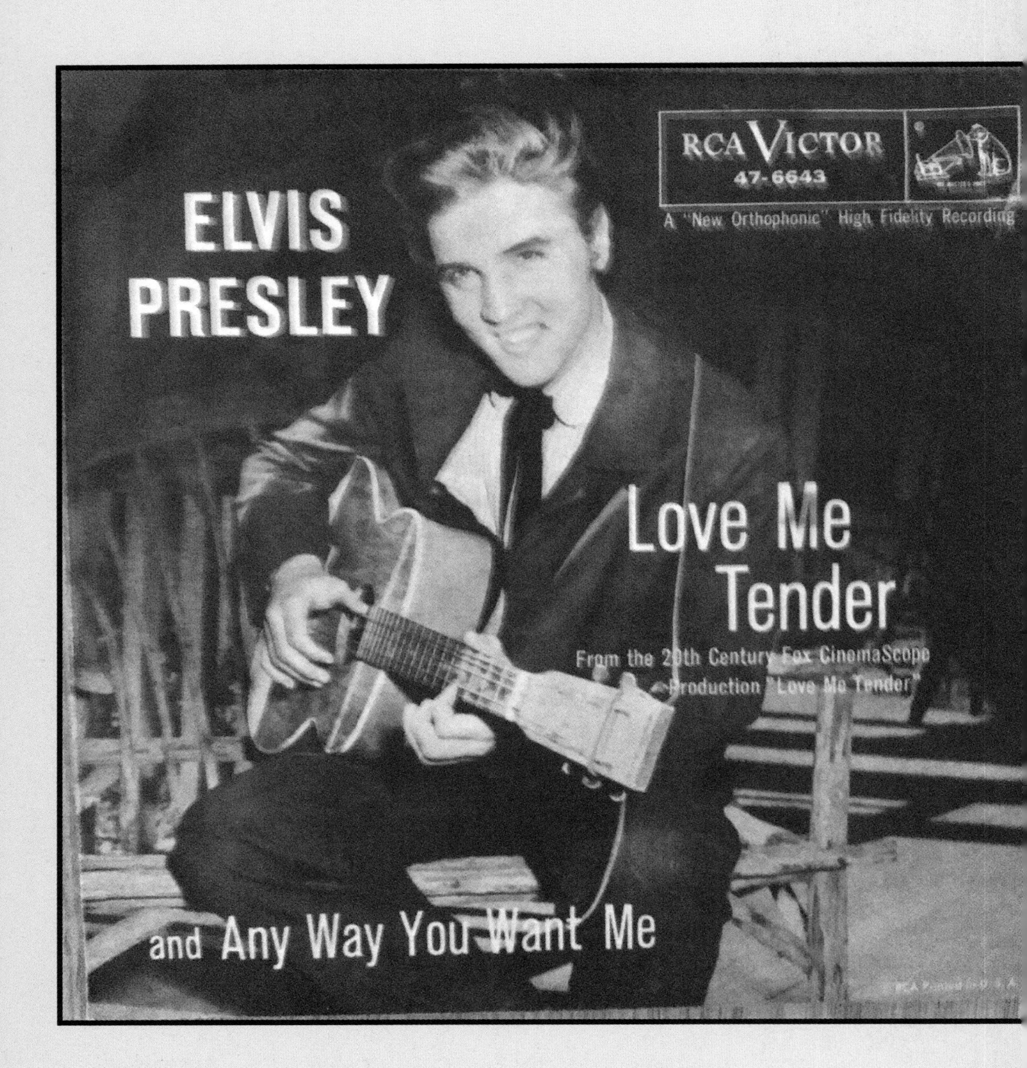
ELVIS
PRESLEY
RCA VICTOR
47-6643
A "New Orthophonic" High Fidelity Recording
Love Me
Tender
From the 20th Century-Fox CinemaScope
Production "Love Me Tender"
and Any Way You Want Me

EIGHT

1957 – STUDIO HIGHLIGHTS

ALL SHOOK UP

Next a song that was America's best-selling single of 1957 and Elvis's first-ever UK number one – the appropriately titled 'All Shook Up'.

Imagine you're already a popular songwriter and you boast that you could probably write a hit about pretty much anything. Well, you're opening yourself up to all sorts of challenges. When fellow lyricist Aaron 'Goldie' Goldmark dropped a Pepsi on the floor, he challenged Otis Blackwell to prove his boast and write a hit song. Blackwell turned that dropped bottle into a hit that crashed into the charts on both sides of the Atlantic – the great 'All Shook Up'.

The song will be forever associated with Elvis Presley – the famous "uh-huh-huh" became a trademark used the world over by Elvis fans and impersonators. In fact, in 1968 when trailing ahead for the forthcoming *'68 Comeback Special*, even Elvis mocked himself.

Eleven years earlier Elvis scored gold with 'All Shook Up' but he wasn't the first to record the track. According to Paul Simpson, writing on the popular Australian website www.elvisinfonet.com, David Hill recorded Blackwell's song on 7 November 1956th. Elvis recorded the track some two months later. Paul Simpson said the track was "Cornily arranged, with a Tin Pan Alley-style vocal backing, and an over-enthusiastic saxophone solo, Hill's rendition is fun but forgettable, although vocally, he gave it all he had. Released on the R&B label Aladdin, it lacks the authenticity that typified its best records." Although he didn't strike gold with 'All Shook Up', Hill later penned a song that would bring in the money – a huge hit for Elvis called 'I Got Stung'. Hill wrote it under his real name, Dave Hess.

Elvis heard Blackwell's demo and loved it, in fact using the demo as inspiration for his own solid gold version.

It was on 12th January 1957 that Presley stepped up to the mic at Radio Recorders in Hollywood to record 'All Shook Up'. The duet vocal part on the record is by Gordon Stoker of the Jordanaires. Within three weeks of its release, 'All Shook Up' had knocked Perry Como's 'Round and Round' off the top spot in the Billboard Hot 100 and stayed there for eight consecutive weeks. It also marked the first time that Elvis hit the number-one spot in the UK Singles Chart, and once it got to the top it wasn't in a rush to leave. 'All Shook Up' remained at number one for seven weeks.

Sales of the single exceeded two-million copies, proving that in 1957 Elvis was continuing to leave his countless fans 'All Shook Up'.

BLUEBERRY HILL

Staying with the *Loving You* album, another song that was on the LP but not in the movie was 'Blueberry Hill'. It became a monster hit for rock and roll legend Fats Domino in 1956.

Antoine Fats Domino had first attracted national attention back in 1949 when he recorded 'The Fat Man', an example of very early rock and roll. It features a rolling piano that Domino would become famous for and Domino vocalising "wah-wah" over a strong backbeat. It was an immediate success. 'The Fat Man' sold one-million copies by 1953. Domino enjoyed great success throughout the '50s and continuing into the 1960s. He released a series of hit songs with the producer Dave Bartholomew who would also co-write many of Domino's biggest hits.

His 1956 recording of 'Blueberry Hill', a 1940 song by Vincent Rose, Al Lewis and Larry Stock, reached number two in the top 40 and was number one on the R&B chart for 11 weeks. Domino's version sold more than five-million copies in 1956 and 1957. He had further hit singles between 1956 and 1959, including 'When My Dreamboat Comes Home', 'I'm Walkin'', 'Valley of Tears', 'It's You I Love', 'Whole Lotta Loving', 'I Want to Walk You Home' and 'Be My Guest'.

Although Domino's version became the definitive hit, he wasn't the first to record it. Gene Autry recorded the original version, which came from the movie *The Singing Hill* in 1940. The Glenn Miller Orchestra with vocals by Ray Eberle enjoyed great success with the song. This was probably the most famous version before Domino recorded the song. Also recording the track in the 1940s were Russ Morgan and His Orchestra, Kay Kyser and His Orchestra (vocal by Harry Babbitt) and then Sachmo himself, Louis Armstrong, recorded this version in 1949 with Gordon Jenkins' Orchestra and Choir.

On the same day, 19th January 1957, that Elvis recorded our previously mentioned song 'Have I Told You Lately that I Love You?' he also recorded his version of 'Blueberry Hill'. There have been rumours over the years that it was actually Elvis himself that played piano on 'Blueberry Hill', but recording documents from the '50s show it was actually Dudley Brooks. However, it's highly likely that Elvis performed it on stage in the 1950s and took to the piano to play and sing the track. In fact in the 1970s on tour, Elvis was quoted as saying "I can't play that anymore man" when talking about 'Blueberry Hill'.

GOT A LOT O' LIVIN' TO DO

We're off to Hollywood for Elvis's second movie *Loving You* and a stand-out track from that film, 'Got a Lot o' Livin' to Do'.

It was on 12th January 1957 at Radio Recorders in Hollywood that Elvis tackled 'Got a Lot o' Livin' to Do'. He recorded it just before attempting what would become his first UK number one – 'All Shook Up'. 'Got a Lot o' Livin' to Do' was written by Aaron Schroeder and Ben Weisman – both prolific songwriters for Elvis. Ben Weisman wrote 57 songs for Elvis which was more than any other songwriter.

Weisman, or the 'Mad Professor' as he was nicknamed by Elvis, worked with Presley writing the first song for him in 1956 ('First in Line') and the last in 1970 ('Change of Habit'). Their early association produced the best songs including 'Follow That Dream', 'Rock-A-Hula Baby', 'Crawfish', 'As Long as I Have You', 'Pocketful of Rainbows', 'Fame and Fortune' and 'Got a Lot o' Livin' to Do'. In a 2005 interview for the Australian website www.elvis.com.au, Ben Weisman said:

> In 1957, I flew to Hollywood to finally meet Elvis. Our meeting was at Paramount Studios where he was recording the soundtrack for his film, *Loving You*. During a break in the session, I noticed Elvis sitting alone in the corner, ad-libbing some blues on the guitar. I wandered over to

> the piano next to him, sat down and joined in. He didn't look up, kept on playing and even changed keys on me, but I followed along. Then he looked up with that smile he was famous for, and asked who I was and what I was doing in the studio. I told him I was invited to the session and that I composed one of the songs he was about to record called 'Got a Lot o' Livin' to Do'. He immediately called out to his musicians, 'Got a Lot o' Livin' to Do', and they recorded it on the spot.

Elvis placed his stamp on the song and no-one has ever beaten it. However, cover versions were done. Country singer Steven Wayne Horton did a version at the end of the 1980s and on the tribute CD *The Last Temptation of Elvis*, the Pogues covered the track.

'Got a Lot o' Livin' to Do' comes from Elvis's second Hollywood movie and the first to be filmed in colour. It is also the first to capture him as a 1950s singer. His first outing *Love Me Tender* had been set at the end of the Civil War. The movie *Loving You* was definitely set in the moment, capturing a 1957 Elvis at the peak of his powers. Along with the scene from *Jailhouse Rock* in which Elvis sings the title track, this movie comes the closest to showing the raw rock 'n' roll excitement Elvis caused during the 1950s.

Loving You was tailored for Elvis as his first leading role in a film vehicle, following his debut the previous year in a supporting role in *Love Me Tender*. Directed by Hal Kanter, the cast included Lizabeth Scott, Wendell Corey and Dolores Hart in her movie debut. Dolores would go on to star with Elvis in *King Creole* the following year.

Dolores Hart made ten films in five years, playing opposite Stephen Boyd, Montgomery Clift, George Hamilton and Robert Wagner, having made her movie debut with Elvis. By the early 1960s she was an established leading lady but 'stunned Hollywood' by announcing that she would be giving up her career to enter a monastery in Connecticut. A documentary film about Hart's life, *God Is the Bigger Elvis*, was a nominee for the 2012 Academy Award for Best Documentary (Short Subject) and was shown on HBO in April 2012. Mother Dolores Hart attended the 2012 Academy Awards for the documentary; her last red-carpet Oscar event had been in 1959 as a Hollywood starlet.

Loving You was the first film to show Elvis sporting his newly dyed hair. Elvis had his natural light-brown hair dyed black. He felt it would look good on film, as did the dark hair of Tony Curtis, one of the actors he had long admired.

During the movie version of 'Got a Lot o' Livin' to Do' when Elvis's character Deke sings the song for a second time, Vernon and Gladys Presley, Elvis's parents, can be seen as extras in the Grand Theatre audience. They are sitting on the aisle and at one stage Elvis goes right up to them, dancing. You can see his proud Mum Gladys enthusiastically clapping along, supporting her son during this movie moment.

HAVE I TOLD YOU LATELY THAT I LOVE YOU?

We're slowing it down a bit now for our next '50s track. This song was written by Scotty Wiseman and was first published back in 1945. 'Have I Told You Lately that I Love You?' was first recorded by Lulu Belle and Scotty and was released on Mercury Records. You can hear it here: https://www.youtube.com/watch?v=kPJzLCQq4h0.

Elvis recorded his version on 19th January 1957, at RCA's Radio Recorders in Hollywood for his *Loving You* album. Session musicians with Elvis that day were Scotty Moore, Bill Black and D.J. Fontana. They were joined by Dudley Brooks on piano, Hoyt Hawkins on the organ and also the Jordanaires.

When the song was included on the *Loving You* album release in July 1957, it prompted cover versions by other stars of the time. Ricky Nelson recorded his version for the B-side of 'Be-Bop Baby'. Eddie Cochran's version was an album cut. Then in 1968 Kitty Wells & Red Foley recorded a version. Countless others have recorded the song including: the Blue Diamonds, Jim Ed Brown, Anita Bryant, Michael Bublé, the Canadian Sweethearts, Tommy Collins, Jill Corey, Floyd Cramer, Bing Crosby with the Andrews Sisters and Bob Hope with Bing Crosby. The list isn't finished – here are some others who have recorded the same song: Curly Joe & his Knights of the Range, Vic Damone, Adrienne Davidsen, Skeeter Davis and Porter Wagoner, Little Jimmy Dickens and UK-rocker Billy Fury, who recorded a live version at the BBC during the 1960s.

‘Have I Told You Lately that I Love You’ appeared on Elvis’s soundtrack album *Loving You* despite not featuring in the movie itself. Songs were added to bring up the running time of the album, including the swing-era favourite ‘Blueberry Hill’, which had been a big hit for Fats Domino in 1956. Even Cole Porter’s ‘True Love’, written for the 1956 musical film *High Society*, made the album. It would become common practice in the mid-1960s for RCA to add ‘bonus tracks’ to Elvis’s soundtrack albums and they were often the stronger tracks.

MEAN WOMAN BLUES

On 13th January 1957 before laying down ‘Peace in the Valley’, ‘I Beg Of You’, ‘That’s When Your Heartaches Begin’ and ‘Take My Hand, Precious Lord’, Elvis attacked a great rocker from the movie *Loving You* – ‘Mean Woman Blues’. The setting was Radio Recorders in Hollywood. Claude DeMetrius wrote the track and it was recorded by Presley as part of the soundtrack for his 1957 movie, his first in glorious techno-colour. The lyrics are about a woman who is so mean, she bruises her lover when she kisses him and can even scare a black cat. All this drives the singer wild.

Fellow Sun Records stable mate Jerry Lee Lewis recorded his take of the song at Sun, which was released in 1957 as part of an EP, *The Great Ball of Fire*. Fast forward to 1964 and Lewis released a live album with the Nashville Teens. Recorded at the Star Club in Hamburg where the Beatles had frequently played before hitting the big time, the LP included a live version of ‘Mean Woman Blues’.

In 1963 the song was recorded as a single on the B-side of ‘Blue Bayou’ by Roy Orbison and charted at number five. Back to the ’50s and in 1959, Cliff Richard and the Shadows recorded a studio version on their *Cliff Sings* album. 1950s rockabilly artist Glen Glen from Los Angeles recorded a version of the song for England’s Ace label that was released on the album *Everybody’s Movin’ Again*.

In recent reviews of the movie *Loving You*, Allmovie defined it as “one of Elvis Presley’s liveliest and most interesting early films… one of the best in [his] output” while MSN Movies called it “a streamlined and sanitized retake on the story of Elvis”. In the movie, the scene where Elvis sings ‘Mean Woman Blues’ perfectly captures the rock 'n' roll Elvis at his best and in colour. From the style of singing, to the movements, it's pure Elvis. It's more like 'Mean Elvis Blues' – his swagger is on full show – his gyrations are exciting and there's a glint in his eye throughout the whole glorious performance.

In the movie, Deke Rivers, Elvis's character, is on a rare break from a busy tour enjoying some food in a local cafe – however, a local is spurred on by his girlfriend to ask 'sideburns' to sing. Deke does the storming version of 'Mean Woman Blues' and ends by punching the rude man out cold. That man was actor Ken Becker. The poor chap also appeared as Elvis's punching bag in other movies including *G.I. Blues* and *Girls! Girls! Girls!* Becker also appeared in *Roustabout* but managed to get away without cuts and bruises in that one. He later starred in the John Wayne film *True Grit* playing Farrell Parmalee. His and Elvis's paths could have crossed sooner than *Loving You*, as he had a part in the Burt Lancaster movie *The Rainmaker*. Elvis had read a scene from that movie as part of his Hollywood audition and even said in an interview that he would be appearing in the film, but sadly that never happened. However, if you'd like to see pictures of Elvis in action during his audition, this can be found here: http://www.elvis-collectors.com/strictly03.html.

Elvis would never watch the fantastic 'Mean Woman Blues' scene or any of the *Loving You* movie after his mother Gladys passed away on 14th August 1958, as she appeared in the movie, along with Vernon, when Elvis sings 'Got a Lot o' Livin' to Do'. Also making their screen debuts in *Loving You* were Scotty Moore, Bill Black and D.J. Fontana.

On the songbase on elvisnews.com, fans speak highly of Elvis's take on 'Mean Woman Blues': ElvisSacramento said: "This is such a splendid, fun, groovy and unique song and the best rendition of it is definitely by Elvis. It should've been a smash hit for Elvis, but sadly it wasn't a hit for Elvis at all. It's a masterpiece of a song and Elvis's rendition of it is a masterpiece too. RCA should've issued Elvis's rendition of it as a single too. It would have certainly been a major hit for Elvis had RCA issued his rendition of it as a single. 5 Stars." And Troubleman wrote: "Definitely one of his best rock/blues songs. Probably would have been another number 1 hit if it had been released as a single."

It really is an underrated but classic slice of rock 'n' roll Hollywood.

1957 – The Early Gospel of Elvis Presley, Part One

IT IS NO SECRET (WHAT GOD CAN DO)

Elvis had spent the entire year of 1956 thrilling his fans and causing panic among parents, middle of the road radio stations, nervous TV executives and church leaders. For the teenagers he was their hero, but to everyone else he was a real threat to the human race. While the controversy eased thanks to the announcement to the country by Ed Sullivan that this was a "real decent fine boy", parents and church leaders were in for another shock when this young threat recorded a gospel EP for Easter 1957. Wow, they never saw that coming, did they! The EP showing a smart, sincere-looking Elvis on the front cover was called *Peace in the Valley*. Elvis was wearing a jacket and tie!

The four recordings were made from sessions that took place at Radio Recorders in Hollywood on 12th, 13th and 19th January 1957. The EP would reach number three on the Billboard EP charts. It may have been a shock for some when the EP came out, but for anyone who knew Elvis, this release was hardly a surprise. Among the earliest music the baby Presley had heard in Tupelo had been that at his local church. Then by the 1950s Memphis had become an important place for gospel music. All four selections on the EP are gospel classics, including 'It Is No Secret (What God Can Do)'. This was a recent gospel song at the time, having been written in 1950 by Stuart Hamblen who actually became one of American radio's first singing cowboys, before turning his hand to Christian music as well as continuing to write pop classics, including 'This Ole House' in 1954.

The first person to enjoy success with 'It Is No Secret' was Bill Kenny, the lead singer of the Ink Spots. His version was the first to make the US pop charts, reaching number 18 in 1951. From the late 1930s to the early 1950s, the original Ink Spots were one of the most popular and influential singing groups. The original group, comprising Ivory 'Deek' Watson, Jerry Daniels, Charles Fuqua and Orville 'Hoppy' Jones, started out singing fast 'jump' tunes beginning in 1934 and their early recordings (RCA Victor, 1935 and Decca, 1936–8) reflected this style. The group became famous after the arrival of Bill Kenny in early 1936 and the group's addition of a ballad style featuring Bill Kenny's high tenor and Hoppy's 'talking' chorus.

The session that yielded these four gospel songs featured Elvis's regular band members, Scotty Moore, Bill Black, D.J. Fontana and the Jordanaires. Piano duties were shared by Floyd Cramer, who would enjoy his own chart success a few years later with tracks like 'On the Rebound', and Dudley Brooks. Elvis would go on to record many gospel tracks as well as performing them live on stage, in the privacy of his own home and backstage in Vegas. Six months after the four songs appeared on their own EP release in April 1957, they were out again in the fall of that same year as part of Elvis's hugely successful Christmas album.

PEACE IN THE VALLEY – THE SONG AND THE ED SULLIVAN SHOW

During 1956, Elvis had generated a lot of criticism from parents, newspaper critics and churches across America. Although Presley had already appeared on *The Ed Sullivan Show* twice, appearing in full view, for his third and final appearance, in January 1957, a decision was taken to only film the star from the waist upwards. As well as singing a selection of shortened versions of his big hits – including 'Hound Dog', 'Don't Be Cruel', 'Too Much' and 'When My Blue Moon Turns to Gold Again' – he toned it right down and started to change the public's perception of him.

Elvis did this, accompanied by the Jordanaires, by singing 'Peace in the Valley'. The song was released as an extended-play single also called *Peace in the Valley*. It also featured 'It Is No Secret', 'I Believe' and 'Take My Hand, Precious Lord'.

'Peace in the Valley' was a hit for Red Foley in 1951. It has been performed by dozens of other artists, including Queen of Gospel, Albertina Walker, and Johnny Cash. It was written by Thomas A. Dorsey in 1937, twenty years before Elvis performed it on the Sullivan show. Dorsey also composed 'Take My Hand, Precious Lord' that Elvis would feature on his April 1957 EP, *Peace in the Valley*.

In 2002, the Library of Congress honoured Dorsey's album *Precious Lord: New Recordings of the Great Songs of Thomas A. Dorsey* by adding it to the United States National Recording Registry.

Elvis had apparently promised to sing 'Peace in the Valley' for his Mother Gladys on *The Ed Sullivan Show*. The producers were against it. Ed Sullivan is quoted as saying, "Let the boy sing the song, let him sing whatever he wants." During this appearance, Elvis dedicated this, his last song, to the people of Hungary who were in the wake of the October 1956 anti-Soviet revolution. Elvis and his manager, Colonel Tom Parker, decided the singer should lend his support to the country's fight against communism.

Ed Sullivan even joined Elvis and asked the TV audience to donate to Hungarian relief efforts. In recognition of Elvis's act and support, Elvis was more recently declared an honorary citizen of Budapest, Hungary, and had a city landmark named after him.

Ed Sullivan calmed the worried parents further when the popular presenter said the following: "I wanted to say to Elvis Presley and the country that this is a real decent, fine boy, and wherever you go, Elvis, we want to say we've never had a pleasanter experience on our show with a big name than we've had with you. So now let's have a tremendous hand for a very nice person!"

Sullivan's show was part of the Sunday-night routine for literally millions of Americans. You knew you had made it if Sullivan came knocking on your door. Among the many who appeared on his show were the Beatles, the Rolling Stones, the Jackson Five, Louis Armstrong and the Doors. The controversy that had followed Elvis everywhere during 1956 seemed to start to disappear after Sullivan's words and Elvis's performance of 'Peace in the Valley'.

Elvis's days as a rock 'n' roll rebel were numbered too – there were still fine moments, like the classic scenes in *Loving You* and *Jailhouse Rock*, but the next time Elvis would appear on national television would be on his return from the army, when Ol' Blue Eyes, Frank Sinatra, welcomed Elvis home. Elvis responded by wearing a tuxedo while singing with Sinatra – how times had changed!

The rebel had become an all-round entertainer.

February–March 1957 – Radio Recorders in Hollywood

I NEED YOU SO

Here's another track from the *Loving You* album, which was a bonus track. 'I Need You So' was written by Ivory Joe Hunter. His own recording of the track was a number-one success on the Billboard R&B chart in 1950, staying there for two weeks. After a series of hits on the US R&B chart starting in the mid-1940s, he became more widely known for his hit recording, 'Since I Met You Baby' (1956). He was billed as the Baron of the Boogie and also known as the Happiest Man Alive.

Elvis recorded 'I Need You So' on 23rd February 1957, meeting its composer Joe Hunter in the same year in Memphis. Hunter recalled in a later interview that the two had spent the day together, singing 'I Almost Lost My Mind' and other songs. In the archive interview, Hunter said: "He is very spiritually minded... he showed me every courtesy, and I think he's one of the greatest."

As well as 'I Need You So', Elvis also recorded other songs by Ivory Joe including 'My Wish Came True' and 'Ain't that Lovin' You, Baby'. Fans of Hunter say he was a prolific songwriter; indeed, he's believed to have written around 7,000 songs! Ivory Joe Hunter died from lung cancer in Memphis at the age of 60, in 1974.

'I Need You So' came from the major recording sessions that were held in January and February 1957. Songs recorded during those sessions were featured in the movie and album *Loving You*, along with the bonus songs. Interestingly, two tracks recorded at the Loving You sessions would remain unreleased for years. 'Tell Me Why' from the same session would finally be released as a single in 1965 and 1966, reaching number six in Canada but only number 33 in the Billboard Hot 100. A remake of the Sun master 'When It Rains, It Really Pours' didn't surface until the 1965 LP *Elvis for Everyone*.

'I Need You So' was a winner with fans commenting on the songbase on www.elvisnews.com: jwedwards835 said 'I Need You So' is "A true classic from one of the greatest albums in history! And that's no laughing matter. I give it the same amount of stars that are in the heavens." NONE000000 said it is "One of those hidden tracks most non-Elvis people don't know. Any time Elvis sang the blues or even something tinged with blues it was pretty much a masterpiece to me and this is no exception. A little reminiscent of 'Don't Leave Me Now' – which is also a great song, but this is just a little better. A real beauty!"

TEDDY BEAR

This is a favourite among many fans and was written especially for Elvis by Kal Mann and Bernie Lowe, for his second movie, *Loving You*. When it was released as a single with the song 'Loving You', 'Teddy Bear' would top the US charts the day before the movie's release, where it stayed for seven weeks.

In the past the song's composers have said they wrote the track after hearing of Elvis's apparent love for cuddly toys. He certainly didn't love them as much as the false rumour claimed he did. The rumour was good enough for Elvis's thousands of female fans who began to send countless teddy bears to Elvis's Memphis home. The ever-generous Elvis donated the collection totalling thousands of teddy bears to the National Foundation for Infantile Paralysis.

If ever Colonel Parker wanted a successful song to calm down the hysteria which had started in 1956, then Teddy Bear was the song to do it. The trick certainly worked. It didn't alienate the fans, but it did show a softer side of Elvis, something we would see much more of after his return from the army in 1960.

Among those who have covered 'Teddy Bear' was Pat Boone on his LP *Pat Boone Sings Guess Who?* (1963) – yeah Pat, we are still guessing! Country singer Tanya Tucker did the song for the Elvis tribute album *It's Now or Never* in 1994. ZZ Top also included it on their 30th anniversary album, *XXX*, in 1999. The band also recorded their own version of 'Viva Las Vegas'.

Elvis himself would go on to include the song on his return to live performance. However, these tended to be throw-away versions and were possibly embarrassing for a 40-year-old Vegas veteran asking to be someone's teddy bear – but it was one the fans always wanted to hear and Elvis always listened to his loyal fans.

The soundtrack for the film *Loving You* was recorded during January 1957 at the Paramount Pictures Scoring Stage, and in two additional sessions at Radio Recorders in Hollywood, and a further session between 23rd and 24th February. 'Teddy Bear' itself was recorded on 24th January 1957. The soundtrack had seven songs composed for the movie by writers contracted to Elvis Presley Music and Gladys Music, the publishing companies owned by Presley and his manager, Colonel Tom Parker.

As always, the reviews were mixed on the release of the movie. *Variety* wrote a favourable review, noting that Presley "shows improvement as an actor... being surrounded by a capable crew of performers". However, *Monthly Film Bulletin* qualified Presley's career as "one of the most puzzling and less agreeable aspects of modern popular music". The review declared: "Presley adopts a slurred and husky style of delivery and a series of grotesque body gestures to impose on his otherwise innocuous material a suggestive meaning. ... in *Loving You* he is allowed more scope and is at times both the cause and sum total of the film's somewhat doubtful entertainment value."

The critics could say whatever they wanted – the parents may have been nodding their approval at the harsh reviews but the teenagers were loving every second of Elvis. And 'Teddy Bear' was certainly a favourite moment from the movie *Loving You.*

May 1957 – MGM Studios in Hollywood

It wasn't just about studio recordings and live performances. The hugely busy Elvis Presley, now aged 22, also found time to make one of his greatest films and fabulous soundtracks – *Jailhouse Rock.*

JAILHOUSE ROCK

Next, one of Elvis's finest moments in Hollywood and arguably one of the world's first-ever pop videos – we're looking at the song 'Jailhouse Rock'.

The song was written by the now-legendary partnership of Leiber and Stoller. The pair had come to New York to check out the music scene and had been asked to write new songs for Elvis's next film project, which was initially to have been called *The Hard Way*. The songwriters were totally star struck by the bright lights of New York and spent valuable song-writing time exploring the sights and enjoying the sounds provided by the clubs in the Big Apple – discovering for themselves why people called New York the city that never sleeps – later to be immortalised by Old Blue Eyes himself, Frank Sinatra in the song 'New York New York'.

However, while Leiber and Stoller were having a ball, Elvis's publishers were nervously awaiting their songs, which were not appearing. They came up with a rather interesting way of ensuring the material was delivered promptly – and it could almost have been a scene in a Hollywood movie. In an archive interview, Mike Stoller explained what focused them on writing songs for *Jailhouse Rock*:

> Jean Aberbach walked in. He said, "Well, boys, where are my songs?" We said, "Don't worry. You're gonna get 'em." And he said, "I know, because you're not going to leave this room until I get them." And then he pushed a big overstuffed chair in front of the door, the only way out. He said, "I'm going to take a nap." He literally went to sleep, and we couldn't get out. So we thumbed through the script and wrote four songs in about four or five hours. ('Jailhouse Rock', 'Treat Me Nice', 'I Want to Be Free' and '(You're So Square) Baby I Don't Care'.) I can't say that the songs were overworked. We didn't have time to overwork them. We were in too much of a hurry to get out of that hotel room.

In his 2002 autobiography, drummer D.J. Fontana explained how he and guitarist Scotty Moore came up with the intro for 'Jailhouse Rock':

> 'Jailhouse Rock' was supposed to be like prisoners breaking rocks on a rock pile. I remembered way back in the '40s they had a song called 'Animal Chorus'. It was a big band thing like Woody Herman or someone like that. I remember someone was beating on what sounded like an anvil, actually. They were playing kind of like a bump, beep, beep, boop. And I said, "That might be good." So Scotty and I got over in a corner and I'd play the first beat and he'd play the one in the middle. We were actually just piddling around with it. They had the mics on and

> they asked what we were doing. So we said, "Well, we don't know. We were just trying to find something that you could use for the soundtrack to make it sound like a chain gang smashing rocks." So they said, "Man, whatever you were doing just then, that's great. Don't touch it. That's exactly what we need." So that's how we originated that one. It was one of those things that we accidentally came up with.

Presley recorded the soundtrack for *Jailhouse Rock* at Radio Recorders in Hollywood on 30th April and 3rd May, with an additional session at the MGM Soundstage on 9th May. The soon to be classic single was released on 24th September 1957 with 'Treat Me Nice', also from the movie, on the flipside.

Among the various artists to have recorded 'Jailhouse Rock' was a deeper-voiced Frankie Lymon. Rod Stewart did a version and the song was performed in another movie – *The Blues Brothers*. The Elvis tribute CD *It's Now or Never* features the unusual pairing of rockabilly legend Carl Perkins with '80s soul star Michael Bolton.

When Elvis's original of 'Jailhouse Rock' was released in 1957, *Billboard* said of the single: "Another sock platter by the phenomenal artist. 'Rock' is a vigorous rocker and is the title tune from Presley's forthcoming flick. Flip ('Treat Me Nice') is an equally strong side somewhat like 'Don't Be Cruel.'"

Also in 1957, 'Jailhouse Rock' was the lead song in an EP (extended play single), together with other songs from the film, namely 'Young and Beautiful', 'I Want to be Free', 'Don't Leave Me Now' and '(You're So Square) Baby I Don't Care' (but with 'Treat Me Nice' omitted). It topped the Billboard EP charts, eventually selling two-million copies.

TREAT ME NICE

Also from the movie *Jailhouse Rock*, 'Treat Me Nice' carries a feel good tune but some of the lyrics have a darker shade, with lines like "I'll be your slave if you ask me to". Elvis then sings that he'll walk out if "you don't behave".

The song was well suited to Elvis Presley, who was familiar with its gently rocking style and could put across the lyrics in a winning way. He recorded the movie version of the song for the soundtrack on 30th April 1957. The official formal studio version was then recorded on 5th September at Radio Recorders in Hollywood. It was released as the B-side of 'Jailhouse Rock' on 24th September 1957. It certainly grabbed the fans attention and got them excited for the premiere of the movie itself on 21st October.

'Jailhouse Rock' became a massive hit, topping the charts and causing the single to sell two-million copies, but let's not forget that the B-side 'Treat Me Nice' got attention as well. It entered the pop and country top 20 and the top ten of the R&B charts.

1960s star Tommy James, who scored big with 'Mony Mony', 'I Think We're Alone Now (later covered by Tiffany in the '80s), 'Crimson & Clover' and 'Hanky Panky', also recorded 'Treat Me Nice'. American rockabilly singer Glen Glenn also recorded a version and more recently the song featured in the Broadway musical *Smokey Joe's Cafe: The Songs of Lieber and Stoller*. Other people who have recorded 'Treat Me Nice' include Lille John and the Rockin' Jupiters, Conway Twitty, the Lincolns, Mac Allen Smith, Ronnie McDowell, and the King Cats. Then in 2016 Mark Summers did the song, with a video that recreated the scene from *Jailhouse Rock* in which Elvis's character Vince Everett was recording the song.

YOUNG AND BEAUTIFUL

We stay with Elvis's third movie for a tender moment taken from the final part of the film. Elvis's character Vince was enjoying his major success and the attention it was bringing but it was turning him into a greedy monster who was isolating himself from the people who really cared about him. Hunk Houghton, who had befriended Vince in the jail, decided to take matters into his own hands and make Vince see sense.

Hunk is not the best negotiator and uses his fists to close deals and finish arguments. Hunk is furious at the way Vince has been treating his business partner, Peggy. He tries to provoke Vince into a fight but he refuses to fight back. In the end, Hunk strikes Vince in the throat (cue the gasps of teenage girls in cinemas around the world!). The punch damages Vince's throat so much he needs emergency surgery, which could damage his vocal chords and singing ability forever.

After nervous days of resting after the operation, Vince is told that his vocal chords are fully recovered. However, his voice might still be affected. The only way to find out is for Vince to try and sing. With the ever-loyal Peggy by his side, Vince starts to sing the song 'Young and Beautiful'. Thankfully, his voice is fine and we're left hoping the incident has made Vince a better and more grateful person.

This tender love song was written by Aaron Schroeder and Abner Silver. We've already mentioned the successes of Aaron Schroeder. His co-writer on 'Young and Beautiful', Abner Silver, started writing with 'You Can't Blame the Girlies at All (They All Want to Marry a Soldier)' way back in 1918! During the 1920s, '30s and '40s, Silver's songs were covered by a galaxy of stars including Frank Sinatra, Billie Holiday, Rudy Vallee, Al Jolson and then in later years by Peggy Lee, Julie London, Etta James and of course Elvis. As well as 'Young and Beautiful', Silver also played a part in the writing of other movie songs for Elvis including 'Lover Doll' from *King Creole* and 'What's She Really Like' from *G.I. Blues*.

Elvis would occasionally return to 'Young and Beautiful' as a live performer in the '70s. He can be heard on the *Elvis on Tour* rehearsals CD singing the track (recently released by the official collector's label, Follow That Dream, a partner label of Sony). He also sang an impromptu version in 1975 when asked to sing it by a member of the audience.

(YOU'RE SO SQUARE) BABY I DON'T CARE

Grab your popcorn and a seat in the back row of the movies as here's another great song from *Jailhouse Rock*. Elvis stars in the film as Vince Everett. The film has gone on to be a fan favourite and even some of the critics commented favourably on Elvis's acting. A reviewer in *Variety* gave some cautious praise saying: "Presley is still no great shakes as an actor but gets by well enough, although the role isn't particularly sympathetic." Hortense Morton from the *San Francisco Examiner* said: "Frankly, I think Presley will turn into quite an actor. It isn't going to happen tomorrow or next year. But, it will happen."

During a spell inside, Presley's character meets Hunk Houghton, previously a successful country music singer who has fallen on hard times. He takes the young Everett under his wing and starts to turn the angry young man into a singer. Hunk convinces Vince to sign a 'contract' to become equal partners in his act. (Was that maybe a slight dig at Old Colonel Tom Parker who took a hefty share of the profits right the way through Elvis career?) Hunk then promises Vince a singing job at a nightclub owned by a friend, where Vince meets Peggy Van Alden (Tyler), a promoter for pop singer Mickey Alba. Vince is surprised when the club owner denies him a job as a singer but offers him a job as a bar boy.

But Peggy sees something special in the young Vince and organises a recording session. But after they get stung by another singer taking Vince's song, the pair form a record company and the records start selling fast. During a garden party packed with Hollywood starlets, Elvis's character sings 'You're So Square, Baby I Don't Care'. The song was written by Jerry Leiber and Mike Stoller. The song marks the only occasion when Elvis plays the electric bass. The backing was recorded on 3rd May, with the vocal track added on 9th May 1957. The song was released on the *Jailhouse Rock* EP and reached number 14 on the R&B charts.

Many artists went on to cover the track, including the great Buddy Holly. The Beatles did a jam-session version during the recording of 'Get Back' in January 1969 and included 'Baby I Don't Care'. Carl Mann, Cliff Richard, Led Zeppelin, Joni Mitchell, Bobby Fuller, Don McLean and Scotty Moore, Elvis's early guitarist, did versions. Queen recorded a version live during *Queen at Wembley*. Others to have recorded the track include Brian Setzer, Ray Condo, Rodney Scott and Bobby Vee.

Back to Elvis's version of 'Baby I Don't Care' – you may have noticed something strange in the movie scenes. In the close ups, Scotty Moore isn't wearing sunglasses – but in the wide shots, mysteriously a pair of sunglasses appear on his face.

5th–7th September 1957 – It's Christmas Time Pretty Baby...

BLUE CHRISTMAS

Whatever the time of year, one thing that can't be denied is that Elvis's 1957 Christmas album was one of the most successful in its genre. It continues to sell well today almost 60 years after it was first released. Over the years, the songs have been re-packaged several times. There's even been a Christmas duets album which saw some of the USA's biggest country stars singing along with the voice of the King.

The song we're looking at today was originally recorded in 1950 by Ernest Tubb. It featured on *Elvis' Christmas Album*. However, it wasn't released as a single until 1964, when in the US it was backed with 'Wooden Heart' from Elvis's soundtrack to his film *G.I. Blues* – the song we're talking about is 'Blue Christmas'.

Nicknamed the Texas Troubadour, Ernest Tubb was one of the pioneers of country music. His biggest career hit song, 'Walking the Floor Over You' (1941), marked the rise of the honky tonk style of music. As well as scoring solo hits, Tubb recorded duets with the then-up-and-coming Loretta Lynn in the early 1960s, including their hit 'Sweet Thang'. Tubb inspired some of the most devoted fans of any country artist – they followed him throughout his career, long after the chart hits dried up. He remained, as did most of his peers, a fixture at the Grand Ole Opry.

In 1980, he appeared as himself in Loretta Lynn's autobiographical film, *Coal Miner's Daughter*, with Roy Acuff and Minnie Pearl. Soon after, he fell ill with emphysema but continued to make over 200 personal appearances a year, carrying an oxygen tank on his bus. After each performance he would shake hands and sign autographs with every fan who wanted to stay. Health problems finally halted his performances in 1982. He died from his illness in 1984 at the Baptist Hospital in Nashville. Tubb is a member of the Country Music Hall of Fame.

After Elvis recorded 'Blue Christmas', several artists have covered the track over the years including the Beach Boys, Bette Midler and UK rocker Shakin' Stevens. It's also been recorded by Bill Haley and the Comets, the Misfits, Freddy Fender, Collective Soul and... Porky Pig.

Recording sessions for *Elvis' Christmas Album* took place at Radio Recorders in Hollywood in September 1957. The four gospel songs on the album were taken from a recording session in January 1957. The album was released in October 1957. Original 1957 copies of *Elvis' Christmas Album* were issued with a red booklet-like album cover featuring promotional photos from Elvis's third movie Jailhouse Rock. Even rarer is a gold-foil price-tag-shaped 'gift giving' sticker attached to the shrink wrap, reading 'TO **********, FROM **********, ELVIS SINGS', followed by a list of the tracks.

More recently, 'Blue Christmas' was the stand-out track on the *Elvis Christmas Duets* album, which featured the voice of the King performing duets with some of Country Music's biggest stars. Martina McBride appeared alongside Elvis on the re-imagined version of 'Blue Christmas'. A very clever video superimposed Martina into the *'68 Comeback Special* where a black-leather-clad Elvis sings 'Blue Christmas' with a very '60s looking Martina McBride – all clever stuff. The official video has notched up almost 12,000,000 hits on Vevo. Here's the link just in case you haven't seen it:

https://www.youtube.com/watch?v=3KK6sMo8NBY.

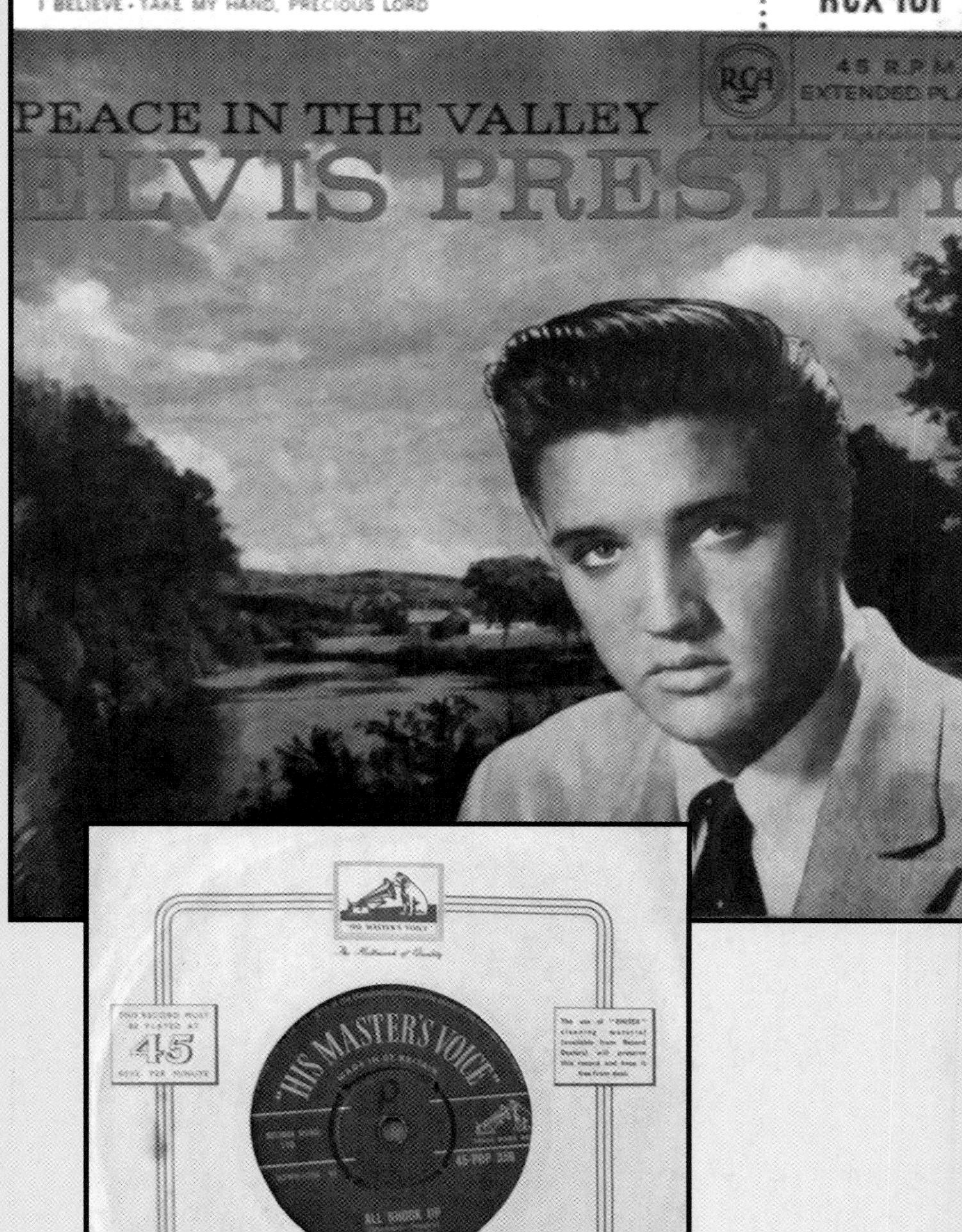
(There'll Be) PEACE IN THE VALLEY (For Me) • IT IS NO SECRET (What God Can Do)
I BELIEVE • TAKE MY HAND, PRECIOUS LORD
RCX-101
RCA
45 R.P.M.
EXTENDED PLA
PEACE IN THE VALLEY
ELVIS PRESLEY
"HIS MASTER'S VOICE"
THIS RECORD MUST BE PLAYED AT
45
REVS. PER MINUTE
"HIS MASTER'S VOICE"
MADE IN GT. BRITAIN
45-POP 359
ALL SHOOK UP
ELVIS PRESLEY
"HIS MASTER'S VOICE"

NINE

1958 – ELVIS STUDIO HIGHLIGHTS

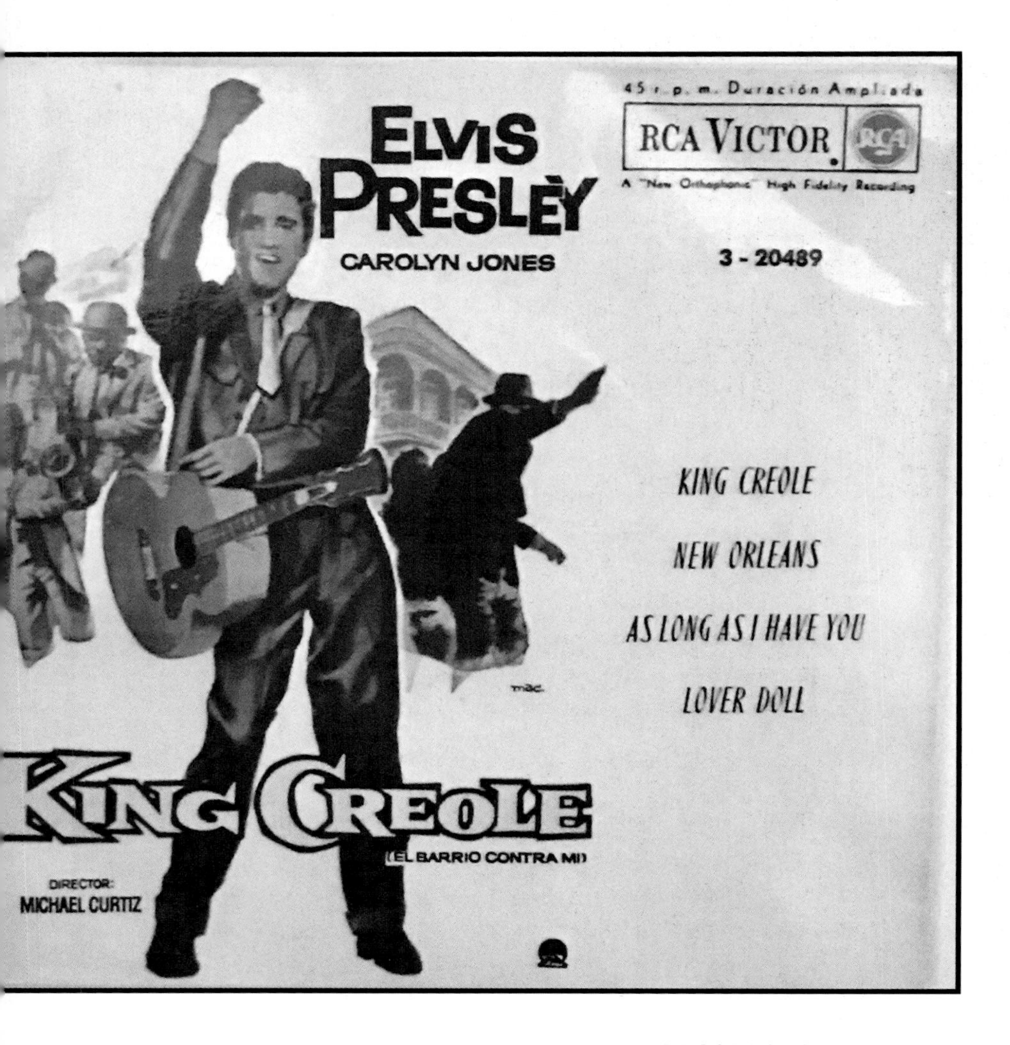

The year of arguably Elvis's greatest movie – *King Creole* – Uncle Sam came knocking and life would never be the same after Elvis's beloved Mum Gladys passes away.

15th January 1958 – Radio Recorders Studio B Hollywood – King Creole Soundtrack

CRAWFISH

Elvis would sing some bizarre songs during his Hollywood years: 'There's No Room to Rhumba in a Sports Car', 'The Fort Lauderdale Chamber of Commerce' and 'The Song of the Shrimp' to name three. But 'The Song of the Shrimp' wasn't the first time Elvis had been captured on film singing about aquatic life. That honour goes to *King Creole* and the song 'Crawfish'.

It was the song featured in the first scene of *King Creole* when the world sees Elvis as Danny Fisher for the first time. Standing on the balcony to his father's apartment he sings 'Crawfish' along with the fish seller in the street. It's Jazz singer Kitty White who can be heard saying those immortal "Craaaaawfiiiiish". This unusual track was written by Fred Wise and Ben Weisman. We've already talked about Weisman, whom Elvis dubbed the Mad Professor. He was responsible for 57 songs that Elvis recorded. Fred Wise contributed towards 'Wooden Heart' for Elvis's movie *G.I. Blues* and many other tracks. His earliest success came in 1948 with a song called 'A – You're Adorable' with Buddy Kaye.

One fan of the song was the frontman of punk band the Clash, Joe Strummer. Surprisingly, given all the rockin' songs he could have chosen by Elvis, Strummer said 'Crawfish' was one of his favourite songs! The song was covered by a few artists over the years including Johnny Thunders and Patti Palladin in 1985.

Crawfish, also known as crayfish or mudbugs, resemble small lobsters and are related to the lobster family. They breathe through feather-like gills and can often be found living where there is fresh water. The fussy little crustaceans cannot tolerate being in polluted waters – and will never know that one of the world's biggest stars sang about them in his finest movie.

'Crawfish' was recorded on 15th January 1958. On the same day Elvis laid down the all-out rocker 'Hard Headed Woman' and the bluesy track 'Trouble'.

HARD HEADED WOMAN

'Hard Headed Woman' is another classic from the *King Creole* soundtrack. However, you only see and hear a bit of it in the movie itself. What a shame there isn't a complete performance in the movie of such an awesome rock 'n' roll song. You can imagine Elvis really throwing himself into the track on stage.

The song, a very tongue in cheek look at women from the Bible, was written by Claude Demetrius, who funnily enough wrote a similar song for New Orleans star Fats Domino, 'Ain't that Just Like a Woman'.

When 'Hard Headed Woman' was released in the USA it was yet another number-one smash for Elvis. However, Elvis wasn't without controversy even in 1958. In the UK, the BBC banned the song from airplay in the country. However, the teenagers rebelled and bought the record anyway. Even with the airplay ban, it still reached number two in the UK charts. No-one could stop Elvis in the 1950s.

Several years later Dolly Parton would record a song that was similar but flipped the genders over. The track was 'Why'd You Come in Here Looking Like That' and includes the line "I'm a soft-hearted woman, he's a hard-headed man."

Elvis's track was recorded at Radio Recorders in Hollywood on the same day as 'Trouble' and 'Crawfish', 15th January 1958. There was a huge ensemble of musicians for the recording of 'Hard Headed Woman'. As well as Elvis's usual musicians and backing singers, there was Ray Siegel on the bass and tuba, and Bernie Mattinson shared drumming duties with D.J. Fontana. Jordanaire Gordon Stoker could be heard on the bongos. Hoyt Hawkins was on the cymbals. Mahlon Clark could be heard on the clarinet, along with John Ed Buckner on trumpet. Justin Gordon was on the saxophone. And Elmer Schneider provided trombone. Wow, what a musical gathering!

'Hard Headed Woman' was released as a single, backed by 'Don't Ask Me Why', on 10th June 1958.

KING CREOLE

Elvis led a hugely talented cast in the movie, which was set in New Orleans and based upon the book *A Stone for Danny Fisher* written by Harold Robbins. The well-respected Michael Curtiz was brought in to direct the film, and what a past he had enjoyed! He was best known for directing *Casablanca* with the legend that was Humphrey Bogart. The *King Creole* cast included some of the finest actors of the time including Walter Matthau as the seedy club owner and gangland boss Maxie Fields. The tormented lover of the gangster who soon catches Danny's eye was Ronnie, played by Carolyn Jones. The movie also featured Dolores Hart who had won Elvis's heart in the movies in the previous year's *Loving You*.

The music brought New Orleans jazz and rock 'n' roll together as one in a way that has never really been repeated. The two completely different sounds appear to merge seamlessly on the soundtrack album to *King Creole*, another huge-selling soundtrack album for Elvis.

As if there weren't enough drama in the movie, there was worrying news off the set too, right before filming was about to start. In December 1957, Elvis received his draft notice. He was ordered to report for duty on 20th January, which would have ended *King Creole* before he even set foot in front of the cameras. Thankfully, Elvis was given a deferment for the filming which was already in pre-production. But the pressure was certainly on to complete everything Elvis was needed for (the soundtrack, the movie, photo shoots and more).

The title track from the movie was 'King Creole'. The entire album was recorded in just four days at Radio Recorders in Hollywood during January 1957. Elvis returned to record one more song for the album, 'Steadfast Loyal and True', in February of that year.

The song 'King Creole' was written by Jerry Leiber and Mike Stoller. However, the songwriters were already feeling the heat of Colonel Parker bearing down on them. He was unhappy with how the pair were trying to influence his client. If only they had been able to be a major influence. The pair pitched an idea to Elvis that he could star in the gritty adaptation of *A Walk on the Wild Side*, from the novel by Nelson Algren. Wow – how good would Elvis have been in that!

Sadly, it never happened.

The 'Colonel' was also angry that the songwriters had 'dared' to approach Elvis with a song without going through the controlling manager. That song was 'Don't'. These incidents saw the song-writing pair go from writing an entire soundtrack for Elvis in *Jailhouse Rock* to seeing just three of their songs in a movie packed with 11 tracks. After 'King Creole', that was pretty much it for the pair when it came to Elvis. He did record other tracks written by the duo, but they were composed for other artists. Elvis would merely cover the tracks. 'King Creole' was released as a single in the UK in 1958, reaching number two in the charts.

TROUBLE

King Creole made a serious effort to reflect the music of the film's location. There's even a song called 'New Orleans' on the *King Creole* album.

The next track we're going to look at had some blues, some jazz and of course the King of Rock 'n' Roll, all thrown together in the mix. The result was the song 'Trouble', which Elvis sang with a glint in his eye in front of gangster Maxie Fields, played by the ultra-talented Walter Matthau. In 1987, Matthau was asked about his feelings on Elvis. He said: "Elvis was an instinctive actor. He was very intelligent. He was very elegant, sedate, refined and sophisticated." Praise indeed from one of Hollywood's finest.

If you ask Leiber and Stoller to write something bluesy – then 'Trouble' is a great example. The duo were no stranger to bluesy tracks – after all, they had written 'Hound Dog' for Big Mama Thornton, and produced the session, while they were still in their teens! The song has received praise over the years. It's certainly in a different league from most of Elvis's Hollywood songs.

Music critic Maury Dean even said: "'Trouble' with Presley's snarl is one of the earliest proto-punk rock songs!" Proto punk would emerge fully in the late 1960s; however, the first proto punk bands, the Sonics and the Monks, were formed at the start of the 1960s. 'Trouble' is almost a movie thriller in a song, with lyrics like "If you're looking for trouble, you came to the right place. If you're looking for trouble then look right in my face... Because I'm evil, my middle name is misery." The lyrics really suited the dark broodiness that is present throughout the whole of the movie. It has a certain edge rarely seen in an Elvis movie.

In 1975, 'Trouble' would be covered by singer and model Amanda Lear. She did a French-language version entitled 'La Bagarre'. Around the same time, Elvis released 'T-R-O-U-B-L-E' – a totally different track – and one that stands out as a rocking track at a time when Elvis was singing quite low-key ballads about lost love. It was a small hit.

Other people to have covered the *King Creole* track 'Trouble' include Jackie De Shannon in 1959. Huge Elvis fan Suzi Quatro recorded the song in 1974. Britney Spears sang the opening lines to 'Trouble' before going into her hit of the time, 'Gimme More', at the 2007 MTV VMA Awards. And Lauren Alaina did 'Trouble' on the tenth season of *American Idol*.

Elvis would return to the song 10 years after he first recorded it for another career-defining moment. He would sing it during the opening moments of the *'68 Comeback Special* which relaunched the King back to rock 'n' roll glory after years in the Hollywood wilderness singing to pretty starlets, cute kids, dogs and of course shrimps and a bull called Dominic. The movie and the soundtrack for *King Creole* were one of those rare moments when Hollywood got it right in Elvis's career. It should be on your 'to watch' list if you have never seen it.

More on *King Creole* in a further volume...

10th–11th June – RCA Studio B, Nashville, Tennessee

This was a last-minute recording session to grab Elvis and hopefully some hits before the army private headed to Germany for his national service. The aim was to have enough material to keep the fans happy without saturating the market. So the material needed to be top notch – Elvis and his musicians did not disappoint. He may have been in the army now, but Presley knew how to turn up the heat and produce some great, albeit highly polished, rock 'n' roll music. Here are two of the highlights from that session.

BIG HUNK O' LOVE

'A Big Hunk o' Love' is a late '50s classic rock 'n' roll track. The driving song was written by Aaron Schroeder and Sid Wyche. Wyche had been best known for composing the jazz standard 'Alright, Okay, You Win' whereas Aaron Schroeder was a rock 'n' roll composer through and through, having written hits for many artists but enjoying his biggest success with Elvis Presley. Other tracks Schroeder would co-write included 'It's Now or Never' and 'Good Luck Charm'.

The 'Big Hunk o' Love' session took place on 10th June 1958 in Nashville, before Elvis headed off to Germany for his national service. Not only did it create some awesome tunes, it must have been a strange session for Elvis as it was his first ever without Scotty Moore and Bill Black by his side. This marked the first time the musicians hadn't worked with Elvis since his very first recordings for Sun four years earlier. Tensions had been mounting for a while. Scotty and Bill had seen Elvis become a millionaire while they were struggling on 200 dollars a week when there were tours and 100 dollars a week when there weren't. It all ended after the September 1957 sessions for Presley's first Christmas album.

Scotty and Bill both said they had been promised a chance to cut some of their own tracks after the session and on Presley's studio time. Both were excited about the opportunities these sessions could produce for them. However, when Elvis's session was done, the producers told Scotty and Bill to pack up as the session was over. Angry and upset, the two wrote a letter of resignation that very night. As well as low wages, they also felt Elvis's manager Tom Parker was working against them and was doing his best to ensure they never got to speak to Elvis alone. (Something Parker would continue to do during Elvis's career.)

It wasn't long before news of the split reached the media. A local journalist in Memphis was the first to interview the duo. Presley responded with a press statement wishing them good luck. However, Elvis was keen to point out that things could have been worked out if they had spoken to him and not the press. Scotty would eventually return to work with Elvis in the 1960s, appearing with Presley for the final time during the sit-down performance of the *'68 Comeback Special*. The legendary guitarist died in 2016. Bassist Bill Black, who enjoyed chart success after the split from Elvis, sadly died of a brain tumour on 21st October 1965, at the age of 39. His death occurred during his third operation, which doctors had hoped would eradicate the tumour once and for all.

After their split from Elvis, Scotty and Bill were replaced by Hank Garland on lead guitar and Bob Moore on the double bass. D.J. Fontana was still on the drums along with Buddy Harman, and Floyd Cramer was sat at the piano. 'A Big Hunk o' Love' was recorded in just four takes; however, the officially released version would be spliced from the last two takes recorded. It was released with 'My Wish Came True' on the B-side on 23rd June 1959. It spent two weeks at the top of the Billboard Hot 100 while the B-side peaked at number 12.

Elvis clearly loved the song as he would return to it during his 1970s live performances, including some pretty high-profile concerts. He first revived 'A Big Hunk o' Love' in February 1972 during his engagements at the Las Vegas Hilton. The song was then featured in the 1972 documentary *Elvis on Tour* and in Elvis's crowning 1970s moment, the *Aloha from Hawaii* show in January 1973.

I GOT STUNG

'I Got Stung' is an upbeat, bouncy rock and roll song written by Aaron Schroeder and David Hill. Elvis recorded the song and released it in 1958. It was then re-released in January 2005 as a series of singles marking what would have been Elvis's seventieth birthday.

'I Got Stung' was the B-side of Presley's number-one UK hit 'One Night'. It was on 10th June 1958 that Elvis managed to squeeze in a two-day recording session at Nashville's Studio B. It was to be his last until March 1960 when he was discharged from active duty, having completed his national service. Elvis had a hugely successful first day recording tracks that would go on to be huge sellers while he was in the army, keeping the fans happy and keeping Elvis hot property even though he was unable to promote any of them due to army life in Germany.

The songs recorded on the 10th June were 'I Need Your Love Tonight', 'A Big Hunk o' Love', 'Ain't that Loving You Baby' and '(Now and Then There's A) Fool Such as I'. Only 'Ain't that Loving You Baby' remained in the can going into the 1960s. On 11th June Elvis and his band recorded 'I Got Stung' with its rapid-fire humorous lyrics. Other people to record I got stung were Little Tony, French rock and roller Johnny Halliday and, more recently, former Beatle Paul McCartney, who covered the track for his album *Run Devil Run*.

In January 2005, Sony released every UK number-one hit by Elvis. Each week a limited-edition CD single and 10" vinyl would come out. The first batch were strictly limited, numbered versions. There was a box to store all the singles in. Collectors and fans struggled for weeks to get the complete set. Some stores literally had five copies of each single every week. Take it from me, it was a nightmare with people queuing outside record shops from the early hours, just to be in with a chance of getting hold of that week's single. The clever marketing certainly worked, with Elvis reaching number one on a handful of occasions during January and February. The song would then disappear from the chart, to be replaced by another Elvis song the following week (which if it didn't make the top slot, would at least be a top-10 hit).

One of those number ones was 'One Night/I Got Stung', but this was an important number one. The CD single and 10" vinyl re-release would become the UK's 1,000th number one since the charts started in 1952. According to the website www.everyhit.com: "By a very odd coincidence, it turned out that Elvis Presley not only had the 1,000th Number One that week but, that very same week, he also became the first artist to have spent 1,000 weeks in the Top 40!" At the time, UK bookmaker William Hill was forced to close the betting that Elvis would take the 1,000th number one after fans backed the price to 14/1 on. Spokesman Rupert Adams said in 2005: "To our knowledge this is the first time that an Elvis bet has taken us to the cleaners as the majority of Elvis bets we take are for him to be found alive – presently offered at 500/1."

Who would have thought that a song recorded by Elvis Presley would become the 1,000th UK number one, 47 years after it was recorded!

I NEED YOUR LOVE TONIGHT

It was essential that this final recording session with Elvis yielded tracks that would keep him high in the charts and deep in the hearts of his loving fans while he was away. The material thankfully was strong and did produce great hits for the famous G.I.

'I Need Your Love Tonight' was written by Sid Wayne and Bix Reichner. Reichner had enjoyed his first success long before rock 'n' roll dominated the charts. In fact, Elvis was just a toddler when 'Stompin' at the Stadium' came out in 1938. It was composed by Reichner and Clay Boland. Reichner would also co-write material for Count Basie, Kay Kyser and his Orchestra and Perry Como. His first taste of rock 'n' roll success came with the track 'Mambo Rock' recorded by Bill Haley and his Comets in 1955.

Sid Wayne was a prolific song writer from the 1950s until the 1980s. Most of Elvis's movies feature a song that Wayne co-wrote with one of his song-writing partners such as Sherman Edwards or Ben Weisman. After Presley's movie career started to dwindle, Wayne went on to pitch songs to other artists. One of his biggest successes came when he wrote the Grammy-nominated song 'It's Impossible'. Perry Como had a massive hit with it. Elvis would also cover the song.

'I Need Your Love Tonight', paired with 'A Fool Such As I', reached number four on the Billboard pop singles chart in 1959. It gained further success when it reached number one in the UK singles chart in May 1959 for five weeks.

We will revisit the 1950s again in a further volume, but before we leave we need to mention possibly the strangest Elvis RCA release of the 1950s – which featured no singing!

ELVIS SAILS…

It was once said that Elvis could sing the telephone book and it would still sell. There is some truth in that as the interview disc *Elvis Sails* sold around 60,000 copies! But then, it captured a moment for Elvis's fans, feeling bereft that their hero was leaving them.

Elvis also had fear in his heart. He was going from being one of the biggest stars of the 1950s to being a young private in the US Army. He was swapping the rock 'n' roll of a stage to the rocking and rolling of a tank. The King confided in his closest friends that he thought the fans would forget him while he was away. This couldn't have been further from the truth. Elvis's manager, 'Colonel' Parker, had a plan to drip music and Elvis news into the minds of his singer's fans. There would be number-one hits and well-selling compilation albums that mopped up the Sun and RCA recordings that hadn't previously featured on an album.

On the *Elvis Sails* EP, Elvis is polite but sounds pretty sombre. It is hardly surprising. He was still raw from the tragic loss of his beloved mother, Gladys. The pair had formed the strongest of bonds since his poverty-stricken childhood in Tupelo. She was his adviser, his friend and now she was gone. Elvis was given little time to grieve. He was soon whisked from the comfort of his Graceland haven to head to a land far away.

The EP itself would eventually rise to number two in the Billboard EP charts. This was an amazing achievement for a recording that was speech only, peppered with boat sound effects of Elvis leaving America for Germany, and on a format that had already passed its sell by date. The cover consisted of a newspaper front page, with a photo of Elvis jumping out of the page as if to say "breaking news". The EP itself featured interviews with Elvis. Side one has an interview with the famous G.I. carried out at the Brooklyn Army Terminal. Side two has a newsreel interview, followed by the most famous track – the interview carried out by journalist Pat Hernon in the library on board the USS Randall as it prepared to sail.

With just minutes to go, Elvis was open and honest about how he was feeling. He said: "Well I'm looking forward to Germany and seeing the country and meeting a lot of the people. At the same time I am looking forward to coming back here." Elvis was also keen to send a message to his fans, saying: "In spite of the fact I am going away and out of their eyes for some time, I hope I am not out of their minds. I will be looking forward to the time when I come back and entertain like I did."

As the USS Randall sailed, Elvis no doubt had the words of Colonel Parker ringing hopefully in his ears. Parker had promised his young star even greater success on his return, telling him that he just needed to "stay a good boy, and do nothing to embarrass your country." As Elvis sailed off to Germany, he had to hope that Parker was right. He was, of course; but Elvis's career would no longer be as the wild and raw rock 'n' roll star. He would return as the world's most famous G.I. – an all-American boy – who would be moulded as an all-round entertainer. The plan would work at first, bringing great riches but also challenges along the way. All this and more to come in *Elvis Presley: Stories Behind the Songs Volume Two*...

The Press Interviews Elvis
RCA
45 E.P.
RCX-131
LATE
EXTRA
LATE
ELVIS SAILS

AFTERWORD

It has been a joy putting this book together. During my research I have read some great Elvis books by Shane Brown, Mike Eder, Trevor Simpson and Robert Matthew Walker. Thank you to all these authors for their awesome books.

The Internet remains an amazing source for Elvis research. Check out the wonderful sites dedicated to Elvis, including the Elvis Information Network. Piers and Nigel have always been a tremendous support and they run a great and regularly updated site. Also check out elvisnews.com, which is also regularly updated with Elvis news. Elvis.com.au is also home to a wealth of information, interviews and fan comments about Elvis's huge catalogue.

In the UK, Andrew Hearn runs a great magazine called *The Elvis Mag* as part of his Essential Elvis company. He has very kindly run some of my interviews in the past.

Trevor Cajiao runs another great magazine called *Elvis: The Man and His Music.*

Strictly Elvis is another great website. The company has been very supportive during my Elvis projects and regularly takes fans to the essential Elvis sites.

Todd Slaughter, a legend in the Elvis world, has also been very encouraging and helped to spread the word about this book and my previous e-book series. Todd runs the Official Elvis Presley Fan Club of Great Britain that has been serving UK Elvis fans since 1957. Here's to many more years Todd!

My thanks must also go to all the Facebook groups that have so kindly posted about my book. Thanks also to the many Instagram accounts dedicated to Elvis. Many are run by youngsters, which is fantastic as it shows that Elvis remains an idol to this generation too.

To all Elvis fans around the world. You are the most loyal fans ever and each one of you keeps the memory of Elvis alive and well.

Finally, my thanks to Becky Hartley Yancey, Elvis's secretary at Graceland in the '60s and '70s who made my year by being one of the first to pre-order my book. Becky, that meant so much. Thank you from the bottom of my heart.

There are countless websites out there dedicated to our legend. Here are a few I have visited for research and over many years as a fan. A quick Google search will help you discover even more.

https://www.elvis.com

https://www.elvispresleyfanclub.co.uk

http://www.essentialelvis.com

http://www.elvisinfonet.com

https://www.elvisnews.com/

http://www.elvismatters.com

https://www.keithflynn.com

http://www.elvis-express.com

http://elvis.co.uk

https://www.nowdigthismagazine.co.uk/about

https://www.memphismansion.dk

https://www.strictlyelvis.net

INDEX